Financing Transit-Oriented Development with Land Values

The Urban Development Series discusses the challenge of urbanization and what it will mean for developing countries in the decades ahead. The Series aims to delve substantively into the core issues framed by the World Bank's 2009 Urban Strategy, *Systems of Cities: Harnessing Urbanization for Growth and Poverty Alleviation.* Across the five domains of the Urban Strategy, the Series provides a focal point for publications that seek to foster a better understanding of the core elements of the city system, pro-poor policies, city economies, urban land and housing markets, sustainable urban environment, and other issues germane to the urban development agenda.

Cities and Climate Change: Responding to an Urgent Agenda

Climate Change, Disaster Risk, and the Urban Poor: Cities Building Resilience for a Changing World

The Economics of Uniqueness: Investing in Historic City Cores and Cultural Heritage Assets for Sustainable Development

Financing Transit-Oriented Development with Land Values: Adapting Land Value Capture in Developing Countries

Transforming Cities with Transit: Transit and Land-Use Integration for Sustainable Urban Development

Urban Risk Assessments: An Approach for Understanding Disaster and Climate Risk in Cities

All books in the Urban Development Series are available for free at https://openknowledge.worldbank.org/handle/10986/2174

Financing Transit-Oriented Development with Land Values

Adapting Land Value Capture in Developing Countries

Hiroaki Suzuki
Jin Murakami
Yu-Hung Hong
Beth Tamayose

WORLD BANK GROUP

ISBN (paper): 978-1-4648-0149-5
ISBN (electronic): 978-0-4648-0150-1
DOI: 10.1596/978-1-4648-0149-5

Cover photo: © Japan Railway Construction, Transport and Technology Agency (2013). Used with permission; further permission required for reuse.

Library of Congress Cataloging-in-Publication Data has been requested.

Contents

Boxes

Figures

Photos

Tables

Maps

Acknowledgments

This book was written by Hiroaki Suzuki of the World Bank, Jin Murakami of the City University of Hong Kong, Yu-Hung Hong of the Massachusetts Institute of Technology, and Beth Tamayose of the University of California, Los Angeles.

It draws on case studies of Hong Kong SAR, China; Tokyo, Japan; New York City, NY, United States; Washington, DC, United States; London, United Kingdom; Nanchang, China; Delhi, India; Hyderabad, India; and São Paulo, Brazil.

Steve Yiu, Rebecca Wong, Lam Chan, and Eureka Cheng (MTR Corporation) provided assistance in preparing the Hong Kong SAR, China, case study.

The Tokyo, Japan, case study was developed with support from numerous individuals and organizations: Takeshi Nakawake, Wataru Tanaka, Kiyoyoshi Okumori, Shigeru Yokoo, Takashi Uchiyama, and Taro Minato (Nikken Sekkei Ltd.); Hironori Kato (The University of Tokyo); Hisao Uchiyama (Tokyo University of Science); Masafumi Ota, Munehiko Shibuya, and Toshiyuki Tanaka (Tokyu Corporation); Katsunori Uchida and Tamotsu Kamei (Tokyu Land Corporation); Hideaki Oohashi, Hiroshi Namekata, Tokunori Tachiki, Takashi Goto, Yoshio Nemoto, Kichiro Watanabe, Hiroshi Ii, and Kimio Higaki (Chiba Prefectural Government); Seiji Nakata (Mitsui Fudosan Co. Ltd.); Kimihiro Kuromizu (City of Yokohama); Hiroyuki Sugata, Mitsutoshi Haniahara, and Hideyuki Kudo (Japan Railway Construction, Transport and Technology Agency); Hiroya Masuda (Nomura Research Institute); Kiyoshi Yamasaki (Value Management Institute Inc.); Takashi Nakamura and Katsuya Amano (Tokyo City University); Seiichiro Akiumura (Japan Transportation Planning Association Research Institute); Ryosuke Fukae

(Japan Ministry of Land, Infrastructure, Transport and Tourism); and Keiichi Tamaki (Asian Development Bank).

Stan Wall (Washington Metropolitan Area Transit Authority) contributed to the preparation of the Washington, DC, case study; Mamoru Sakai (Japan International Cooperation Agency) provided research assistance for the Washington, DC, and London case studies.

The Nanchang, China, case study was prepared with assistance provided by Jianyang Liu (vice mayor, Nanchang), and Shunmao Mao (Urban Rail Company). Additional support was provided by Jie Lin and Xuan Yang (Nanchang Railway Transit Group Co. Ltd.).

Berenice Bon (Centre for South Asian Studies at L'Ecole des Hautes Etudes en Sciences Sociales) and Shirley Ballaney (Environmental Planning Collaborative) coordinated the case study preparation in Delhi and Hyderabad, India, respectively, and supported the World Bank team's field research. The Delhi, India, case study was developed with support from Romi Roy (UTTIPEC); Rakhi Metra, Marco Ferrario, and Swati Janu (Micro Home Solutions); Gaurav Wahi (Jones Lang LaSalle); Sanjeev Jain, Er. R. K. Ganjoo, Bijendra K. Jain, and Deepak Mowar (Parsvnath Developers Ltd.); Naini Jayaseelan and Syed Aqeel Ahmad (NCR Planning Board); K. Jayakishan and Ashvini Parashar (DIMTS); Mangu Singh, Anuj Dayal, U. C. Mishra, Ashok Kumar Gupta, P. S. Chauhan, Kaushal Kumar Sahu, and R. M. Raina (Delhi Metro Rail Corporation Ltd.); Pritam Kumar and Dheeraj Kumar (IL&FS Rail Limited); and Kuldip Singh (Kuldip Singh & Associates).

The Hyderabad, India, case study was developed with support from N. V. S. Reddy, Vishnu Reddy, D. Surya Prakasam, and Y. Murali Mohan (Hyderabad Metro Rail Ltd); Sri M. T. Krishna Babu, Dhanajay Reddy, and Navin Mittal (Greater Hyderabad Municipal Corporation); Purshottam Reddy, Neerabh Kumar Prasad, and Madhava Raja (Hyderabad Metropolitan Development Authority); Devender Reddy, Mallikarjun Setty, T. S. Reddy, Vivek Gadgil, and P. Ravishankar (L&T Metro Rail [Hyderabad] Limited); Sunil Srivastava (Balaji Railroad Systems Limited); Sista Viswanath (Warangal Urban Development Authority); Srinivas Chary Vedala (Centre for Energy, Environment, Urban Governance, and Infrastructure Development); S. P. Shorey (Urban Poverty Reduction/SNPUPR); C. Ramachandraiah (Centre for Economic and Social Studies); and Utpal Sharma (CEPT, Ahmedabad).

Domingos Pires de Oliveira Dias Neto, Camila Maleronka, and Mariana Yamamoto Martins (P3urb) coordinated the case study preparation for São Paulo, Brazil, and supported the World Bank team's field research. The São Paulo, Brazil, case study was developed with support from Celso Petrucci and Flavio Prando (SECOVI); Alberto Epifani (Companhia do Metropolitano de São Paulo—Metrô); Ciro Biderman (SPTrans); Alexandre Rodrigues Seixas and Marcelo Fonseca Ignatius (São Paulo Urbanismo); Paulo Henrique Sandroni (Getulio Vargas Foundation); Vitor Hugo dos Santos Pinto (Caixa Economica Federal); João Teixeira and Joshua Pristaw (GTIS Partners); Carlos Henrique Malburg and André Luiz Teixeira dos Santos (BNDES); Julio Lopes (Rio de Janeiro State Secretary of Transport); Vicente de Paula Loureiro (Rio de Janeiro State Secretariat of Public Works); and Waldir Peres (AMTU-RJ).

The Tokyo Development Learning Center (TDLC) assisted with the organization of the workshop on Financing Transit with Land Values and the interviews in Tokyo with support from Tomoyuki Naito and Rumi Horie.

Peer reviewers included Valerie Joy Eunice Santos (World Bank), Francesca Medda (Quantitative and Applied Spatial Economic Research Laboratory, University College London), Robert Cervero (University of California, Berkeley), and P. Christopher Zegras (Massachusetts Institute of Technology). Additional comments were provided by Om Prakash Agarwal (World Bank) and Joshua Gallo and Lauren Wilson (PPIAF).

This book was supported by the following World Bank operational staff: Bernardo Guatimosim Alvim, Georges Bianco Darido, Nupur Gupta, Fabio Hirschhorn, Holly Krambeck, Paul Kriss, Augustin Maria, Barjor E. Mehta, Satoshi Ogita, Gerald Paul Ollivier, Xuan Peng, Shigeyuki Sakaki, Yi Yang, Ruifeng Yuan, and Jingyi Zhang.

Adelaide Barra, Fernando Armendaris, and Vivian Cherian (World Bank) provided logistical and administrative assistance. This work was supported by the World Bank Urban and Disaster Risk Management Department under the overall guidance of Zoubida Allaoua, Sameh Wahba, and Ellen Hamilton.

Preparation of this book was funded by the Public-Private Infrastructure Advisory Facility (PPIAF) and the Cities Alliance. PPIAF is a multidonor technical assistance facility aimed at helping developing countries improve the quality of their infrastructure through private sector involvement. For more information on the facility, visit http://www.ppiaf.org. The Cities Alliance is a global partnership for urban poverty reduction and the promotion of the role of cities in sustainable development. The overall strategic objectives of the Cities Alliance are to support cities in providing effective local government, an active citizenship, and an economy characterized by both public and private investment. For more information on its activities, visit http://www.citiesalliance.org.

The publication of *Financing Transit-Oriented Development with Land Values* was managed by the World Bank's Publishing and Knowledge Division under the supervision of Patricia Katayama and with the help of Mark Ingebretsen. Michael Alwan provided layout and graphics support. The book was edited by Communications Development Inc., led by Bruce Ross-Larson and including Jonathan Aspin and Jack Harlow.

About the Authors

Principal Authors

Hiroaki Suzuki is the former lead urban specialist of the Urban and Resilience Management Unit of the Urban and Disaster Risk Management Department at the World Bank. Currently, he is a lecturer at the Graduate School of Engineering, University of Tokyo; the National Graduate Institute for Policy Studies (GRIPS); and the Graduate School of Politics, Hosei University. He has more than 30 years of operational experiences within the infrastructure and public sectors and at the World Bank and the Overseas Economic Cooperation Fund, Japan (now the Japan International Cooperation Agency [JICA]). He specializes in the areas of sustainable urban development, transport and land use integration, municipal finance, and innovative urban infrastructure financing. He is the lead author of *Eco² Cities: Ecological Cities as Economic Cities* (2010); its implementation guide, *Eco² Cities Guide: Ecological Cities as Economic Cities* (2012); and *Transforming Cities with Transit: Transit and Land-Use Integration for Sustainable Urban Development* (2013), all published by the World Bank. He earned a master of science degree in management from the Massachusetts Institute of Technology (MIT) Sloan School of Management.

Jin Murakami is an assistant professor in the Department of Architecture and Civil Engineering at City University of Hong Kong. He specializes in the areas of transportation and economic development, development strategy and spatial planning in globalization, and public finance and land policy. His research focuses principally on spatial and financial matters to increase city-regions' global competitiveness and local livability. He earned his PhD in city and regional planning from the University of California, Berkeley. He is a lead author, Working Group III, of chapter 12, "Human

Settlements, Infrastructure and Spatial Planning," for the Fifth Assessment Report of the Intergovernmental Panel on Climate Change (IPCC).

Contributing Authors

Yu-Hung Hong is a lecturer of Urban Planning and Finance at the Massachusetts Institute of Technology (MIT) and a visiting fellow at the Lincoln Institute of Land Policy. He is the founder and executive director of the Land Governance Laboratory where he studies the use of land tools to facilitate open and inclusive decision-making processes for land resource allocation in developing countries. He earned his PhD in urban development from the Department of Urban Studies and Planning at MIT.

Beth Tamayose is a visiting researcher in the Department of Urban Planning at the University of California, Los Angeles. Her research focuses on land use planning, governance structures, and land and resource access and allocation in the Pacific. She earned her PhD in urban planning from the University of California, Los Angeles.

While this book is the product of a collaborative effort, primary authors for the sections are as follows:

Overview	Hiroaki Suzuki and Jin Murakami
Chapter 1	Hiroaki Suzuki
Chapter 2	Hiroaki Suzuki, Yu-Hung Hong, and Jin Murakami
Chapter 3	Jin Murakami
Chapter 4	Jin Murakami
Chapter 5	Jin Murakami and Beth Tamayose
Chapter 6	Yu-Hung Hong and Hiroaki Suzuki
Chapter 7	Jin Murakami and Hiroaki Suzuki
Chapter 8	Jin Murakami and Hiroaki Suzuki

Abbreviations

BRT	bus rapid transit
CEPAC	Certificates of Additional Construction Potential
CDA	comprehensive development area
DBLVC	development-based land value capture
DDA	Delhi Development Authority
DfT	Department for Transport (UK)
DFI	development financial institution
DIF	District Improvement Fund
DMRC	Delhi Metro Rail Corporation
EWS	economically weaker sections
FAR	floor area ratio
GHMC	Greater Hyderabad Municipal Corporation
GLUP	General Land Use Plan (Arlington)
GoAP	Government of Andhra Pradesh
HKSAR	Hong Kong Special Administrative Region
HMDA	Hyderabad Metropolitan Development Area
HS1	High Speed 1
HSR	high-speed rail
JD	joint development
JnNURM	Jawaharlal Nehru National Urban Renewal Mission
JNR	Japanese National Railways
KCRC	Kowloon-Canton Railway Corporation
LCR	London and Continental Railways
LVC	land value capture

MPD-2021	Master Plan for Delhi-2021
MRTS	Mass Rapid Transport System (Delhi)
MTA	Metropolitan Transportation Authority (NYC)
MTR	Mass Transit Railway (Hong Kong SAR, China)
NCTD	National Capital Territory of Delhi
NMG	Nanchang municipal government
NMT	nonmotorized transport
NRTG	Nanchang Railway Transit Group Co., Ltd.
OODC	additional building charge (Outorga Onerosa do Direito de Construir)
O&M	operation and maintenance
ORR	Outer Ring Road
PFI	private finance initiative
PDE	Plano Diretor Estratégico (Strategic Development Plan)
PITU 2025	Integrated Urban Transport Plan 2025 (São Paulo)
PPP	public-private partnership
R+P	Rail Plus Property (program implemented by MTR Corporation, Limited, Hong Kong SAR, China)
SAR	Special Administrative Region
TAD	transit-adjacent development
TDR	transfer of development rights *or* transferable development rights
TOD	transit-oriented development
UMTA	Urban Mass Transportation Act
UO	Urban Operation
UTTIPEC	Unified Traffic and Transportation Infrastructure Planning and Engineering Centre
VGF	viability gap fund
WMATA	Washington Metropolitan Area Transportation Authority

Note: Unless otherwise noted, dollar amounts are in U.S. dollars.

Glossary

Air right sale. One of the development-based LVC instruments. Governments sell development rights extended beyond the limits specified in land use regulations (e.g., FAR) or created by regulatory changes to raise funds to finance public infrastructure and services.

Bus rapid transit (BRT). High-quality bus-based services that mimic many of the features of high-capacity metrorail systems but at a fraction of the cost. Buses most closely resemble metrorail services when they operate on specially designated lanes or have physically separated lanes for their exclusive use. Grade separation of busways at critical intersections and junctures also expedites flows. BRT systems often include bus stations instead of stops to provide weather protection and allow passengers to pay before boarding.

Central business district (CBD). Areas where cities' major businesses (financial institutions, stores, major convention and sport facilities, hotels, etc.) are concentrated. CBDs produce agglomeration economies.

Eminent domain. Regulatory power granted to governments or public agencies, which allows them to take private property for public projects or interests, subject to appropriate compensation.

Floor area ratio (FAR). Ratio of a building's total floor area to the size of the land on which it is built. The higher the FAR, the higher the density. Also referred to as floor space ratio (FSR) or floor space index (FSI).

Greenfield development. New development that takes place on lands that were not previously developed as urban land including agricultural, rural, and unused land.

Land readjustment scheme. Landowners pool their land together for reconfiguration and contribute a portion of their land for sale to raise funds to partially defray public infrastructure development costs. This can be used as a development-based LVC instrument to finance transit and TOD-related investments.

Land value capture (LVC). LVC is defined as a public financing method by which governments (a) trigger an increase in land values via regulatory decisions (e.g., change in land use or FAR) and/or infrastructure investments (e.g., transit); (b) institute a process to share this land value increment by capturing part or all of the change; and (c) use LVC proceeds to finance infrastructure investments (e.g., investments in transit and TOD), any other improvements required to offset impacts related to the changes (e.g., densification), and/or implement public policies to promote equity (e.g., provision of affordable housing to alleviate shortages and offset potential gentrification). There are two main categories of LVC: development-based LVC and tax- or fee-based LVC. Development-based LVC can be facilitated through direct transaction of properties whose values have been increased by public regulatory decisions or infrastructure investment. Tax- or fee-based LVC is facilitated through indirect methods, such as extracting surplus from property owners, through various tax or fee instruments (e.g., property taxes, betterment charges, special assessments, etc.).

Market freehold system. Land holding system under which landowners have absolute ownership of land. Its conditions are full right of transfer, right to bequeath, right to mortgage, full use rights (unless restricted by law), and unlimited duration.

Mixed use. Pattern of development characterized by a mixture of diversified land uses, typically including housing, retail activities, and private businesses, either within the same building space (e.g., vertical mixing) or in close proximity (e.g., horizontal mixing).

Nonmotorized transport (NMT). Any type of transport mode that is not motorized, such as walking or bicycling. NMT has gained popularity as not only a clean, carbon-free form of mobility with a very small footprint but also as a means to improve public health through increased physical activity.

Public-private partnership (PPP). Formal partnership between a public sector entity and a private corporation often used to construct and operate infrastructure facilities or develop certain urban areas.

Redevelopment/regeneration. Type of development that seeks to reinvest in already developed areas, typically targeting parcels that are underutilized (e.g., vacant or abandoned properties); often considered part of an economic development scheme.

Sprawl. Pattern of development characterized by uniform low density, lack of a distinctive core, poor accessibility, dependence on automobiles, and uncontrolled and noncontiguous land expansion.

State leasehold system. Land holding system under which lands are owned by the states and the lands are leased by the states to individuals or firms for a fixed duration, with lease fees and other conditions. The rights enjoyed by lessees can vary with specific lease conditions, but terms frequently allow for the right to assign the lease to another or allocate the residual value of the lease. Development and use rights are likely to be restricted by the States.

Transfer of development rights (TDR). Ability to effectively buy and sell "air rights" (i.e., rights to fully develop the maximum allotted vertical envelope—or "air space"—of properties) within the limit of their FAR allotment or the unused development rights that remain when a particular building does not use up its FAR allotment; typically applies only to certain parcels, and the rights often can only be transferred to specific "receiving" parcels.

Transit-adjacent development (TAD). Development that is similar to TOD in that it is located within the vicinity of a transit node but is not actually connected with transit in the absence of pedestrian-friendly development organized around a transit station.

Transit-oriented development (TOD). Compact, mixed-use, pedestrian-friendly development organized around a transit station. TOD embraces the idea that locating amenities, employment, retail shops, and housing around transit hubs promotes transit usage and nonmotorized travel.

Urban redevelopment scheme. Development-based LVC instrument mainly used in Japan. Landowners together with a developer establish one cooperative entity to consolidate piecemeal land parcels into a single site that they then develop (e.g., high-rise building and/or mixed-use building) with new access roads and public open spaces. The local government modifies zoning codes and increases maximum FARs in the targeted redevelopment district (typically around rail transit stations).

Message to City Leaders

Would you like to reduce traffic congestion, promote business, improve public services, and boost revenues? How about making your city more livable, economically competitive, and environmentally and socially sustainable?

One way that cities can achieve these goals is by creating and capturing the benefits of higher land values around urban transit stations and corridors. Needless to say, land has its own intrinsic value. Private investors pay to obtain property rights and develop the land, further pushing up its value. These developers rightly deserve to profit from their investments, but shouldn't your city, too? Taxes and fees certainly have a role, but in this book, other approaches are explored which will enable cities to reap the benefits of increases in land value attributable to public policies and actions—such as changes in land use regulations and investments in infrastructure, specifically transit-oriented development.

How can your city do this? Cities typically use land sale or lease, joint projects, and air rights deals. For example, a joint project can ensure that the development of transit stations and adjacent private properties is well coordinated, with the developers contributing financially or physically to the construction of the stations because property values will rise, thanks to the new transit facility. Under an air rights deal, governments can sell development rights that allow for higher densities or taller structures beyond the limits specified in land use regulations to raise revenue for public infrastructure and services.

Such deals have many advantages for cities. They help clearly connect increased value from regulatory changes and related investments to funding for transit infrastructure. In addition to obtaining direct revenues resulting from creating and sharing higher land values, you will also get more sustainable revenues in the long run—not just from higher ridership but from new retail shops, parking garages, leisure facilities, and residential buildings around the station.

These deals can be explored not only as financing instruments but also as ways to pursue planning and public policy that is good for both the local economy and the environment and that encourages more inclusive urban growth. By using some of the proceeds to invest in parks, sidewalks, street lights, and bike lanes, you can work with transit agencies, developers, and communities to jointly develop efficient, attractive, and safe public places, further increasing property values. By offering bonus floor area ratios and other regulatory incentives, you can require developers to provide affordable housing and daycare centers in their new facilities.

One kind of method for capturing land value does not preclude others. They can be applied separately or jointly in ways that best suit the conditions in your city and country. So in choosing how to proceed, you should consider the project's objectives, its regulatory and administrative feasibility, and its political acceptability.

The perception of land transfers from the public to private sector may be negative in countries where there is a lack of transparency. For this reason, governments or transit companies often find it difficult to secure public support, especially from those living in the targeted property development areas. To build support, your city government can introduce a transparent monitoring and recording system for transactions. All stakeholders need to have access to information on how the private partner has been selected, what public revenues are projected, and how the revenues will be used. Perhaps most important is to require that transactions be at market prices based on independent assessments using established and neutral land valuation principles and practices. It is also important to involve civil society organizations in front-end planning and post-project development activities.

We invite you to consider this book's examples of how some cities have created and captured higher land values through a strategic mechanism coupled with supportive regulatory changes for sustainable urban finance and development. Hong Kong SAR, China; Tokyo; New York; Washington, DC; and London have generated funds for their transit systems and promoted sustainable urban development. Nanchang, Delhi, and Hyderabad are adapting such an approach for their metro construction.

The majority of cities, especially in developing countries, have not yet fully explored the possibilities. These cities will need to develop their legal and institutional framework and build technical expertise, capacity, and experience under a consistent vision, policy, and strategy. We hope this book will help you find a strategic approach for urban finance and planning that works in your local context. By creating and capturing higher land values around urban transit stations and corridors, cities can recoup some of the costs of building, operating, and maintaining mass transit systems, as well as support transit-oriented development in ways that make them more appealing places to live, work, and do business.

Ede Jorge Ijjasz-Vasquez
Senior Director
Social, Urban, Rural and Resilience
    Global Practice
The World Bank Group

Pierre Guislain
Senior Director
Transport and ICT Global Practice
The World Bank Group

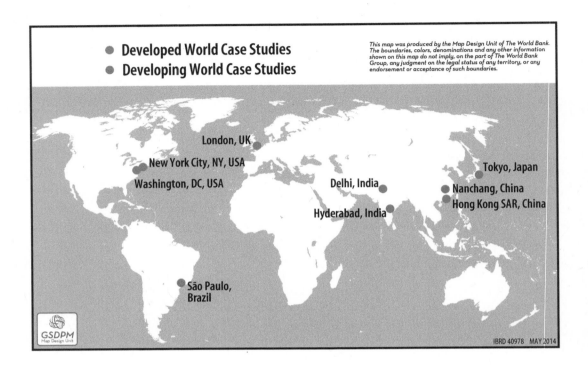

● Developed World Case Studies
● Developing World Case Studies

This map was produced by the Map Design Unit of The World Bank. The boundaries, colors, denominations and any other information shown on this map do not imply, on the part of The World Bank Group, any judgment on the legal status of any territory, or any endorsement or acceptance of such boundaries.

London, UK
New York City, NY, USA
Washington, DC, USA
Delhi, India
Hyderabad, India
Tokyo, Japan
Nanchang, China
Hong Kong SAR, China
São Paulo, Brazil

GSDPM
Map Design Unit

IBRD 40978   MAY 2014

Overview

Cities in developing countries are experiencing unprecedented growth. But this is often accompanied by the negative impacts of car-dependent urbanization such as congestion, air pollution, greenhouse gas emissions, inefficient use of energy and time, and social inequality of accessibility. The World Bank's *Transforming Cities with Transit: Transit and Land-Use Integration for Sustainable Urban Development* (Suzuki, Cervero, and Iuchi 2013) concluded that compact, mixed-use, pedestrian-friendly development organized around a transit station is one of the most effective strategic initiatives to address the negative effects of motorization.

Despite increasing recognition of transit-oriented development as an effective strategic approach for sustainable urban development, most cities, particularly those in developing countries, do not have the practical know-how and expertise to make transit-oriented development happen. Because these cities are almost always under a severe fiscal constraint, they face great challenges in financing capital-intensive mass transit systems to reverse car-dependent urbanization. Development-based land value capture (LVC) in Hong Kong SAR, China; Tokyo; New York; Washington, DC; and London allows these cities not only to generate funds for transit investment and operation and maintenance but also to promote sustainable urban development. If adapted well to local contexts, such schemes have great potential to become an effective finance and planning apparatus for cities in developing countries.

Many rapidly growing cities in developing countries, particularly those in emerging middle-income countries, are endowed with macro conditions for development-based LVC schemes. Strong economic growth, rising real incomes, increasing motorization, and congestion all cause land values to appreciate near transit stations or corridors. And some forward-looking cities in middle-income countries such as Nanchang, Delhi, and Hyderabad are adapting development-based LVC for their metro systems. But the majority of cities in developing countries have not yet fully explored these favorable conditions to adapt locally-specific development-based LVC schemes. Why? Because they lack a consistent vision, strategy, and policy. They also lack legal and institutional frameworks. And they lack technical expertise, capacity, and experience. This book can help them fill these gaps and adapt their own development-based LVC scheme as a strategic apparatus for urban finance and planning.

Car-Dependent Urban Development in the Developing World

The 21st is the century of cities. More than half the world's people, or 54 percent of the world's population (UN Department of Economic and Social Affairs 2014), reside in urban areas, and 7 of every 10 people will live in cities by 2050, with about 90 percent of the growth in developing countries (UN-Habitat 2013). Cities globally generate about 75 percent of gross domestic product. But urbanization also bears social, economic, and environmental costs. Cities consume about 67 percent of energy and produce about 70 percent of greenhouse gas emissions. And the problems of car-dependent urban development—congestion, air pollution, greenhouse gas emissions, lengthy commutes, and social inequality in accessibility—have been increasing in rapidly growing cities in developing countries. Enrique Peñalosa, former mayor of Bogotá, said (in 2002), "Transport differs from other problems developing societies face, because it gets worse rather than better with economic development" (Peñalosa 2002). As wealth increases, people shift from walking to bicycling, and then from bicycling to riding motorbikes and to driving cars. By 2050, China is projected to have 900 million cars, or more than the number in the world today (Fulton and Cazzola 2008).

Recognizing the problems of car-dependent urbanization, many cities in developing countries have started to invest in metrorail, light rail, bus rapid transit, and commuter and heavy rail transit. But these systems are extremely intensive in capital. Beyond the upfront construction costs, operation and maintenance also require substantial cross-subsidies from other revenue sources because fare revenues in most cities are insufficient (Murakami 2012). Such operational deficits are due in large part to the weak integration of transit infrastructure with urban development. And suitable development schemes are often unavailable for transit and planning agencies in developing countries (Suzuki, Cervero, and Iuchi 2013).

These constraints have stimulated interest in development-based LVC for transit financing and sustainable urban development. Indeed, Hong Kong SAR, China; Tokyo; Osaka; and Singapore have been using it to finance transit costs and promote sustainable urban development.

Development-Based Land Value Capture as a Strategic Apparatus for Transit Financing and Urban Planning

The notion of land value capture is to "mobilize for the benefit of the community at large some or all of the land value increments (unearned income) generated by actions other than the landowner's such as public investments in infrastructure or administrative changes in land use norms and regulations" (Smolka 2013) (figure O.1).

Unlike taxes and fees, development-based instruments capture land value increments by selling or leasing land, development rights, and air rights. Under such schemes, governments, transit agencies, developers, and landowners jointly increase land values by exploring development opportunities of transit station areas and sharing increments in land values.

Development-based LVC has the following advantages over taxes and fees in financing transit and transit-oriented development related investments (table O.1):

- It has greater potential to finance capital-intensive transit and transit-oriented development related investments without significant fiscal distortion or public opposition to additional taxes or fees.
- It can generate not only direct revenues from incremental land value increases attributed to transit investments but also more sustainable long-term revenues from higher transit ridership and retail shops, leisure facilities, parking, and residential buildings in the precinct of station areas.

Figure O.1 Land values and their attribution

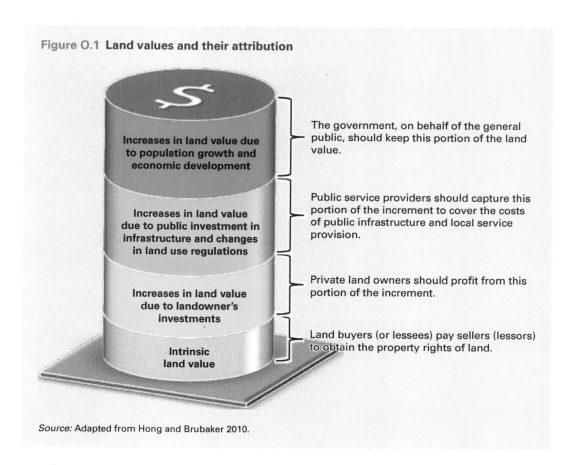

Source: Adapted from Hong and Brubaker 2010.

Table O.1 Selected land value capture instruments

	Instrument	Description
Tax- or fee-based	Property and land tax	Tax levied on estimated value of land or land and buildings combined, with revenues usually going into budgets for general purposes.
	Betterment charges and special assessments	Surtaxes imposed by governments on estimated benefits created by public investments, requiring property owners who benefit directly from public investments to pay for their costs.
	Tax increment financing	A surtax on properties within an area that will be redeveloped by public investment financed by municipal bonds against the expected increase in property taxes. Mainly used in the United States.
Development-based	Land sale or lease	Governments sell developers land or its development rights, whose values have increased thanks to a public investment or regulatory change, in return for an up-front payment, leasehold charge, or annual land rent payments through the term of the lease.
	Joint development	A well-coordinated development of transit station facilities and adjacent private properties between transit agencies and developers, where the latter usually contribute physically or financially to the construction of the station facilities, as their property value will increase thanks to the transit investment. Used in Japan, the United States, and other countries.
	Air rights sale	Governments sell development rights extended beyond the limits specified in land use regulations (such as floor area ratios [FARs]) or created by regulatory changes to raise funds to finance public infrastructure and services.
	Land readjustment	Landowners pool their land and contribute a portion of their land for sale to raise funds and partially defray public infrastructure development costs.
	Urban redevelopment schemes	Landowners and a developer establish a cooperative entity to consolidate piecemeal land parcels into a single site that they then develop (such as a high-rise mixed-use building) with new access roads and public open spaces. The local government modifies zoning codes and increases maximum FARs in the targeted redevelopment areas (typically around rail transit stations) and finances the infrastructure. Mainly used in Japan.

- It involves transacting land rights, development rights, or air rights whose values have increased due to public investment or regulatory changes. It establishes a clear link between creating value and capturing value. In addition, the increment in land value is calculated using a method agreed by stakeholder consensus. By contrast, taxpayers often contest the coverage and amount of taxes or fees because the definition of benefits created by public intervention is often vague, the accuracy of the estimated incremental value is often challenged, and the calculation methods are not well defined.
- It has a much better chance of working well administratively in places with an inadequate property tax system (outdated cadasters, weak capacity for assessing value), as in most cities in developing countries.

Governments can explore development-based LVC not only as a financing instrument but also as an urban planning and public policy instrument to promote economic competitiveness, environmental sustainability, and social equity:

- By changing land use regulations, such as allocating higher floor area ratios (FARs) and converting land from single to mixed use, governments can increase densities in station areas for diverse uses while increasing revenues.
- By using proceeds for investments in station areas (such as parks, street lights, bike lanes, and pedestrian sidewalks), governments, transit agencies, developers, and communities can jointly develop efficient, attractive, and safe public places, further increasing property values.
- By providing bonus FARs or other regulatory incentives, governments can require developers to include social facilities and affordable housing in exchange for the additional rights.

This is not to deny the usefulness of tax- or fee-based schemes, which have their own advantages. For instance, the revenues from property taxes can be sustainable because their collection does not deplete finite land resources. Nor does adopting one category of LVC preclude adopting another. Taking into account the different objectives, the regulatory and administrative feasibility, and the political acceptability of public infrastructure finance, these different instruments can be applied separately or jointly in ways that suit the conditions of countries and cities.

Global Good Practices for Development-Based LVC

Two global cities in Asia—Hong Kong SAR, China, and Tokyo—provide cases of successful large-scale development-based LVC as a strategic apparatus for sustainable urban finance and development. They have been applying development-based LVC not only to recoup the costs of mass transit construction, operation, and maintenance but also to support transit-oriented development for sustainable urban development.

Hong Kong SAR, China's, R+P Program

Hong Kong SAR, China, is one of few global cities whose rail transit sustains the world's densest urban form productively. The 218-kilometer Mass Transit Railway (MTR) network consists of 10 railway lines with 84 stations serving Hong Kong Island, Kowloon, and the New Territories, with more than 4 million passenger trips a day. Due to the high ridership, MTR generated a net operating profit of HK$6.694 billion (US$869 million) from its transit operation and achieved farebox recovery of 185.5 percent for 2012. This financial success is thanks to the Rail Plus Property (R+P) program implemented by the MTR Corporation (map O.1).

Under the R+P program, the Hong Kong SAR, China, government gives exclusive property development rights of government-owned land at a "before-rail" market price. MTR then captures the land value increment created by R+P, such as accessibility and agglomeration benefits thanks to transit and transit-oriented development related investments, by partnering with private developers in developing the land and selling the completed

Map O.1 Hong Kong SAR, China: MTR's operating network and future lines with property developments

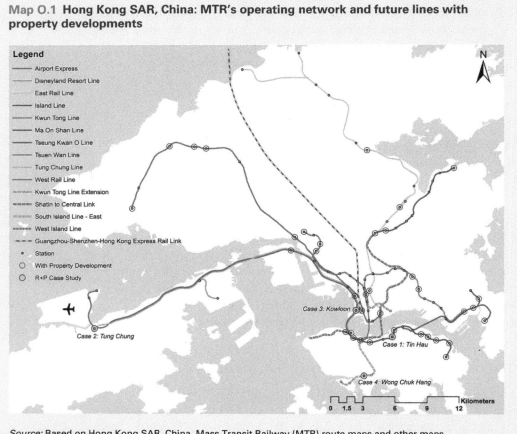

Source: Based on Hong Kong SAR, China, Mass Transit Railway (MTR) route maps and other maps.
Note: R+P = Rail Plus Property.

development at an "after-rail" market price. It recoups the capital, operating, and maintenance costs of railway projects through sharing profits (figure O.2). R+P also allows MTR to integrate different phases of rail and property development projects, ensuring smooth project implementation and reducing transaction costs.

From 2000 to 2012, property development produced 38 percent of MTR's corporate income, related businesses (such as commercial and property lease and management business) 28 percent, and transit operations 34 percent. From 1980 to 2005, the government received $18 billion equivalent in net financial returns, with earned income from land premiums, market capitalization, shareholder cash dividends, and initial public offer proceeds of $22.2 billion equivalent, minus the equity capital injected of $4.2 billion equivalent. Although MTR is entitled to capture land value increments, its financial benefits are distributed to the government through dividends and appreciation of the value of its shareholding. MTR also contributes to sustainable urban development and economic development by providing efficient transit services and high quality property development.

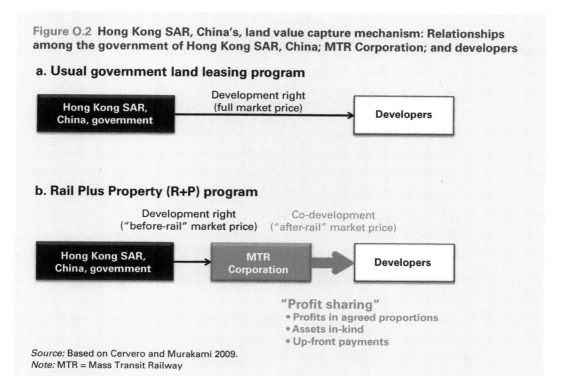

Figure O.2 Hong Kong SAR, China's, land value capture mechanism: Relationships among the government of Hong Kong SAR, China; MTR Corporation; and developers

a. Usual government land leasing program

b. Rail Plus Property (R+P) program

Source: Based on Cervero and Murakami 2009.
Note: MTR = Mass Transit Railway

The following key principles ensure the program's effectiveness:

- Master plans and policy documents consistently state the importance of an MTR network as a "backbone" of urban and regional development, particularly during a rapid growth period.
- A public leasehold system controls urban land supply, attracts private resources, and ensures public interests around new railway corridors.
- The Comprehensive Development Area zoning sets special FARs around key stations to attract private investment to strategic locations, while providing flexibility for private developers to negotiate and design.
- Property development rights are exclusively granted at a pre-rail market price for a business-oriented rail corporation to cover the capital and running costs of a rail project and to master multiple functions and phases of rail and property development at lower transaction costs.
- The granting of development rights starts with small parcels above stations or depots primarily to generate project revenue and later evolves into large-scale, high-quality new towns, iconic business centers, and local community hubs.
- Private developers cover land premiums and bear project risks for higher financial returns, whereas the government and rail corporation (to some degree) are protected from market and development risks.
- The rules for sharing costs and profits among public agencies, the railway corporation, and private developers are clear and sound, easing project uncertainties and public opposition.

- Development parameters for rail stations vary by locations based on market demand and socioeconomic conditions.
- After project completion, the railway corporation stays on as an asset manager not only to capture the upfront profits of property development but also to maximize management-related recurring revenues from the long-term business portfolio.

Tokyo's Diverse and Inclusive LVC Schemes

A 3,500-kilometer extended railway network with about 2,000 stations operated by 48 transit agencies serves Tokyo, the world's largest metropolis with 37 million inhabitants (map O.2). Tokyo provides one of the best

Map O.2 The Tokyo metropolitan area

a. Polycentric regional structure

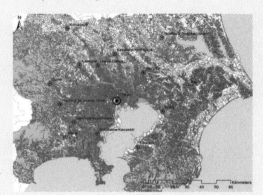

b. Urban regeneration special districts

c. Railway network built, operated, and owned by multiple public-private agencies

Source: Based on data from National Land Information, Ministry of Infrastructure, Land, and Transport (MILT), Japan.

experiences in applying development-based LVC to finance railway investments with the revenues from real estate development. Unlike Hong Kong SAR, China's, state leasehold system, Tokyo's schemes operate under a market freehold system.

Land readjustment is mainly used on urban fringes, and urban redevelopment schemes in built-up areas especially, where property rights are fragmented (boxes O.1 and O.2). Both instruments, however, require either

Box O.1 Integrated land readjustment for Tsukuba Express

Under the Housing-Railway Integration Law, municipal governments and housing agencies can designate special land readjustment areas along future railway lines. In this scheme, several landowners within the designed areas give up and reserve percentages of their land for public uses, including the transit facilities or land sales to generate funds for public investments (figure BO.1.1). The economic rationale is that although the original landowners receive smaller land parcels, these parcels would have higher land values thanks to a new station and other local infrastructure and service provision. Railway companies can smoothly acquire the rights of way for their transit investment and promote transit-supportive housing developments through the land readjustment practices.

Figure BO.1.1 Integrated land readjustment

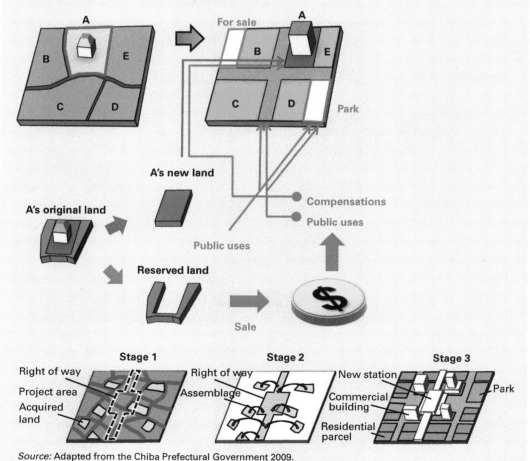

Source: Adapted from the Chiba Prefectural Government 2009.

strong community ties or sufficient economic incentives. The consent of all landowners is typically sought, though the laws allow project agencies to implement schemes once they secure the consent of more than two-thirds of landowners.

Box O.2 Inclusive urban redevelopment scheme, Japan

Under the Urban Redevelopment Law, landholders, tenants, and developers can create development opportunities in built-up areas, typically where a transit station exists or has newly opened. To capture the potential accessibility benefits conferred by the transit station, the local government first converts zoning codes from single use to mixed use with higher floor area ratios (figure BO.2.1).

Figure BO.2.1 Inclusive urban redevelopment scheme, Japan (hypothetical)

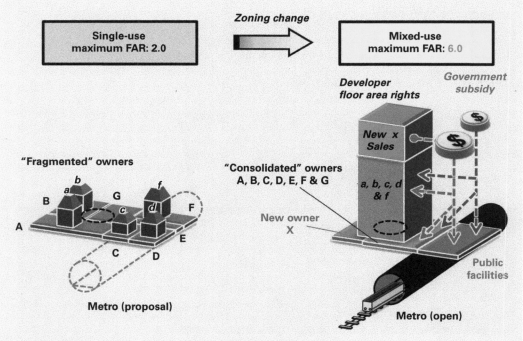

Source: Adapted from Ministry of Land, Infrastructure, Transport, and Tourism 2013.
Note: FAR = floor area ratio.

Before the urban redevelopment project, the site consisted of several small parcels owned by individual landowners and occupied with different tenants. Most houses are one- or two-story structures because each parcel is too small to replace the old building with a taller building, and the landowners do not have the capital or expertise to do so. This urban redevelopment project consists of construction of a taller, higher-quality building on land prepared by assembling small parcels; construction of an underground metro station; and provision of public infrastructure (such as wider roads, a station plaza, and amenities). The national government finances a third of site survey, land assembly, and open space foundation costs, using the national general budget, and half the public infrastructure costs using the roadway special fund. Through this process, the original landholders and building

(continued next page)

Box O.2 **Inclusive urban redevelopment scheme, Japan** *(continued)*

owners are entitled to keep the property rights of floor spaces in the new building that are valued as equal to their original property (though sometimes one developer will purchase all the property rights from the original owners to accelerate the redevelopment). The "surplus" floor area permitted by the municipal government is sold to new property owners to substantially cover the costs of land assembly, new building(s), and public facilities within the district.

Table BO.2.1 presents respective stakeholder's contribution to the land value and their benefit received through the urban redevelopment undertaking.

Table BO.2.1 **Stakeholder contributions and benefits**

Stakeholders	Contribution	Benefit
Landholders (A, B, C, D, E, F & G)	Land parcel for the new building	Joint ownership of land for the new building (sections A, B, C, D, E, F & G) with higher access and better local infrastructure and service provision
Building owners (a, b, c, d & f)	Old buildings and housing units	Ownership of the new building (sections a, b, c, d & f) with higher access and better local infrastructure and service provision
Developer	Capital and property development expertise	Profit from section X and from surplus FAR
Transit agency	Construction of transit station	Transit-supportive environment/increased ridership
National government	Subsides for land assemblage and road construction	Save road and other public infrastructure construction costs
Local government	Change in zoning code (from single use to mixed use with higher FAR)	Yields higher property tax revenue; promotes local economic development; builds townships resilient to natural disasters

Note: FAR = floor area ratio.

The world's largest metropolis has adapted LVC to match the variety of stakeholders, locations, time periods, and scales over the world's most expansive railway network. Tokyo's rich transit-oriented experiences offer the following lessons:

- The national government's master plan leads to polycentric regional development and railway extension strategies, even though multiple public, private, and semi-private entities use different development approaches and LVC techniques in the same metropolitan area. All stakeholders need to share a clear vision and take collective actions.
- Both the land readjustment and urban redevelopment schemes require a consensus building that is often very thorough and time-consuming. And smooth implementation relies on traditional social ties and adequate economic incentives. The power of eminent domain can help practitioners speed land assembly, but careless application could generate long-lasting social tensions and feelings of mistrust.
- Entrepreneurial railway agencies should also acquire expertise not only for conventional system engineering but also for real estate investment,

town planning, and marketing to set appropriate development parameters, analyze market profiles, offer multiple services, and maximize value increments in their station properties and wider catchment areas. Essentially, railway agencies need to be entitled to keep the long-term ownership and stewardship of properties to generate recurring revenues from both development and service activities around stations.

- The rights of way for a new railway line can be assembled cost-efficiently by railway agencies and local governments through land readjustment projects, especially in areas where local residents are waiting for new railway access. This approach can promote property development along the new line to achieve targeted ridership and fare revenues.
- Major landholders or developers in a designated district can foster land readjustment projects. With their real estate knowledge and resources, they are more likely to invest in local infrastructure, take strong initiatives in planning, and maximize the value of their land around a new station.
- To create high-quality built environments around a station, substantial density bonuses should be provided. Private transit agencies and developers are encouraged to supply social infrastructure and services, maximize synergies, and mitigate redistributive impacts through inclusive urban redevelopment. They can provide human-scale built environments within the superblocks already constructed in many developing countries.

Tokyo's multiple techniques provide lessons for the rapidly growing cities of developing countries.

Critical Factors for Success in Developing Countries

Case studies of cities that have creatively pursued development-based LVC to finance transit and transit-oriented development in both developed and developing countries highlight the unique contexts and challenges of creating and sharing land values for transit financing and transit-oriented development. The insights from these experiences point to policy recommendations and implementation measures that deserve careful consideration at different levels of strategic decisions. They also highlight policy decisions, planning exercises, and project development in applying development-based LVC in developing countries.

Key Findings

Inclusive Value Creation

The rationale behind development-based LVC is creating and sharing incremental value among the governments, transit agencies, developers, businesses, and residents in and around stations. This obviously differs from tax- or fee-based capturing of "windfalls" from private property owners, as practiced in North America and other parts of the world. The Japanese expression of development-based LVC ("開発利益還元") literally means "returning profit generated by development," rather than having the government or transit company unilaterally capture the land value increments from landowners or developers. Development-based LVC is designed and implemented around the incentives of various stakeholders. This shared interest facilitates various complex property development processes such as acquiring land and authorizing land use change and zoning codes. Unlike most tax- or fee-based LVC instruments, evaluating increment value in development-based LVC is not a unilateral decision by municipalities. The land price is agreed on by all parties up-front based on market trends, and the distribution of profit is decided though negotiations, based on the contribution of each stakeholder.

Public Land Ownership Is Important but not Absolutely Necessary
Development-based LVC is a value creation exercise rather than a simple sale of public land or lease of land use rights. Even under a market freehold system, municipalities and transit agencies that do not own land can acquire land through incentive-based techniques such as "land readjustment" or "urban redevelopment," as applied in Tokyo. These can generate land values exceeding the land purchase costs by exploring undeveloped economic opportunities through densification, transit, and other transit-supportive investments. New York City and São Paulo are also exploring vertical development opportunities by leveraging air rights of the lands owned by private landowners in densely built-up districts (box O.3).

Box O.3 Air rights sales in São Paulo

Brazil is a pioneer in air rights sales, but these sales have rarely been adapted to finance transit or transit-oriented development related investments in São Paulo.

In Brazil, a private landowner cannot freely develop air rights above a certain floor area ratio (usually between 1.0 and 2.0 in São Paulo) without paying for the costs of the impact of the air rights use. The logic behind selling air rights is that owners should contribute to infrastructure construction costs in proportion to the volume of their air rights use, as higher densities require additional infrastructure investments. Certificates of Additional Construction Potential (CEPACs) are sold by auction as a tradable financial security, and they are applicable only to designated urban districts, with the revenues to finance predetermined urban infrastructure. Through the issue of CEPACs, municipalities can raise infrastructure investment funds by selling the bearer additional building rights—such as a larger floor area ratio and possible land use changes—that would induce private investments to adjust to the transformations desired in urban development policy.

São Paulo's highly indebted financial position forced city authorities to generate funds for infrastructure without increasing debt. Unlike many cities in developing countries, São Paulo cannot raise revenue by selling land because it possesses little developable land. So, air rights sales are one of a few possible measures for São Paulo to raise funds for infrastructure investments. By auctioning CEPACs, the city can allocate limited air rights according to market needs at a price to be fixed by market demand.

(continued next page)

Box O.3 Air rights sales in São Paulo   *(continued)*

Except for a few minor investments, CEPAC revenues have not been used for metro construction. Nor have allocations of CEPACs been linked to railway station areas. So, CEPACs have not always captured the increments of land value attributable to metro construction. Further, the state government and the city government are not controlled by the same political party, making coordination between transit agencies and the urban planning department difficult. Even in the same transport sector, railway transit companies owned by the São Paulo State and bus companies owned by the municipality seem to compete rather than collaborate. Due to lack of coordination between transit agencies and city planning bureaus as well as agencies' railway-centered engineering approaches, transit agencies often miss out on great opportunities to explore the use of air rights above stations to generate revenues. Given the tight budget situation and legal restrictions, metro company engineers tend to design metro stations according to minimum structural specifications requiring the least investment costs. But these developments cannot support the type of multipurpose use terminal building that could generate sizable lease revenues and increase transit ridership.

Although São Paulo currently faces these planning and institutional challenges, there is great potential to adapt development-based LVC for transit investment and to shape urban form and develop articulated densities suitable for future transit-oriented development. This approach has already been adapted in the "Linha Verde" (Green Line) Urban Operation in Curitiba, where a major national highway was converted into an urban avenue with the extension of a bus rapid transit green line and higher density land uses. CEPAC revenues partially financed the investment costs of this transit-oriented development project (Smolka 2013). In São Paulo, the Metro has already started to study the possibility of using air rights sales to finance new metro construction in the Vila Sonia Urban Consortia (Fróes and Rebelo 2006).

In addition, São Paulo's city planners are now considering to reduce the overcrowded commuting movement between suburbs and city centers by developing subdevelopment centers to balance business and residential densities across the city area (Região da Jacu-Pêssego as a new commercial center and Região da Cupecê for both commercial and residential use), based on the transit-oriented development concept where developable lands are still available. As the demand for good quality housing at the mid-market segment is very high because of rapid household income increase in Brazil, land prices close to transit stations could increase due to good accessibility and connectivity. If the municipal government and transit agencies collaborate and coordinate with investors and developers, as their counterparts in Hong Kong SAR, China, and Tokyo have been doing, they would be able to raise revenues to recoup a portion of the transit and other transit-oriented development related investment costs.

For cities with a state leasehold system, strategic public land use is imperative for successful development-based LVC implementation. Public land is a finite resource in cities—especially growing ones—and would be hastily exhausted if municipalities sold it for short-term cash flow. Municipalities as landholders must therefore strategically manage limited public land, taking into account long-term development benefits. The Hong Kong SAR, China, MTR captures the land value increment created by R+P not by selling the development rights, but by partnering with private developers, selling the completed property units, and finally capturing the value through the sharing of profits. In this sense, regardless of the differences between the respective landholding systems, both the Hong Kong SAR, China, MTR and the Japanese railway companies have been undertaking development-based LVC, based on creating and sharing value.

Sound Planning Principles

Revenue maximization is important because developable land is scarce in rapidly growing cities, but development-based LVC should be based on sound planning principles that increase the benefit of society as a whole. If these schemes are co-opted by cities to simply raise money, and not to try to plan cities sustainably, they may "distort the purposes of planning by putting the focus on benefits extracted from developers rather than on the actual needs of new residents and businesses" (Rahenkamp 2013). In this context, policymakers and practitioners should design development-based LVC so that the transaction generates land value increments that benefit society to the greatest extent possible (box O.4). In a different context, the unintended negative impact of São Paulo's planning regulation on free FAR limit (between 1.0 and 2.0), combined with its air rights sales on its spatial development pattern (urban sprawl and shortage of affordable housing stocks in the city center), should be carefully analyzed. So should the impact of Hong Kong SAR, China's, land lease policy on the affordability of local housing.

Enabling Factors

Macro Fundamentals

Demographic and economic fundamentals are paramount when applying development-based LVC. Generally, it works well when rapid urban population and strong economic growth create high demand for land and property prices increase. But even under slow economic growth, municipalities and transit agencies can adapt it to maximize accessibility and agglomeration premiums around selected station areas where the economic potential has not yet been fully realized due to inadequate land uses and outdated zoning codes.

The emergence of middle-income households—and high housing demand—can justify large-scale investment in rail extensions to suburbs

---

Box O.4 **Development rights leases in Nanchang, China**

Chinese cities have long converted rural agricultural land to urban land equipped with infrastructure and then leased the development rights for a premium. And as in many other Chinese cities, revenues from development rights leases are the major public finance source of infrastructure investments in Nanchang. But Nanchang, one of several forward-looking Chinese cities, is using development-based LVC schemes to promote transit-oriented development by creating articulated densities around major metro station areas. The idea is to maximize development rights lease revenues to recoup new metro investment costs by promoting efficient land use around stations through zoning changes for mixed use with higher floor area ratios—and to promote sustainable urban development through transit-oriented development.

Nanchang's practice is more sustainable than the typical rural-urban land conversion, which runs the risk of unnecessarily expanding cities outward, leading to urban sprawl. As this scheme has not yet been fully implemented, it is still too early to know whether it will generate the desired financial and urban development outcomes. But if successful, Nanchang's scheme could provide a good model for other Chinese cities.

and generate up-front value increments along new corridors. The metro corporations in Nanchang and Hyderabad are taking advantage of their growth, as Japanese private railways exercised development-based LVC for the initial infrastructure investments in the 1960s and Hong Kong SAR, China's, MTR Corporation in the 1980s.

Both Tokyo and Hong Kong SAR, China, could generate steady recurring revenues, even during periods of slow economic growth, since their instruments were well positioned for long-term development benefits rather than short-term financial gain. Tokyo's development-based LVCs are still being undertaken, thanks to market demand to consolidate land parcels for redevelopment and regenerate property values in selected strategic built-up areas with high economic potential.

Economic restructuring from low-cost manufacturing to knowledge- and service-based industries, as in Nanchang and Hyderabad, also provides greater opportunities to capture accessibility and agglomeration benefits around stations, where firms and workers can explore value-added business opportunities through agglomeration. Indeed, the competitive advantage of international and regional businesses in Tokyo, New York, and London has shifted toward central locations thanks to recent urban regeneration programs, taking advantage of strong infrastructure reinvestments, land use deregulation, and tax incentives.

Visionary Master Plans

A master plan needs to provide a long-term vision of development shared among all members of a city. Policymakers must emphasize transit infrastructure as the spine of spatial development strategies in their visionary plans, helping guide planning, funding, construction, and operations in a way that supports transit. This long-term development vision should be consistently reflected in other planning instruments such as diverse sector plans and local master plans.

Master plans from the past decades of global good practice cities clearly identified rail transit systems as the backbone of urban development. Hong Kong SAR, China's, territorial development strategies in the 1980s and 1990s anticipated growth areas along with a series of MTR extensions. Tokyo's latest national capital region master plan also stresses the formation of business cores and nine satellite centers that are well served by multiple rail lines. Nanchang's comprehensive development plan considers the metro railway system redirecting industrial and housing development from the old center to newly planned areas on a metropolitan scale. The location of key corridors and nodes for future development should be specified based on this vision, taking into account the feasibility of transit investment, market demand, and availability of developable land.

To formulate and revise master plans in a pragmatic way, national governments, metropolitan bodies, and city authorities need to invite multilevel stakeholders and cross-sectoral professionals to come together to share key information and address mutual interests. The National Capital

Region Plan of Tokyo has long coordinated potential development areas and authorized specific transit projects among multiple local governments and railway corporations. By contrast, the Master Plan for Delhi as the national capital region has been unable to resolve many conflicting bureaucratic interests and unfavorable land use regulations, which significantly blocks development-based LVC practices for the new metro system.

Master plans should not be too prescriptive. Development parameters depend on diverse site conditions and changing market demands, though transit-oriented development in general has a certain set of design principles. The overly standard and impractical criteria stipulated in the master plans of Delhi (maximum FAR of 1.0 at metro stations) have reduced or completely negated the opportunities for developers to coordinate better layout plans and maximize accessibility to their real estate.

In addition to the metropolitan master plans, there are various sector or local master plans across government departments and agencies. Such subplans must be consistent vertically among national, metropolitan, and local governments—and horizontally among departments of urban planning, land administration, transport, economic development, and housing—all under one consistent vision. For example, new transit investments cannot create enough ridership and associated land value if subplans encourage public spending on massive roadway systems and automobile-dependent housing development. In Hong Kong SAR, China, and Tokyo, transit-supportive policies and investment have been endorsed throughout a subset of sector plans or local master plans.

Flexible Zoning

Development-based LVC facilitates negotiations among planning authorities, transit companies, developers, landowners, and local stakeholders for mutual interests and benefits. So zoning codes and site design parameters around stations should be flexible enough to meet changing market demands and diverse local needs.

Zoning systems can provide flexible and negotiable codes with minimum standards to target station areas, allowing transit companies and developers to adjust site-design parameters. In Hong Kong SAR, China, Comprehensive Development Areas have been designated around key stations as set out in the MTR Corporation's Master Layout Plan to coordinate more complex, integrated mixed-use development packages and to flexibly exercise the financially viable R+P program. Tokyo's urban regeneration districts were designated to attract private real estate investments with generously relaxed development codes around the former rail yard sites (maximum FAR over 10.0, height deregulation, and expedited approvals).

In many developing countries, outdated land use plans or inconsistent regulations enforced by planning and statutory authorities deter transit agencies and real estate companies from exploring development opportunities in and around stations. For example, the Delhi Development Authority has strictly fixed maximum building coverage at 25 percent, with a FAR of

1.0 for any development activities at metro station areas. But under the new draft master plan (MPD-2021), it is proposing to allocate a higher FAR in the metro influence zones outside metro station sites. One official justification for the strict development regulations in Delhi is that increasing the maximum FAR around stations generates additional trips and exacerbates traffic congestion. But newly attracted travelers are more likely to choose transit and nonmotorized travel modes in origins and destinations near stations. Indeed, the most typical issue preventing flexible land use is the conflict of development interests inside and outside station areas.

Relaxing development regulations around stations alone does not ensure transit-supportive land use. To achieve this, municipalities and transit agencies need to coordinate the physical integration of rail station facilities with private property development and surrounding neighborhoods. Such integration can enhance a transit's accessibility and produce greater revenues from both transit farebox collections and development-based LVC schemes. In Delhi, nevertheless, a residential condominium project undertaken by a private developer along the metro depot is filled predominately with luxury 3–5 bedroom units having about four parking spaces per household. This can be regarded as transit-adjacent development rather than transit-oriented development (box O.5).

Box O.5 Government-led development-based land value capture for India's first metro system in Delhi

The Delhi Metro Rail Corporation (DMRC) is India's first metro system, extending over 190 kilometers with 144 stations. It has enjoyed very strong political and financial support from the national government, which leased land owned by various ministries and public agencies to DMRC for metro construction over a 99-year period at an intergovernmental transfer rate lower than the market rate. The government provided the land for property development to finance 11 percent of the construction costs of the first two phases. The government also provided the remaining financing, including budgetary support, together with the Delhi government, and secured yen loans from the Japan International Cooperation Agency by providing a sovereign guarantee. DMRC reports only to the Ministry of Urban Development, which coordinates with other relevant ministries and agencies, while DMRC holds all the decision-making power for metro construction and operation.

But Delhi's complex governance and regulatory framework is a direct result of multiple layers of government stakeholders—the national government, Delhi government with three municipalities, and the Delhi Development Authority (DDA; a state enterprise in charge of land management and policies, under the Ministry of Urban Development)—which has adversely affected the implementation of development-based LVC. While the national cabinet mandated DMRC to carry out property development projects to finance its construction cost, DMRC had difficulty obtaining development approval from different authorities such as DDA and the municipal government for the floor area ratio modification, the land use change for property development, and the construction permits. Effectively, the decision of the national government is being blocked by lower governments and planning and land management agencies that have statutory approval powers over the change of land use or construction permit. While DDA approved the land use for the right of way, it often rejected DMRC's applications for the land use change for property development.

Multiple Funding Sources

Development-based LVC should not be regarded as a single funding source to fill any funding gaps. In theory, the primary funding source for transit systems must be the fare revenue that can be increased by adopting transit-oriented development principles around stations. But few transit agencies in the world can cover even their operation and maintenance costs with fare revenues alone. The capital intensity of transit investment further increases the financing challenges for municipalities and transit agencies. Given the broader economic, environmental, and social roles of transit systems, including a range of externalities and social benefits, governments should help transit agencies close their financial gaps by mobilizing diverse funding sources.

Development-based LVC accounts for a substantial portion of transit finance in Hong Kong SAR, China, and Tokyo. But it should not be considered as a single financing source to cover expensive transit costs. As transport economists have long argued, the primary funding source for transit systems should be fare revenue, which should ideally increase with effective transit-oriented development. Railway finance models in Hong Kong SAR, China; Tokyo; Nanchang; Delhi; and Hyderabad assume that fare revenues will fully cover operation and maintenance costs and partially cover construction costs, primarily thanks to adequate passenger demand driven from their high-density passenger catchment areas. But even in such an exceptionally high-density area as Hong Kong SAR, China, the MTR Corporation sometimes relies on government cash grants when the R+P scheme cannot fill a funding gap, especially because of the scarcity of developable land parcels along new lines.

Land prices by their nature are volatile in response to changing economic and political climates, which are beyond the control of local governments or transit agencies. So a variety of alternative funding sources should be available to mitigate the risks of volatile land prices, through diversification of funding sources, and to prepare contingent financing sources in case of lower revenues from development-based LVC. Diversified funding arrangements can ensure the provision of transit infrastructure and services for the long term.

Any special funds run the risk of being captured by special interests—sometimes for economically unjustifiable investment, as with economically nonviable highway construction funded by a road fund. But if designed well, special funds could support governments' planning objectives and address externalities. For example, governments could apply a gasoline tax or automobile charge as strategic funding arrangements to supplement transit and transit-oriented development related investments and discourage automobile use. Tokyo's Roadway Special Fund—comprising earmarked gasoline charges and vehicle registration fees—financed one-third of transit-related bridge and underpass construction to reduce traffic congestion and upgrade station facilities to improve local feeder access, pedestrian circulation, and street amenities, along with the land readjustment and urban redevelopment schemes.

Among several funding sources, property taxes are particularly important for municipal governments, transit agencies, developers, landholders, and commercial entities around stations. Such taxes not only support the provision of infrastructure and services but also determine the distribution of development benefits in and around station facilities. Indeed, the special exemption of property tax for railway development and railway-associated businesses have been debated in Tokyo and Delhi, since railway corporations take advantage of the exemption without considering the redistributive effects of railway and property development in and around stations.

Intergovernmental Collaboration

Development-based LVC requires multiple government entities to work together to deliver innovative transit-related projects and programs, and that is one of the biggest challenges in many cities of developing countries. One recommended approach would be for a single local government body—which includes transit agencies—to coordinate planning, design, land acquisition, construction, operation, and asset management to sustain collaborative relationships and actions.

The culture of transit agencies is traditionally engineering-oriented, with a focus on narrowly defined performance criteria, even though development-based LVC needs expertise and intergovernmental collaboration beyond transit facilities. It is crucial for transport officials to recognize the financial potential and social importance of dealing with land and property around their transit stations. In both Delhi and São Paulo, the national or state transport bureaus have been less involved in adapting development-based LVC due in part to their technical focus, the multiple layers of governments (sometimes controlled by different political parties, as in São Paulo), and the complicated land and development right transfers from one agency to another.

Development-based LVC usually involves a wide range of government agencies to create greater development opportunities, generating conflicts of intergovernmental interests in lands and properties around stations. In many capital cities, such as Delhi and São Paulo, multiple layers of governments have long adopted their own legislative policies and design parameters. Delhi planning authorities and statutory bodies have used their regulatory instruments to block property development projects mandated by their national government around metro stations and to prevent the full exploration of development opportunities the new metro investment could bring.

Trusted political leaders may be able to remove such intergovernmental barriers and regulatory constraints by bringing all stakeholders together. But such a top-down approach might not always work well in democratic cities. In addition to political support, it is important that one government body acts as a coordinator to deal with land-related legislative tasks across agencies. In Hyderabad, a transit agency is a liaison to ensure that a private partner can smoothly obtain land for metro construction and property development by coordinating with several municipalities, traffic and police departments, and utility agencies for multiple statutory clearances (box O.6).

Entrepreneurship

Transit agencies need to become entrepreneurial as they manage development-based LVC's evolving process from a simple tool of short-term corporate or project finance to a strategic model of long-term urban finance and development—mainstreaming property development and asset management around stations as a part of their businesses. To ensure the sustainability of these property-related businesses, transit companies have to develop a consensus with other stakeholders on the ownership of and responsibilities for land and property management in and around stations.

Development-based LVC was originally an entrepreneurial undertaking in the mid-19th century in the United Kingdom and the United States. Around the turn of the 20th century, a few entrepreneurs in Japanese cities began adapting the classic private railway and land development business model. Since then, more railway corporations have evolved development-based LVC from a simple tool of short-term project finance to a strategic

---

Box O.6 World's largest public-private metro project in Hyderabad

Hyderabad, the largest historical city of southern India, home of 7 million citizens and prosperous information technology industries, is implementing the world's largest public-private partnership (PPP) for a metro project, extending 77 kilometers and with 66 stations. The PPP project is being implemented in the form of design-build-finance-operate-and-transfer under a 35-year concessionary agreement between Hyderabad Metro Rail Ltd. (HMR) and Larsen and Toubro Limited (L&T; one of the largest contractors and developers in India). HMR is a Special Project Vehicle set up by the state government of Andhra Pradesh (GoAP) to coordinate and manage the project. Through HMR, the state government and the municipality provided L&T with the right-of-way for metro construction and land for property development (109 hectares) close to the metro stations.

L&T will finance most of the metro construction costs ($2.7 billion) and expects to recover them over a 35-year concession, extendable for 25 years. Revenue sources include fare revenues (50 percent of the total), property development (45 percent of total revenues from 109 hectares of leased land), and a viability gap fund (VGF), which receives subsidies from the national government to fill the financial gap of the PPP project and others. The criterion for selecting the concessioner was the amount of VGF requested by the bidders. L&T, which requested the smallest VGF ($320 million), won the award. The Hyderabad Metro Project is a unique example of a PPP using development-based LVC as its financing scheme.

Hyderabad's institutional and regulatory framework is less complicated than Delhi's and more straightforward. On the government's side, stakeholders such as the heads of various departments of GoAP—including the Chief Secretary, the Commissioner representing Greater Hyderabad Municipal Corporation, and the Managing Director of HMR—sit on the board of HMR. HMR is assuming the role of a one-stop-shop representing the governments vis-à-vis L&T, the PPP concessionaire. This well-coordinated institutional framework ensures that a consistent vision, strategy, and policy facilitates various steps of the project, such as provision of state land, acquisition of land, and permission for land use changes. And the Chief Minister of Andhra Pradesh provides strong leadership and political support.

model of long-term urban finance and development across the Tokyo Metropolitan Area.

Transit agencies are typically established as public sector entities in cities of both developed and developing countries since urban transit on its own is seldom profitable enough. This is due in part to high land acquisition costs and competition with other transport modes, particularly automobiles. Even so, encouraging private entrepreneurship through different degrees of privatization in the provision of transit infrastructure and services could support such a public sector undertaking. In Hong Kong SAR, China, the MTR Corporation is highly entrepreneurial in exercising its R+P program, though the government as a beneficial owner keeps 76.7 percent of the MTR shares issued under the control of the Financial Secretary to ensure broader public interests. The privatization of the Japanese National Railways in 1987 brought a more business-oriented corporate culture and entrepreneurial business model, exemplified by large-scale private redevelopment of rail yard sites near strategic terminal stations.

In the portfolios of entrepreneurial transit agencies or private railway companies, real estate and other related business practices have accounted for more than one-third of their recurring profits over the last decade—38 percent between 2000 and 2012 for Hong Kong SAR, China's, MTR Corporation and 34 percent between 2003 and 2013 for Tokyo's Tokyu Corporation. The diversification of corporate portfolios also reveals that railway companies can be passenger service providers, real estate developers, and town planners through the implementation of development-based LVC in broader urban contexts. Indeed, high-profile railway agencies in progressive cities such as Hong Kong SAR, China; Tokyo; Washington, DC; Nanchang; and Hyderabad have accumulated knowledge by recruiting not only transport engineers, but also real estate experts and urban planners and designers.

The MTR Corporation is an example of an entrepreneurial transit agency with sufficient expertise to propose site-level layout plans in and around stations and control development parameters/design standards that maximize the accessibility benefits conferred by stations on a case-by-case basis. To assure the public interest in the private provision of infrastructure and services, the innovative public-private partnerships (PPPs) in cities of developing countries should clearly specify the obligations of private partners in each of the project phases. In Hong Kong SAR, China, and Tokyo, public requirements are also set up along with market incentives for entrepreneurial private entities to meet local community needs through the exercise of development-based LVC.

Clear, Fair, and Transparent Rules
The underlying principle of development-based LVC as practiced by Hong Kong SAR, China, and Tokyo is the joint creation and sharing of land value increment. Creating development opportunities among voluntary public-private contributors in a collaborative effort can generate additional values

and greater synergies. Thus, it is essential to establish clear and fair rules for sharing costs, benefits, and risks among stakeholders to ensure the long-term commitment of public agencies and private entities to deliver transit projects, promote transit-supportive activities, and maximize benefits in and around stations.

The rationale behind development-based LVC is incremental value creation and sharing among governments, transit agencies, developers, businesses, and residents in and around stations. This obviously differs from tax- or fee-based LVC capturing "windfalls" from private property owners, as practiced in North America and other parts of the world. Tokyo illustrates the need for some voluntary contributions to create greater development opportunities for both the public and private sectors. So, in adapting development-based LVC for local contexts of the developing world, the rules for sharing costs, benefits, and risks must support the collaborative actions of multiple stakeholders.

The rules should be clear. In Hong Kong SAR, China, for example, the MTR Corporation's R+P model offers three options for benefit sharing to private developers: profits in agreed proportions from the sale or lease of properties, assets in kind, and up-front payments from developers. The case-by-case arrangements are made according to development locations and market conditions, but rules of thumb make it easier for developers to work with the MTR Corporation on more complex and higher risk mixed-use development projects for greater returns on investment around stations. The government has also reaped substantial rewards through the transfers of development rights to the MTR Corporation, which can be shared with multiple departments and agencies for other social welfare programs.

The rules must be fair and transparent. As in Delhi, the land granted exclusively to a transit agency for development-based LVC is likely to produce intergovernmental conflicts of interest in capital cities with complex multilayered governance structures, unless other agencies can also obtain some development benefits in proportion to their resource contribution. To establish a win-win relationship among stakeholders, the innovative PPP scheme in Hyderabad attempts to ensure that the rules for sharing costs, benefits, and risks are adhered to by clearly specifying the obligations of government agencies and a private partner in the concession agreement.

Key Instruments

Policymakers and practitioners need to understand the basic features of various instruments and adopt appropriate combinations of development-based LVC techniques for the landholdings, stakeholders, periods, scales, and localities in their cities. Among the various instruments, land readjustment and urban redevelopment financing schemes—through the inclusive process of land resource allocation and urban planning—are particularly important for cities with a market freehold system.

Cities under a state leasehold system can generally use development rights sales with public requirements, as well as development incentives, to achieve their planning objectives. Cities in developing countries—such as China—have limited experience in property development in conjunction with transit investment. As a consequence, disproportionately large-scale layout plans have sometimes been adopted in station catchment areas. To set up realistic site parameters and attain intended spatial outcomes around stations, the MTR Corporation in Hong Kong SAR, China, maintains staff expertise in property development and town planning and has updated the property market profiles since the 1980s. These capacity building efforts can be seen as steps for adopting development-based LVC techniques in the developing world.

Cities under a market freehold system may be able to auction off public land with development conditions for public interests as well as development incentives for developers. In so doing, government agencies can raise up-front capital for infrastructure development, but they do not generate recurring revenues for operation and maintenance activities. Rail yard redevelopment in Tokyo and London shows that either local development agencies or private railway corporations should remain as stakeholders to directly control the public domain and sustain property management incomes in and around station facilities.

Land readjustment can efficiently assemble the rights of way for guided transit extension projects and simultaneously promote transit-supportive property development around new stations (mainly in suburban areas) if all landholders agree. Similarly, inclusive urban redevelopment schemes should become available with sufficient market incentives to consolidate private land parcels in target built-up urban areas, and create development opportunities in and around existing underused stations. Adopting inclusive instruments in developing countries requires entrepreneurial transit agencies to engage in lengthy negotiation processes, acquire knowledge about the options, and establish close relationships with multiple local stakeholders. The multiple development experiences in Tokyo highlight the need for active involvement and commitment of major landholders—who are often large real estate developers as well—to create greater development opportunities and maximize the land value added by transit investment.

FAR distribution requires special attention as it is associated with development rights sales, land readjustment projects, and inclusive redevelopment schemes. FARs can be used as a market incentive to achieve multiple policy objectives. These include the provision of infrastructure and services, public open space and amenities, affordable housing units, and mixed land uses in private development packages or urban regeneration districts near target stations.

The sale of tradable air rights can raise up-front cash for cities in developing countries where local governments face increased public debt and acute land constraints. But New York and São Paulo reveal that it is very difficult to estimate the value of air rights and to control land use parameters that could directly result in transit-supportive urban forms through market-based air rights transfers.

Challenges and Risks

Development-based LVC is a powerful financing and planning apparatus, unlocking unexplored land value to finance transit and promote transit-oriented development, but the risks of overreliance, corruption, and gentrification should be carefully addressed.

Overreliance

Overreliance on development-based LVC exposes municipalities and transit companies to excessive risk in real estate markets. While a robust real estate market and rising land prices are good for development-based LVC, both governments and transit agencies should adopt sound funding strategies and financial management, especially when property markets indicate excessive speculation. Given the unpredictability of the real estate market, municipalities and transit companies should estimate the revenue to be generated from development-based LVC schemes based on cautious and realistic assumptions, taking market trends into account. But in the face of rapid urbanization, transit investment cannot wait for the market. So, governments should prepare contingent plans in case revenues are lower than projected—preparing alternative funding sources or adjusting the sequence of investments based on technical and economic consideration.

Corruption

In general, the perception of land transfers from the public to private sector is negative among citizens in many developing countries because of a lack of transparency. For this reason, governments or transit companies often find it difficult to secure public support for development-based LVC, especially from those living in the targeted property development areas. To secure public support, governments should raise public awareness of the chosen scheme and its objectives, principles, rules, and regulations. It is also important for governments to involve civil society organizations in front-end planning and postproject development activities.

Governments should also introduce a transparent monitoring and recording system for development-based LVC transactions. Stakeholders and citizens should have access to information on how the private development partner has been selected, what are the projected actual revenues, and how the revenues will be used. Probably the most important way to prevent potential corruption is to require that transactions be at the market prices based on independent assessment. For example, in Hong Kong SAR, China, the land price assessed by the government is not arbitrary—it is a market price based on independent, highly sophisticated land valuation principles and practices. Transparent information systems will also help governments, transit agencies, and developers prepare future development-based LVC schemes, by making the relevant market data available for them.

Gentrification

Land prices in and around transit stations typically rise, often displacing low-income households. But transit-oriented development should not just create economically efficient and environmentally friendly urban spaces. It should also address urban poverty and deprivation. Where possible, city authorities should pursue affordable housing and provide developers the incentives to ensure that affordable housing is built close to transit stops. A FAR density bonus for constructing social housing is such an incentive and can be built into development-based LVC agreements.

Roadmap for Development-Based LVC Implementation through a Gradual Approach

Development-based LVC is a complex operation where various public and private stakeholders jointly maximize and share increments in land value around transit station areas, exploring the accessibility and agglomeration benefits of transit investment. It requires favorable macro conditions, a strategic vision, a supportive regulatory and institutional framework, and considerable expertise. Its adoption and implementation depend on the conditions and needs of each city. The roadmap for development-based LVC implementation shows the critical decisions and steps for governments and their transit agencies in designing and implementing development-based LVC—and the factors related to their decisions and actions (figure O.3).

Adapting and implementing development-based LVC requires consistent policies, a strong institutional framework, a clear and transparent regulatory framework, strong planning and financial management, effective design, and efficient property management. Many policymakers and practitioners likely feel that what Hong Kong SAR, China's, MTR Corporation and Japanese railway companies have done is unmanageable in developing countries. But both organizations developed expertise over many years, through trial and error. Other policymakers and practitioners might hesitate to adopt development-based LVC schemes because of the lack of available lands or the difficulty in acquiring them. Even in these situations, however, transit agencies can explore the possibilities for their own land, such as underground or above-station areas or depots, just as Nanchang Metro and Hyderabad Metro are doing. On land under their control, municipalities or transit agencies could start with a simple development-based LVC property development such as a single tower office building above a transit station. They could next develop a mixed-use complex, possibly with private developers. And they could eventually apply land readjustment or urban redevelopment schemes to develop areas adjacent to transit stations owned by

Figure O.3 Roadmap for development-based land value capture implementation

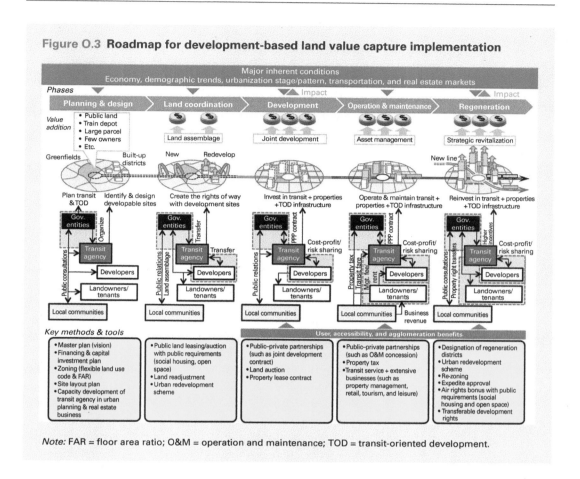

Note: FAR = floor area ratio; O&M = operation and maintenance; TOD = transit-oriented development.

private owners. To do this, the national or any upper-level government may need to adjust the regulations for railway properties to allow their commercial development. The key is to take incremental steps that make sense for each municipality and to leverage internal and local assets.

What International Development Financial Institutions Can Do

At the 2012 Rio+20 Conference, international development financial institutions including the World Bank announced a joint commitment to provide more than $175 billion in loans and grants to develop sustainable transport systems in developing countries over the coming decade. While encouraging this commitment, it can cover only a fraction of total urban transit investment needs. For example, the total financial needs (for investment, operation, and maintenance) for the next two decades in Latin America are estimated at $308 billion (Ardila-Gomez, Ortegón, and Rubiano forthcoming). Given this financial gap, international development financial institutions can help national and local governments develop policies and institutional capacities to tap financial resources other than public sources, through unconventional financial and project development schemes. They could also help countries develop their institutional and regulatory frameworks and implementation capacities. And they could finance prototype projects to demonstrate the effectiveness of development-based LVC. Given the expertise needed for development-based LVC implementation, they should collaborate with experienced transit companies like Hong Kong SAR, China's, MTR Corporation and various Japanese railway companies. The institutional support also requires "bridge financing," which allows transit agencies and their partner developers to start construction before development-based LVC revenues begin to flow.

Conclusion

High-quality transit is indispensable for sustainable urban development. Well-integrated transit and land use fosters cities' economic competitiveness, environmental sustainability, and social equity. More specifically, transit-oriented development—which creates articulated densities around transit hubs by locating amenities, employment, retail, and housing in close proximity—is one of the most effective ways to achieve sustainable urban development. Properties in well-designed areas gain a price premium thanks to their accessibility and agglomeration benefits. Collaborative efforts of municipalities, transit agencies, developers, landowners, and communities can maximize this premium. In this joint value-creating exercise, municipalities and transit agencies can contribute significantly to value creation either through zoning changes (FARs and land use) or through transit investment. And by adapting various development-based LVC schemes in their respective local context, they can recoup some of their transit investment, operation, and maintenance costs.

The rapid population increase and robust economic growth in rapidly growing cities in developing countries, particularly in middle-income countries, are certainly favorable for development-based LVC. Regardless of diverse political, institutional, and regulatory frameworks, regardless of different economic development stages and financial positions, and regardless of state leasehold or market freehold systems, all cities are endowed with invaluable land resources that have made them what they are. Policy makers, government officials, transit practitioners, developers, landowners, and citizens can together decide their cities' future—whether they continue to let cars dominate their places or whether they reclaim those places for the benefit of society. To reverse unsustainable development trajectories caused by rapid motorization, cities can unlock unexplored land values to finance transit investments and promote transit-oriented development for the well-being of people today and for their sustainable future.

References

Ardila-Gomez, Arturo, Adriana Ortegón, and Leonardo Canon Rubiano. Forthcoming. "Comprehensive Urban Transport Finance: Financing Capital, Operation, and Maintenance from the Sidewalk to the Subway." Washington, DC: World Bank.

Cervero, Robert, and Jin Murakami. 2009. "Rail and Property Development in Hong Kong: Experiences and Extensions." *Urban Studies* 46 (10): 2019–43.

Chiba Prefectural Government. 2009. "Human- and Environment-friendly Town Planning: Kashiwa North Central District." Chiba City.

Fróes, Marilda, and Jorge M. Rebelo. 2006. "Urban Operations and São Paulo Metro Line 4." Working Paper, World Bank, Washington, DC.

Fulton, Lew, and Pierpaulo Cazzola. 2008. "Transport, Energy, and CO_2 in Asia: Where Are We Going and How Do We Change It?" Presented at "The Better Air Quality 2008 Workshop," Bangkok, Thailand, November 12.

Hong, Yu-Hung, and Diana Brubaker. 2010. "Integrating the Proposed Property Tax with the Public Leasehold System." In *China's Local Public Finance in Transition*, edited by Joyce Y. Man and Yu-Hung Hong, 165–90. Cambridge, MA: Lincoln Institute of Land Policy.

Ministry of Land, Infrastructure, Transport, and Tourism. 2013. "Urban Redevelopment Project." Tokyo. www.mlit.go.jp/crd/city/sigaiti/shuhou/saikaihatsu/saikaihatsu.htm.

Murakami, Jin. 2012. "Transit Value Capture: New Town Codevelopment Models and Land Market Updates in Tokyo and Hong Kong." In *Value Capture and Land Policies*, edited by Gregory K. Ingram and Yu-Hung Hong, 285–320. Cambridge, MA: Lincoln Institute of Land Policy.

Peñalosa, Enrique. 2002. "The Role of Transport in Urban Development Policy." In *Sustainable Transport: A Sourcebook for Policy-Makers in Developing Cities*. Eschborn, Germany: Deutsche Gesellschaft für Internationale Zusammenarbeit (GIZ).

Rahenkamp, J. Creigh. 2013. "Letters to the Editor: LVR? Think again." *Planning Magazine* 79, no. 6 (July): 46.

Smolka, Martim O. 2013. *Implementing Value Capture in Latin America, Policy Focus Report*. Cambridge, MA: Lincoln Institute of Land Policy.

Suzuki, Hiroaki, Robert Cervero, and Kanako Iuchi. 2013. *Transforming Cities with Transit: Transit and Land-Use Integration for Sustainable Urban Development*. Washington, DC: World Bank.

UN-Habitat (United Nations Human Settlements Program). 2013. *The State of the World's Cities 2012/2013: Prosperity of Cities*. New York: Routledge.

UN Department of Economic and Social Affairs. 2014. *World Urbanization Prospects: the 2014 Revision Highlights*. New York.

PART I

Introduction

CHAPTER 1

Development-Based Land Value Capture for Financing Transit-Oriented Development

As cities in developing countries expand rapidly, their sprawl brings traffic congestion, air pollution, greenhouse gas emissions, poor use of energy and time, and socially unequal accessibility. Many of them have therefore turned to transit systems, yet costs of investment, as well as of operation and maintenance (O&M), are high and often beyond their fiscal means, even though per capita economic costs of transit may be lower than that of private cars. And so fiscal constraints have boosted interest in new sources of revenue, including "capturing" the increase in land value created by investing in transit systems through, for example, development-based land value capture (LVC). This approach seems to have strong potential, not only to raise funds for investing in transit, but also to guide sustainable urban development, leveraging synergies with transit-oriented development (TOD).

The objective of this book is to provide these cities with strategies and methods for applying development-based LVC for transit and TOD-related investments, based on lessons learned primarily from the world-class transit systems of Hong Kong SAR, China, and Tokyo and from other cities in developed and developing countries alike.

Car-Dependent Urban Development in the Developing World

The 21st century is the century of cities. More than half the world's people, or 54 percent of the world's population (UN Department of Economic and Social Affairs 2014), reside in urban areas, and 7 of every 10 people will live in cities by 2050, with about 90 percent of the growth in developing countries (UN-Habitat 2013). The urban areas in developing countries newly built in 2000–30 will equal the total built-up urban area worldwide in 2000 (Angel, Sheppard, and Civco 2005).

Cities globally generate about 75 percent of gross domestic product (World Bank 2009), but while urbanization is an engine of growth, it also has socioeconomic and environmental costs. For example, cities globally consume about 67 percent of energy and account for about 70 percent of greenhouse gas emissions.[1] Due to the rapid urban population increase, one-third of urbanites are living in slums (UN-Habitat 2010); their number is projected to hit 2 billion by 2025 (UN-Habitat 2003).

The problems of urbanization caused by car-dependent urban development or "urban sprawl"—such as congestion, air pollution, greenhouse gas emissions, lengthy commutes, and socially unequal access to various urban services—are mounting in the developing world's fast-growing cities. Enrique Peñalosa, former mayor of Bogotá, Colombia, has said that "Transport differs from other problems developing societies face, because it gets worse rather than better with economic development" (Peñalosa 2002). Essentially, motorization in developing countries accelerates with economic growth—as wealth increases, people shift from walking to bicycling to riding motorbikes and to driving cars. By 2050, China is projected to have 900 million motor vehicles, or more than the total number in the world a few years ago (Fulton and Cazzola 2008).

Recognizing the problems of car-dependent urban development, many cities in developing countries have started to develop mass transit systems such as bus rapid transit (BRT), light railways, and metrorail. In particular, the BRT approach first applied in Curitiba, Brazil, is gaining popularity among many secondary cities in the developing world due to its relatively low cost and short period of construction relative to rail transit. However, although BRT's capital costs are a fraction of rail transit's, they are still a financial burden for many cities. For example, after the success of TransMilenio BRT in Bogotá, the Colombian government supported the construction of BRTs in several secondary cities such as Barranquilla, Cali, and Cartagena, subsidizing 70 percent of the capital costs. Most cities cannot, however, cover BRTs' O&M costs simply with fare-box receipts. Policymakers where the majority of urbanites are poor have little room for cost recovery, as seen in the 2013 unrest in São Paulo and Rio de Janeiro in Brazil, which was triggered by the government's decision to increase transit fares. They also have little capacity to subsidize transit costs due to other funding demands.

As these cities continue to grow, the next transit systems, such as metros and suburban railways, which are extremely capital intensive, need to meet ever-increasing traffic demand.[2] While comprehensive data on worldwide metro construction costs are scarce, metro construction costs seem to range from $43 million a kilometer (Seoul Subway Line 9) to $600 million a kilometer (Singapore Thomson MRT Line).[3] And beyond these costs are high O&M costs, often exceeding cities' fiscal means. Transit investment requires long-term financing, but the financing schemes are rarely available in developing countries.

These constraints have stimulated interest in new revenue sources, including capturing the increase in land value created by transit investment. In fact, a few mega- and large cities in Asia such as Hong Kong SAR, China; the Tokyo metropolitan area; the Osaka-Kobe metropolitan areas; and Singapore have either fully or partly financed transit investment costs (and sometimes some O&M costs) by capturing the land value increase attributable to transit investment in corridor precincts or station areas (or both) for a long time (Murakami 2012; Cervero and Murakami 2009; Cervero 1998).

Development-Based LVC as a Strategic Financing and Planning Apparatus for Transit and TOD-Related Investments

LVC is defined in this book as a public financing method by which governments[4]:

- Trigger an increase in land values via regulatory decisions, such as a change in land use or floor area ratio (FAR), or infrastructure investments, such as transit.
- Institute a process to share this land value increment by capturing part or all of the change.
- Use LVC proceeds to finance infrastructure investments, such as transit and TOD-related investment (box 1.1); fund any other improvements required to offset impacts related to the changes, such as densification; and implement public policies to promote social equity, such as provision of affordable housing to alleviate shortages and offset potential gentrification.

LVC instruments vary widely and have been applied by local governments and related agencies in different parts of the world. They can be classified into two major types: tax- or fee-based and nontax- or nonfee-based—what we call "development-based LVC."

Tax- or fee-based instruments capture land value increases through, for example, property taxes, betterment charges, special assessments, and tax increment financing. In contrast, development-based LVC instruments capture these increments through land transactions such as selling or leasing land, development rights, and air rights; making land readjustments; and redeveloping urban areas. (More complete definitions of some LVC instruments are in chapter 2.)

Development-based LVC has the following advantages over tax- or fee-based LVC in financing transit and TOD-related investments:

- It has greater potential to finance capital-intensive transit or TOD-related investments without major fiscal distortions or public opposition to additional taxes or fees.
- It can generate not only direct revenues from land value increases attributed to transit investments but also more sustainable long-term revenues from properties (such as retail shops, leisure facilities, parking, and residential buildings to be developed around station areas) and increased transit ridership due to TOD.

Box 1.1 What is transit-oriented development?

Transit-oriented development (TOD) has two main characteristics:

- Proximity to and a functional relationship with transit stations and terminals, with service provision by high-quality public transit (such as metro and bus rapid transit).
- Compact, dense, mixed-use buildings and neighborhoods that are designed to encourage walking, cycling, and use of public transit by residents, employees, shoppers, and visitors.

The ingredients of successful TOD include strategic (macro-) and design (micro-) elements such as a strong development climate and master plans for multiuse, high-intensity developments supported by implementation plans.

They also include investments that promote:

- Easy and direct pedestrian, bicycle, and public transit access (figure B1.1.1)
- Good signage and a pleasant environment to attract substantial pedestrian flows
- Substantial regional accessibility to major job and activity centers
- Short, direct connections between transport modes and transit facilities
- Bicycle lanes and parking facilities that feed stations
- Attractive facilities that are well integrated with the surroundings (such as public spaces and street furniture)
- Safe and secure designs, including adequate lighting
- Effective parking management around stations
- Environmentally friendly technology, such as shared fleets of alternative (electric) vehicles in neighborhoods

Figure B1.1.1 **Key features of the eco-block concept**

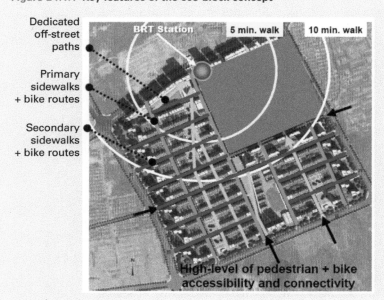

Source: Fraker 2009.
Note: BRT = bus rapid transit. The eco-block concept maximizes pedestrian access to transit stations. It is illustrated here using a location in China.

- Taxpayers often contest the coverage and amount of tax- or fee-based LVC instruments because the definition of benefits created by public intervention is often vague, the accuracy of the estimated increment is often challenged, and calculation methods are not well defined. As development-based LVC involves transactions of land, development rights, or air rights whose values have risen due to public investment or regulatory change, it establishes a clearer linkage between value creation and capture. Also, under development-based LVC the land value increment is calculated from a method that the stakeholders have agreed on consensually.
- It has a much better chance of administratively working well in places with inadequate property taxes (for example, outdated cadasters or weak value assessment capacity), as in most cities in developing countries.

Governments can explore development-based LVC not only for infrastructure financing but also for urban planning and public policy. Ideally, it should promote cities' economic competitiveness, environmental sustainability, and social equity:

- By changing land use regulations (by, for example, granting higher FARs and converting single land use into mixed land use), governments can develop articulated densities in station areas for diverse uses while increasing development-based LVC revenues (as higher FARs and mixed land use generally raise property values).
- By using development-based LVC revenues for TOD investments in station areas (such as parks, street lights, bike lanes, and pedestrian sidewalks), governments, transit agencies, developers, landowners, and communities can jointly develop efficient, attractive, and safe public places in TOD areas. Development of such prime public spaces, in turn, increases property values in TOD areas.
- In exchange for bonus FARs or other regulatory incentives, governments can require developers to provide social facilities, such as affordable housing units, daycare centers, and green spaces.

The authors are not denying the usefulness of tax- or fee-based LVC, as it has its own advantages. For instance, the revenues generated from property taxes can be sustainable, as collection does not deplete finite land resources. Moreover, using one category of LVC does not preclude using another.

With a range of objectives, regulative and administrative feasibility, and political acceptability of public infrastructure finance, these LVC instruments can be applied separately, or together, to suit countries' and cities' own conditions.

Objectives, Methods, and Readership

This book is intended to extend the authors' publication "Transforming Cities with Transit: Transit and Land Use Integration for Sustainable Urban

Development" (Suzuki, Cervero, and Iuchi 2013). In that publication, the authors concluded that integrating transit and land use—which can be achieved through a combination of TOD and LVC—is one of the most important strategic initiatives for developing more sustainable urban development. Thus, this book revisits LVC as a powerful financing and planning apparatus to promote such development, leveraging synergies between transit and TOD-related investments.

A more specific objective of this book is to provide cities in developing countries with strategies and practical methods for adapting development-based LVC, based on the experiences of Hong Kong SAR, China, and the Tokyo metropolitan area, as well as other cities in developed and developing countries. While the authors analyzed mainly metros, development-based LVC can be applied to different types of "fixed-guideway transit" (BRT, light railways, monorail, metro, urban rail), even though their economic and financial impacts differ by type: larger and nonreversible transit investments tend to have higher impacts.[5] Given the wide range of conditions of developing countries' cities, this book does not aim to generate a single standard model but rather to identify key enabling factors for development-based LVC adaptation, to introduce these to policymakers and practitioners, and then to encourage them to develop their own tailor-made development-based LVC schemes.

This study combined secondary source data and information review with in-depth field research on case study cities and projects. It first reviewed the experiences of development-based LVC mechanisms in transit investments in Hong Kong SAR, China, and the Tokyo metropolitan area, both of which are very good models for developing countries. Both areas have a long history of applying development-based LVC as a strategic financial and planning apparatus for large-scale transit and TOD-related investments. The Hong Kong SAR, China, case represents a development-based LVC mechanism under state leasehold, the Tokyo case under market freehold. The research also reviewed developed-country cities in other continents—New York City and Washington, DC, in the United States and London in the United Kingdom. Looking at several transit investment projects (including station areas funded under development-based LVC), the study analyzed historical and socioeconomic backgrounds, urban context, legal and regulatory systems (including planning systems and institutional framework and capacity), financial mechanisms, methods of LVC, and individual project cases.

Second, to make the recommendations relevant to realities in developing countries, the study investigated three transit project cases—Nanchang in China and Delhi and Hyderabad in India—using the same research framework applied to the cities in developed countries (to the extent possible). Background papers on the case cities were prepared by national consultants, except for Nanchang, China, due to availability of data and information collected for the World Bank's lending operations.

These two developing countries are large, rapidly growing middle-income countries with sizable transit investments. China has a state lease-hold system, India a market freehold system. Nanchang is applying a development-based LVC scheme for its new metro system, with financial and technical support from the World Bank. Two cities in India have also used development-based LVC, learning from the experiences of Hong Kong SAR, China, and Tokyo. The capital city, Delhi, partly financed its metro system using development-based LVC, but its metro agency has faced regulatory and institutional constraints in implementing it even with strong backing from the national government. Hyderabad is constructing new metro lines under public-private partnerships in which development-based LVC is important.

São Paulo, Brazil, was also studied, because of high potential for applying an innovative scheme of air rights sales, called CEPACs (Certificates of Additional Construction Potential), to transit and TOD-related investments, even if CEPACs have rarely been applied to these investments so far.

In selecting all these case studies, the authors also considered the demands of the World Bank's operational staff, as they hope that this book will contribute to applying development-based LVC to transit and TOD-related investments in their client countries.

The concluding sections of the chapters mostly highlight and distill the key findings and lessons learned for policymakers, planners, and practitioners.

This book should interest a wide and diverse readership, including mayors, city council members, national and local policymakers, urban and transportation planners, transit agency officials, developers, local financiers and investors, development financial institutions, and others involved in transit and TOD-related projects in rapidly growing and motorizing cities in the developing world.

Development Finance Context

Tax- or fee-based LVC instruments have already been well explained in many academic papers and government reports.[6] A few researchers have documented development-based LVC cases, but the information remains scattered and has not been evaluated within a coherent framework focusing on applying it to transit-related investments, and even less so to fast-growing cities in developing countries. Further, international development financial institutions (DFIs) like the World Bank have not yet seriously explored the international transfer of development-based LVC techniques across cities in developing countries, which are making sizable transit investments. Increasing demand for transit investments in DFIs' operations provides excellent opportunities to help municipalities and transit companies in developing countries apply development-based LVC to their transit and TOD-related projects, to leverage DFIs' financial support.

Structure of the Book

This book is divided into four parts: Overview; Part One—Introduction (chapters 1 and 2); Part Two—Lessons Learned from Global Development-Based Land Value Capture Practices (chapters 3, 4, and 5); and Part Three—Emerging Development-Based Land Value Capture Practices in Developing Countries (chapters 6, 7, and 8).

Major findings and recommendations are synthesized in the Overview. It presents key findings of the study and enabling factors for developing-country cities to establish their own development-based LVC schemes. After this chapter, chapter 2 presents the theory of transit-induced land capitalization and various LVC instruments used in different parts of the world.

In Part Two, chapter 3 describes the Rail Plus Property program of MTR Corporation Limited in Hong Kong SAR, China, as a successful development-based LVC practice under state leasehold. Chapter 4 introduces inclusive and diverse schemes involving multiple stakeholders in the Tokyo metropolitan area as an example of successful development-based LVC practices under market freehold. Chapter 5 highlights such practices in the United States—New York City and Washington, DC—and in the United Kingdom—London.

In Part Three, chapter 6 reviews development-based LVC practices associated with Nanchang's new metro line. Chapter 7 analyzes the institutional and regulatory frameworks that affect the performance of LVC schemes in metro projects in Delhi and Hyderabad, India. Chapter 8 discusses the application of air rights sales in São Paulo, Brazil, highlighting innovations and challenges and their potential for financing transit and TOD-related projects.

Notes

1. The data vary depending on sources and methodologies. These are from the International Energy Agency.
2. Upgrading the transit system (such as BRT to metro on the same route) does not easily occur because of problems of "lock in"—once a technology is adopted, it is hard to change it due to institutional resistance and political inertia, beyond a weak fiscal capacity.
3. According to a report on selected metro projects posted on June 3, 2013, to the Pedestrian Observation website (http://pedestrianobservations .wordpress.com/2013/06/03/comparative-subway-construction-costs -revised/).
4. However, governments as well as their public transport agencies undertake LVC. In a still wider definition of LVC, public and private transit agencies can recoup the land value increase created by their transit investments regardless of ownership.

5. In general, the economic and financial impacts of metro investment are higher than those of BRT as BRT lines are reversible.

6. See, for example, "Tax Increment Financing: A Tool for Local Economic Development" (Dye and Merriman 2006); "Infrastructure Financing Options for Transit-Oriented Development" (U.S. Environmental Protection Agency 2013); and "Unlocking Land Values to Finance Urban Infrastructure" (Peterson 2009).

References

Angel, Shlomo, Stephen C. Sheppard, and Daniel L. Civco. 2005. *The Dynamics of Global Urban Expansion.* Washington, DC: World Bank.

Cervero, Robert. 1998. *The Transit Metropolis: A Global Inquiry.* Washington, DC: Island Press.

Cervero, Robert, and Jin Murakami. 2009. "Rail and Property Development in Hong Kong: Experiences and Extensions." *Urban Studies* 46 (10): 2019–43.

Dye, Richard F., and David F. Merriman. 2006. "Tax Increment Financing: A Tool for Local Economic Development." *Lincoln Institute of Land Policy Land Lines* 18 (1): 2–7.

Fraker, Harrison. 2009. "Sustainable Neighborhood 'Eco-Blocs' in China: Qingdao Sustainable Neighborhood." http://www.slideshare.net/geoff848/harrison-fraker-ecoblocks.

Fulton, Lew, and Pierpaulo Cazzola. 2008. "Transport, Energy, and CO_2 in Asia: Where Are We Going and How Do We Change It?" Paper presented at "The Better Air Quality 2008 Workshop," Bangkok, Thailand, November 12.

Murakami, Jin. 2012. "Transit Value Capture: New Town Codevelopment Models and Land Market Updates in Tokyo and Hong Kong." In *Value Capture and Land Policies*, edited by Gregory K. Ingram and Yu-Hung Hong, 285–320. Cambridge, MA: Lincoln Institute of Land Policy.

Peñalosa, Enrique. 2002. "The Role of Transport in Urban Development Policy." In *Sustainable Transport: A Sourcebook for Policy-Makers in Developing Cities.* Eschborn, Germany: Deutsche Gesellschaft für Internationale Zusammenarbeit (GIZ).

Peterson, George E. 2009. *Unlocking Land Values to Finance Urban Infrastructure.* Washington, DC: World Bank. www.ppiaf.org/sites/ppiaf.org/files/publication/Trends%20Policy%20Options-7-Unlocking%20Land%20Values%20-GPeterson.pdf.

Suzuki, Hiroaki, Robert Cervero, and Kanako Iuchi. 2013. *Transforming Cities with Transit: Transit and Land-Use Integration for Sustainable Urban Development.* Washington, DC: World Bank.

UN Department of Economic and Social Affairs. 2014. *World Urbanization Prospects: the 2014 Revision Highlights*. New York.

UN-Habitat (United Nations Human Settlements Program). 2003. *The Challenge of the Slums: Global Report on Human Settlements 2003*. London: Earthscan Publications.

————. 2010. *The State of the World's Cities 2010/2011: Bridging the Urban Divide*. London: Earthscan Publications.

————. 2013. *The State of the World's Cities 2012/2013: Prosperity of Cities*. New York: Routledge.

U.S. Environmental Protection Agency. 2013. *Infrastructure Financing Options for Transit-Oriented Development*. Washington, DC: U.S. Environmental Protection Agency. www.epa.gov/dced/infra_financing.htm.

World Bank. 2009. *The World Bank Urban and Local Government Strategy*. Washington, DC: World Bank.

CHAPTER 2

Theory of Land Value Capture and Its Instruments

*Many cities around the world are facing fiscal stress. One perennial prob-
lem is the disagreement between governments and their citizens on the taxes
and fees the latter should pay for public services. Attempts by governments
to raise them to cover the costs of public infrastructure and local services
often face public opposition, as in Brazil in 2013. Fiscal challenges have
stimulated governments' interest in nontax or nonfee revenue sources, such
as capture of land value increments created by public infrastructure investments to defray the costs of providing public services. Tapping into publicly
created land value increment can be an efficient way to allocate resources
by exploiting positive externalities—or windfalls. It is also rational because
landholders who have capital gains from these windfalls should partly
cover public costs under the "beneficiary pays" principle.*

*This chapter introduces the theory of land value capture (LVC), particu-
larly that of transit-induced land capitalization and associated empirical
evidence. Within the transit finance framework, LVC hinges on accessibility and agglomeration benefits of transit infrastructure investment along
with transit-oriented development (TOD), which in turn get capitalized
into land prices. Since TOD can also boost such benefits, governments and
transit agencies could use some of the LVC-generated revenue for TOD-
related investments, ideally increasing overall LVC-related revenues. This
chapter also presents the features of major LVC instruments, some of which
are further discussed in the case studies in later chapters.*

Rationale for Land Value Capture (LVC)

LVC is an idea dating back to David Ricardo (1821) and to Henry George
(1879). It is founded on the principle that land value is determined not only

by its intrinsic value and private investment but also by other external factors including changes in land use regulations, public investment in infrastructure and local services, and general population and economic growth (figure 2.1). There seems to be a consensus among scholars and development institutions like the United Nations (UN 1976) that "the beneficiaries of the public investments or the public decisions that increase their land values should partly cover public investment costs or return their benefit to the public."

Transit-Induced Land Capitalization

LVC hinges on land price increases around transit stations or along transit corridors. Yet transit investment alone does not always cause land price appreciation. LVC is feasible only if external economic benefits of transit investment are capitalized into nearby land under prevailing market conditions and transit-supportive public policies. This section, therefore, introduces the theory of transit-induced land capitalization, its empirical evidence, and factors other than transit investment that may influence the land values of the transit station areas or corridors.

Figure 2.1 Land values and their attribution

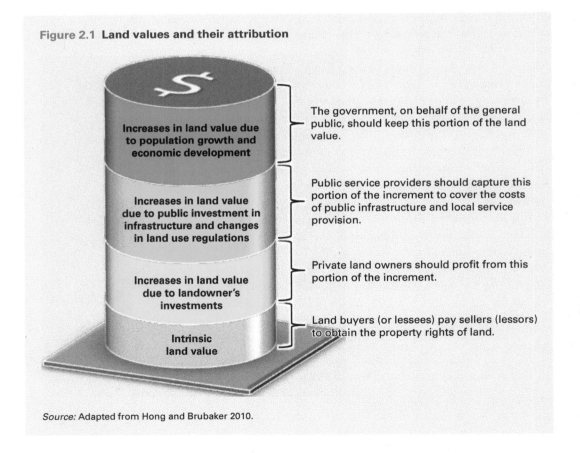

Increases in land value due to population growth and economic development

The government, on behalf of the general public, should keep this portion of the land value.

Increases in land value due to public investment in infrastructure and changes in land use regulations

Public service providers should capture this portion of the increment to cover the costs of public infrastructure and local service provision.

Increases in land value due to landowner's investments

Private land owners should profit from this portion of the increment.

Intrinsic land value

Land buyers (or lessees) pay sellers (lessors) to obtain the property rights of land.

Source: Adapted from Hong and Brubaker 2010.

Theory of Transit-Induced Land Capitalization

The impact of transport investment on land value[1] has long been debated, due in large part to the complex mechanism of transit-induced capitalization under differing urban conditions. Conceptually, accessibility and productivity increases are key external economic gains from transport investment, which are capitalized into land values near transit facilities.

Accessibility benefits. Accessibility can be defined as the ability to reach economic resources and social opportunities (Hansen 1959; Ingram 1971; Wachs and Kumagai 1973). This means that the degree of access is determined by a combination of travel congestion and activity location in cities and regions. Under this definition, contemporary urban planning attempts to coordinate locations between activities for proximity, whereas conventional transport engineering and economics tend to maximize speeds between activities for mobility (Levine and others 2012; Black, Paez, and Suthanaya 2002). The type of activities depends on each individual, household, or firm, so accessibility is often addressed from homes to workplaces, schools, shopping, and leisure sites. All other things equal, households and businesses prefer to locate their houses, shops, offices, and factories with wider travel "sheds" around higher accessibility nodes of urban and regional transport networks. These typically include transit stations, highway interchanges, and airport terminals in cities' key locations (Giuliano 2004). Without negative externalities from transport facilities (such as congestion, noise, and air pollution), willingness to pay for higher accessibility locations could be revealed, as development density/land value increases in the proximity of nodes or development density/land price gradients from nodes in a bid-rent curve. In this sense accessibility can be regarded as a surrogate for measuring external economic benefits of transport investment (Banister and Berechman 2000).

Agglomeration benefits. In recent years, agglomeration benefits have been increasingly discussed in academic and policy circles (for example, Cervero 1995; Cervero, Aschauer, and Cambridge Systematic Inc. 1998; Chatman and Noland 2011; Graham 2007; UK Department for Transport 2005), though conceptually it is more elusive and indirect than accessibility benefits, and its mechanism is yet to be fully comprehended. Agglomeration economies generally address increases in economic productivity of, singly or combined, workers, firms, or cities, stemming from higher densities of economic and social activities that can be explained by locational advantages such as sharing production inputs, sharing infrastructure, sharing consumer services and amenities, matching labor pools to jobs, matching firms in production processes, and capturing knowledge spillovers through face-to-face communication. Some of these explanations may be strongly related to changes in accessibility, though others may not (Cervero, Aschauer, and Cambridge Systematic Inc. 1998; Chatman and Noland 2011). The net agglomeration benefit of transport investment alone is often questionable because of the double counting issue with cost-benefit analysis,[2] which we do not deeply investigate in this book. Our work refers to the synergistic agglomeration benefit of transit investment along with the provision of TOD-related infrastructure, which can be seen as transit-induced land capitalization beyond accessibility benefits.

Empirical Evidence for Transit-Induced Land Capitalization

Much of the last few decades' literature draws on North American (especially U.S.) case studies (table 2.1). Many papers identified land premiums caused by transit investment in station areas (Lari and others 2009; Dunphy and others 2004; Smith and Gihring 2006; and other authors in table 2.1). However, researchers sometimes found a weak correlation between transit and land value, or even inverse correlations (Gatzlaff and Smith 1993; Medda 2011).

This variance is due partly to methodological differences and quality of data, but it could be more fundamentally explained as multiple trends in contemporary urbanization. One is the localization of the transit investment impact: research in U.S. and European cities indicates that transit investment impacts on land values have become more localized (microgeographic) as cities and transport networks developed well. In particular, the highest impact can be found downtown (where knowledge- and service-based business entities, such as finance and insurance, real estate, and advanced business services, concentrate around high-accessibility transit facilities) rather than in suburban areas' bedroom communities.

Yet some argue that local development effects of transit investment are likely to be redistributive rather than generative within cities and regions, though the net economic impacts of business relocation are not a zero-sum game for society as a whole (Cervero, Aschauer, and Cambridge Systematic Inc. 1998; Weisbrod and Weisbrod 1997; Murakami 2010). Another important finding is that the impact of transit investment on land value could be synergistic with TOD infrastructure provisions and supportive public policies under favorable market conditions (Duncan 2011; Cervero and Murakami 2009).

Table 2.1 Summary of empirical findings of transit-induced land value capitalization

Author (date)	Location (United States unless otherwise flagged)	Dataset	Findings
Armstrong and Rodriguez (2006)	Eastern Massachusetts	1,860 SFR	Properties within ~1/2 mile of commuter rail sell for a ~10% premium; each additional minute driving distance from the station associated with a 1.6% decline in price
Benjamin and Sirmans (1996)	Washington, DC	250 rent observations (July 1992) from 81 apartment complexes	Rent decreased 2.4–2.6% per tenth of a mile distance from the metro station

Table 2.1 Summary of empirical findings of transit-induced land value capitalization *(continued)*

Author (date)	Location (United States unless otherwise flagged)	Dataset	Findings
Bowes and Ihlanfeldt (2001)	Atlanta, GA	SFR sales from Atlanta region, 1991–94	More than a quarter mile from station: negative effects primarily restricted to low-income neighborhoods; positive direct effects quarter to three miles of station
Cervero and Duncan (2002)	Santa Clara County, CA	Metroscan* data from 1998–99; 1,197 observations	23% capitalization for typical commercial parcels near a light rail transit stop; 120%+ for commercial land in a business district within quarter of a mile of a commuter rail station
Cervero (1994)	Washington, DC, and Atlanta, GA	Five rail stations in both cities, 1978–89	Office rents near stations increased; joint developments added $3+/gross square foot to annual rents
Chen and others (1998)	Portland, OR	1992–94	LR has a positive effect (accessibility) and negative effect (nuisance) on SFR values; at 100 meters from stations, each additional meter results in $32.20 reduction in average home price
Dewees (1976)	Toronto, Canada	Sale prices of residential properties and description characteristics	$2,370 premium per hour of travel time saved for sites within 20 minutes (walking) of Bloor St.
Dueker and Bianco (1999)	Portland, OR	Pre-/post-1980 and 1990 (LR east-side opening in 1986)	Property value declines $1,593 every 200 feet from station
Fejarang (1994)	Los Angeles, CA	1980–90	$31/square foot premium for properties within quarter of a mile of station
Grass (1992)	Washington, DC	Control and impact neighborhoods, 1970–80	Significant direct relationship between metro opening and residential properties; increase around station area
Gatzlaff and Smith (1993)	Miami, FL	Property sales, 1971–90 (912 observations)	Weak correlation between rail development and housing values; impact does not vary upon property distance from station but does vary across neighborhood types
Gu and Zheng (2008)	Beijing, China	New residential projects within 4 kilometers of No. 13; January 1999–September 2006	Housing prices higher by nearly 20% within 1,000 meters; encourages development intensity around stations

(continued next page)

Table 2.1 Summary of empirical findings of transit-induced land value capitalization *(continued)*

Author (date)	Location (United States unless otherwise flagged)	Dataset	Findings
Hess and Almeida (2007)	Buffalo, NY	2002 assessed value of properties (City of Buffalo, 1990–2000)	Average residential property values increased by an average of $2.31 for every foot closer to a rail station (geographic straight line) and $0.99 (network distance); homes within quarter of a mile of LR station can earn $1,300–$3,000 premium
Knaap and others (2001)	Washington County, OR	All sale transactions of vacant residential parcels within urban growth boundary, January 1992–August 1996 (1,537 observations)	Plans had positive effects on land values in proposed station areas; discouraged low-density housing, encouraged high-density TOD
Landis and others (1995)	San Diego, CA	Five City Study (California)	$272 increase in home sale price for every 100 meters closer to LR station; no effect for commercial properties
Landis and others (1995)	San Francisco, CA	Five City Study (California)	$51,000 sale discount for houses within 300 meters of train tracks
Lewis-Workman and Brod (1997)	Portland, OR; San Francisco, CA; New York	Portland: property tax rolls, 1995 cross sections; San Francisco: home sale prices 1.6 kilometer radius of station, 1984–96 sales in regression; New York: 18 years of sale data	Portland: $2.49 increase for every meter closer to rail, within 762–1,609 meters to transit; $760 (average) premium for homes 305 meters closer to transit; San Francisco: nonuser benefits account for 50% of observed premium, 1% increase in distance from Bay Area Rapid Transit reduces home prices by 0.22%; New York: $75 decline in home price for every meter from subway stations, $37,000 average home premium within subway station areas (as opposed to outside)
Lin and Hwang (2004)	Taipei, Taiwan, China	1993–95 (before subway); 1997–99 (after subway)	Subway opening significantly influences hedonic prices of floor space, building age, and distance from public facilities; second influence of system opening on hedonic price varies significantly according to different submarkets such as subway construction, location in city, position of property relative to subway stations, land use, zoning, and building type

(continued next page)

Table 2.1 Summary of empirical findings of transit-induced land value capitalization *(continued)*

Author (date)	Location (United States unless otherwise flagged)	Dataset	Findings
Nelson (1992)	Atlanta, GA	Office commercial property sold in study area, 1980s–94 (30 sales)	Negative effect on home values in high-income areas, positive in lower; premium on property values in low-income areas ($0.96 per foot distance to station)
Voith (1991)	Philadelphia, PA	1970–88	7.5–8.0% price premium for SFR with access to rail
Weinberger (2001)	Santa Clara County, CA	Lease transactions, 1984–2000 (3,701 records)	Higher lease rate for properties within 0.8 kilometers of a rail station
Yankaya (2004)	Izmir, Turkey (subway)	December 2003–March 2004 (360 observations)	Proximity to subway stations cause higher property values due to accessibility and commuting reduction

Source: Adapted from Lari and others 2009.
Note: LR = light rail; SFR = single family residential property; TOD = transit-oriented development.
* Metroscan data encompass all real estate transactions that are recorded in country assessor offices.

Other Factors

Factors other than transit investment may influence land values in transit station areas or corridors, categorized under four heads, as now discussed. Those adapting LVC for transit and TOD-related investment financing should also consider these factors.

Macro Factors

- Population and economic growth: Both areas of growth are fundamental to creating demand for land with accessibility and agglomeration benefits. In the metropolitan context, we should observe both regional trends (the metropolitan area as a whole) and local trends (specific locations), as not all areas experience the same growth rate. These factors include different stages of economic development (such as deindustrialization, shifting from manufacturing to knowledge- and service-based industries) and emerging demographic patterns (such as international migration and population aging).
- Degree and pattern of urbanization: These are important to the potential impact of path-dependency, which may limit land value appreciation.
- Real estate: Transit can only enhance land values where market demand exists. Similar to population and economic growth, real estate has submarkets, according to differing uses (shops, offices, residential-single detached houses, apartments/condominiums, and so on) and different locations, and transit investment influences each submarket differently.

- Developing countries: Many cities, particularly in middle-income developing countries, have favorable macro conditions (strong economic growth and rapid population increase), leading to strong demand for land in prime locations with good accessibility.

Regulatory and Institutional Factors

- Land administration and availability of developable land (such as under leasehold or freehold systems).
- Regulations: Government planning regulations such as a floor area ratio limit and land use also influence land values. As accessibility and agglomeration benefits are appreciated differently by each real estate submarket, the government's decision on land use also influences land values in transit station areas. Regulations on public parking supply and pricing also affect accessibility in transit station areas.
- Institutions: Competent local governments and transit agencies with strong planning capacity and real estate knowledge are critical to maximize land values with private developers. This factor includes the degree of privatization or private participation in transit investments, TODs, and LVC implementations.
- Developing countries: Few governments and transit agencies have either adequate regulatory frameworks or institutional capacity, and both are typically required to implement transit and TOD-related investments with LVC.

Transit Technologies, Networks, Alternatives, and Nuisance Factors

- Technologies: Heavy or metro rail usually has a bigger impact on land values than light rail or bus rapid transit as it provides greater accessibility benefits due to higher speeds and larger transit capacity than light rail or bus rapid transit (which often shares road space with automobiles).
- Networks: Transit networks—including connectivity with other transport modes—are important for accessibility. Hence, the larger the network, the greater the accessibility benefits. For example, the accessibility benefits of the well-connected metro system with 304 kilometers of lines serving 285 stations in Tokyo is much higher than that of the Porto Alegre metro system in Brazil with 44 kilometers serving only 22 stations. However, the incremental accessibility impact of transit on land values will gradually diminish as the impact becomes saturated and more redistributive over the entire network as it expands.
- Alternatives: Transit impact on land values is less when transit catchment areas have access to other competing transport modes. For example, San Francisco's Bay Area Rapid Transit (BART) system had

a smaller impact than anticipated on land values in suburban station areas. Fewer residents than anticipated shifted from car to transit as the area had been served by a well-developed highway system long before BART's construction.

- Nuisance from transit: Transit often reduces the value of residential properties very close to transit stations or corridors because of, for example, air and noise pollution, which may override accessibility benefits. Commercial properties are less sensitive, and close proximity to stations or corridors is not a liability.
- Developing countries: Transit investment may have a greater impact on land value than in developed countries with a large stock of transport infrastructure, due to underinvestment in transport infrastructure despite increased congestion and motorization.

Local Socioeconomic and Market Factors

- Socioeconomic disparities: In some U.S. cities, residential land values in wealthy suburban neighborhoods have declined after transit construction. Many high-income residents or shop owners do not want transit-dependent people coming to their neighborhood, as their presence might increase the costs for onsite security or discourage more affluent shoppers.
- Developing countries: Socioeconomic and local market factors are path dependent and context sensitive. Social segregation and spatial divisions of labor markets within cities and regions are often emerging trends or potential concerns, which would shape transit-oriented or car-dependent trajectories at some point.

Nonlisted Factors

There are likely more factors influencing the degree of transit-induced land capitalization than these. For example, Knight and Trygg (1977) presented about 30 factors, including transit, that influence land-use impacts and their complex interactions. However, a similar analysis is beyond this book's scope.

Little research has been done on transit-induced land capitalization and its empirical findings in developing countries.[3] This may be due to the relatively short history of transit development and paucity of data. Similar to the U.S. empirical findings, the above transit-induced land capitalization theory cannot be applied to all situations in developing countries. In addition, many of these countries have even more difficult conditions, such as inadequate land registration and sizable illegal settlements. More in-depth research is thus needed, which would help developing-country policymakers and practitioners implement better transit and TOD-related investments, in combination with LVC schemes.

Situating LVC in Urban Transport Finance

Elucidating LVC instruments' similarities and differences may help those actors select the best combination of financial instruments for their situation.

The beneficiary pays principle applies to urban transport finance. Beneficiaries of transport improvements fall into three categories: the public, transport users, and property owners and developers (Lari and others 2009). Governments assign different financial instruments to recover capital investment and service costs according to the characteristic of benefits received by each group and the timing of these benefits (table 2.2). LVC is the financial instrument highlighted to recover costs from property owners or developers by capturing increased land value attributable to transport infrastructure investment (and related efforts). As the land value increase is realized at the end of transport infrastructure construction, LVC is suitable to recover capital investment costs.

To show the roles of LVC instruments for transit and TOD-related investments, we apply the above transport finance framework to transit and TOD-related investment finance (table 2.3).

Based on the beneficiary pays principle, governments and transit agencies should first recover their investment and operation and maintenance costs from transit fares as user fees. However, transit fares are regulated because of their public nature. Fares alone rarely allow transit agencies to fully recover their capital investment and operation and maintenance costs, as fares are usually set at lower than the full cost recovery level to mitigate the externalities created by car users and to keep transit fares affordable.

Table 2.2 Application of the beneficiary pays principle to urban transport finance

Beneficiary categories	Benefits of transport improvement	Financial instrument	Rationale for use	Cost recovery area[a]	
				Capital	Services
Public	Broad economic and social return, such as economic development and growth	Government's general fund	Broad economic growth provides the base for general taxation	A	A
Transport users	Reduced travel time and costs; improved travel comfort and enhanced safety	Direct or indirect user charges	Benefit attributed to the users of transport facilities	B	A
Property owners and developers (restricted nonusers)	Increased property values	Various value capture or development charges	Benefits are land value increase due to public investments for transport	A	B

Source: Adapted from Lari and others (2009).
a. A implies principal, B secondary.

Table 2.3 Beneficiaries of investments and key features of financial instruments

Beneficiaries and bearers	Types of instruments	Instruments	Investment to be funded		Delivered typically by	Cases studied
			Transit	TOD Infra.		
Public	Nonuser based general budget	General fund/tax	Y	Y	Government	
Polluters	Charges	Environmental fees	Y	Y	Government	
Car users	User-based fees	Fuel tax	Y	Y	Government	
		Car registration fees	Y	Y	Government	
		Parking fees	Y	Y	Government agencies	
		Toll	Y	Y	Government agencies	
Transit users		Fare	Y	N	Transit agencies	
Property owners	Tax- and fee-based LVC	Property tax	Y	Y	Government	
Property owners and developers		Betterment charges and special assessment	Y	Y	Government	
		Tax increment financing	Y	Y	Government	
	Charges	Exaction/impact fee	Y	Y	Government	
Property owners and developers	Development-based LVC	Air rights sales	Y	Y	Government	New York City, São Paulo
		Land sales	Y	Y	Government transit agencies	Tokyo, London
		Development rights leases	Y	Y	Government transit agencies	Hong Kong SAR, China; London; Nanchang; Delhi; Hyderabad
		Joint development	Y	Y	Government transit agencies and private sector	Washington, DC; Hong Kong SAR, China; Tokyo
		Land readjustment	Y	Y	Government transit agencies and private sector	Tokyo
		Urban redevelopment schemes	Y	Y	Government transit agencies and private sector	Tokyo

Note: LVC = land value capture; N = no; TOD = transit-oriented development; Y = yes. The table includes TOD under "supported investments," with the idea that governments and their private partners can increase development-based LVC revenues by financing TOD-related investments due to the higher land value appreciation in station areas.

Governments have to fill public transit deficits by providing capital or operational subsidies from their general budget, based on the justification that transit provides broad economic and social benefits.[4]

Governments also transfer the tax and fee revenues generated from car users or environment fees to mitigate the car-use externalities. But as they find it hard to fill their deficits (given their fiscal constraints), they have looked to alternative sources, including development-based LVC, based on the beneficiary pays principle.

Types of LVC Instruments

Techniques similar to LVC have been practiced in many countries for a long time, some dating back to Roman times (Smolka 2013). The two major LVC categories are tax- and fee-based LVC and development-based LVC.

Tax- and Fee-Based LVC Instruments

Land and property tax. The oldest and most common form of a tax-based LVC instrument is land and property taxation. Most of these taxes are levied on the estimated value of land or of land and buildings combined. The distinction between solely taxing land and levying on land and buildings together has significant efficiency underpinnings. In theory, a land tax encourages high-density development, enhancing land use efficiency. Because urban land supply is relatively inelastic in the short run, taxing land will not alter the amount available for development but will take away the unearned land rent retained by landowners. Hence, many practitioners and analysts view land tax as a fiscal instrument that creates the least amount of distortions (or deadweight losses) to the market. Some have proposed a split-rate property tax that taxes land more heavily than buildings (England 2003). Despite these recommendations, the empirical evidence of the practicality and effectiveness of land or split-rate property tax is mixed (Dye and England 2011).

Most developed countries have property taxes, and their weight in municipal budgets varies greatly. In some Organisation for Economic Cooperation and Development countries like the United States, United Kingdom, and Japan, local governments rely heavily on property taxes to fund public expenditure—16–25 percent of local revenue comes from them. In many continental European cities, however, sales or value-added tax is far more important.

Property taxes in developing countries are not as advanced (Smoke 2008), partly because they require a good cadastral system and huge financial commitments to establish a computer system and training for tax assessment and enforcement. Most important, the notion of paying a property tax when property rights in some countries are not yet well defined presents a major challenge (Hong 2013). It is also because many local governments in developing countries still rely on central transfers to finance local spending, giving officials little incentive to develop local fiscal bases (Bahl 2008). That said, many decentralization programs have led local governments to search for their own revenue sources.

Betterment charges and special assessments. These were introduced in the 1970s as a major LVC instrument in the United States and United Kingdom. For betterment charges, payments could be collected ex post, that is, after the construction of public infrastructure, or ex ante, as with, in Brazil, Certificates of Additional Construction Potential (see chapter 8). Betterment charges and special assessments are basically the same instrument—the term *special assessment* is used in the United States, while *betterment charges* or *levies* are used in other countries like the United Kingdom (or Colombia). By using this kind of surtax, governments attempt to require property owners who benefit directly from public investments to pay for their costs. Misczynski (2012) identifies the Mello-Roos Act in the United States as one such mechanism that has financed parks, open spaces, gymnasiums, swimming pools, landscaping, rail transit, and other public facilities. Special assessments allow tax-exempt status on government bonds to finance public services and infrastructure investments. Initial funding for the Los Angeles subway system came from special assessments on properties within a one-mile radius of downtown stations and a half-mile radius of other stations. This is considered to be LVC because public investment will increase property values.

The largest assessment district in the United States, encompassing nearly all of Los Angeles County and more than 2 million parcels, was created to fund parks and open space. The use of special assessments in California has not been problem-free, however. The rapid expansion of special assessment districts triggered the passage of Proposition 218 in 1996, which added new requirements for special assessments to the state's constitution. It called for a more rigorous definition of and distinction between special and general benefits generated by projects financed by special assessments.

Owing to the ambiguity of the language in Proposition 218, special assessments are now subject to a wide range of interpretations. In some situations, it is almost impossible for public officials to deploy this instrument because they cannot adequately define and distinguish the special and general benefits of their proposed projects. In other cases, when the distinction can be made explicitly, special assessment projects have renewed legitimacy. Misczynski (2012) predicts that it will take much time and many lawsuits to define the range of permissible uses of special assessments in California.

A similar instrument, betterment levies, has been used in other countries in an attempt to capture as much as 30–60 percent of land value gains attributable to public investment from property owners (Peterson 2009). Public resistance to these extra levies on top of existing property taxes has made implementation difficult. The major challenge is to estimate the land value increments with precision. For instance, estimates of land value created by the extension of the London Underground's Jubilee Line ranged from £300 million ($484 million) to £2.7 billion ($4.4 billion), according to the commission report.

Colombia has for a long time had a betterment levy, *contribucion de valorizacion* (valorization contribution), for infrastructure investment. The levy is usually charged in proportion to the total capital investment and operating costs at the early stages of investment. When construction is completed, the levy rate is reset in proportion to the land value increments. Between 1980 and 1990, public opposition, chronic underestimation of investment costs, and high administrative expenses reduced the share of *valorizacion* revenue in the local government budget from 15 percent to 5 percent (Peterson 2009, 62). Yet a more recent study by Borrero and others (2011) found that revenues from betterment levies in Bogotá had increased from 7.7 percent of property tax collections in 2003 to 60.3 percent in 2008.

Tax increment financing (TIF). This is another tax-based mechanism that originated in California, in 1951, to encourage redevelopment of blighted areas. It is essentially a surtax on properties within an area to be redeveloped by public investment financed by municipal bonds. After a municipality has declared a qualified area a TIF district, assessment values of all dwellings within the district are frozen. Any future change in the assessed tax base is subject to an extra tax on top of the existing property tax. TIF collections are earmarked for servicing and repaying the municipal bonds issued against such expected increases in tax revenue. In Illinois, more than 500 TIF districts have been created since the inception of the technique.

To the authors' knowledge, TIF is not widely used in developing countries, or the same name has not been used to describe similar LVC mechanisms outside the United States. This may be because TIF collections piggyback onto a property tax—an instrument not used effectively in developing countries for the reasons mentioned earlier.

A summing up. A general observation from practitioners and analysts of the tax- and fee-based instruments is that they lack a clear link between benefits and costs, which is particularly problematic for property taxation whose revenues are not necessarily tied to investment in infrastructure or social services for specific neighborhoods (or blocks) where the taxes are collected. This is one reason for their unpopularity. Although later instruments such as betterment levies and TIFs have tried to create a stronger cost-benefit link by defining more explicitly where revenues will be applied, there remains the problem of accurately estimating the cost of public goods provision. More important, in some cases, poor neighborhoods have challenged these practices on the grounds that the government provides public services only to areas where residents have the ability to pay taxes and fees. That said, tax- and fee-based LVC can still generate supplementary revenues to fund citywide infrastructure and social services.

Development-Based LVC Instruments

Development-based LVC approaches rely on one or more of public or private control over land and increment of land value by infrastructure investment, better site-level plans, and regulatory changes. The government, transit agency, or private investor will then capture the land value increment by either selling the serviced land or leasing the development or land use rights to other parties. They may invest directly in property development solely or in partnership with other parties. Being an investor or co-developer, the government, transit agency, or private investor can recoup some of the future increases in land value for further public infrastructure investment. As discussed in Part Two, Hong Kong SAR, China, and Tokyo have used this approach to finance the construction, operation, and maintenance costs of their urban rail transit systems. Some developing cities in China and India have also started to adapt development-based LVC instruments for their new metro systems, as introduced in Part Three.

Land sale or leasing. Governments can capture the land value increments created by public infrastructure investment or regulatory changes (such as floor area ratio and land use) by selling their public lands or lands acquired from private landowners to developers. The use of public land leasing to finance infrastructure investment has been extensively used in China (Peterson and Kaganova 2010). Rithmire (2013) argues that encouraging local governments to sell development rights to raise investment funds is a deliberate policy of the Chinese central government and an implicit strategy to encourage self-financing of local government expenditures. Unfortunately, the use of land lease revenue by local governments in China is sometimes unrestricted and not tied to any improvements of specific parcels of land (Anderson 2012). In addition, relying on leasing fees to finance municipal spending might create incentives for governments to convert rural land to urban use, thereby promoting sprawl in China. Lessees are required to pay the majority of the leasing fee up-front and sometimes an annual land rent through the term of the lease (Bourassa and Hong 2003).

Peterson (2009) states that lease revenues have been the primary source of highway infrastructure finance in the wealthier coastal provinces in China for the past 15–20 years. Yet this source of revenue has been exhausted, and municipalities must explore other means. Thus, for other municipalities that still depend on lease revenue to pay for local expenditures, governments should auction off land use rights instead of assigning them through negotiated contracts. This will ensure the transparency of the land leasing system and collect the highest possible leasehold charges through competitive bidding. Mandating the establishment of a land fund account in the municipal budget will help cities achieve this goal, with other fiscal reforms.

Land leasing is also practiced in India, as its public sector owns a lot of land. The Bandra-Kurla complex in India is a new business center in Mumbai that was created out of marshland by the Mumbai Metropolitan Development Authority (MMDA) in the 1990s. Covering 553 acres, the site has been enormously successful as a new business location, housing the Bombay Stock Exchange and the majority of bank headquarters. Initially, the MMDA developed the site and collected proceeds from developers in the form of annual rents and development fees. In 2003, it changed the system in response to the added responsibility of building infrastructure. In 2006 and 2007, the MMDA auctioned 80-year leases on 13 hectares of land, raising $1.2 billion (five times the amount of annual infrastructure investment by Mumbai's municipal authorities). The motivation for the switch to long-term land leasing was to fund ambitious infrastructure projects, including a new metro rail system and a 23-kilometer bridge spanning Mumbai's harbor (Peterson and Kaganova 2010; Peterson 2009).

Joint development. As the name indicates, this is well-coordinated development of transport facilities (such as a transit station) and adjacent private property between public agencies and developers. Private developers usually contribute to the development by constructing a facility (such as a station) or financing a part or all of the constructions costs. Joint development is a development-based LVC instrument practiced in the United States, Japan, and elsewhere. In the United States, the joint development program of the Washington Area Transit Authority (WMATA) is one of the most successful, even though its contribution to WMATA's annual operating revenues is small (less than 2 percent). According to WMATA: "Metro defines joint development as a creative program through which property interests owned and/or controlled by Metro are marketed to private developers with the objective of developing transit-oriented projects."[5]

Air rights sale. Development-based LVC can also be adopted in countries where land is publicly or privately owned. Market freehold lands are normally subjected to land use regulations, such as height and use restrictions. Any development rights beyond these legal limits are sometimes referred to as air rights. By relaxing land use controls, land value will increase, creating opportunities for the government to capture the economic benefit. In principle, exactions and planning gains discussed earlier are also based on a similar principle, but on an ad hoc basis. Thus, the basic idea has been practiced in many countries.

The best known air rights sales are in São Paulo, Brazil. The city government uses them, called Outorga Onerosa de Direito de Construir (Additional Building Charge; OODC) and Certificates of Additional Construction Potential (CEPACs), as LVC instruments to finance local infrastructure investment (see chapter 8). The OODC is applied to all city areas and the revenues go to the city's Urban Development Fund, which finances urban infrastructure investments across the city. CEPACs are applicable only to designated urban areas (called Urban Operations), and their revenues should be used to finance predetermined urban infrastructure. CEPACs entail hybrid features of development-based LVC and tax- and fee-based LVC, as their selling prices consist of the price for air rights and for benefits to be generated from future infrastructure investments funded by CEPAC revenues.

A key impetus for the innovations in São Paulo was the need to avoid further debt financing. Blanco (2006) states that 70 percent of municipal debt in Brazil was attributed to São Paulo, and its net debt in 2004 was over twice as large as total revenue. The municipality has established three Urban Operations that are empowered with legislation and regulatory tools to enable LVC from private investments (Sandroni 2011; Biderman, Sandroni, and Smolka 2006; Smolka 2013). Density was increased from a floor area ratio of 1.0 to 2.0, and the newly created development rights were auctioned off to private developers, with the proceeds going to public infrastructure investment within the perimeter of the Urban Operation.

In New York City, the government has also tried to apply sales of air rights to direct high-density development and redevelopment, most often around major transit nodes. The approach is based on the city's transferable development rights program that was originally designed for preserving historic buildings. Owners of such properties were prohibited from redeveloping them, and to compensate them, the government allowed them to transfer their unused development rights to other land parcels for high-density development. Recipients of the transferable development rights then paid owners for these rights at market value (see chapter 5).

A similar approach in the city was proposed (though not passed) to allow property owners to transfer their unused air rights to designated areas surrounding a major regional transit hub. New York City's stated intent was to incentivize higher density, competitive land development potential to increase land value, thereby allowing the developer to use the financial gains to compensate the original owners of the transferred development rights and to defray a portion of the area's station maintenance costs and pedestrian space reinvestments.

Land readjustment. Land readjustment originated in Germany, where supporting legal structures were enacted in 1902 (Hong and Needham 2007; Lozano-Gracia and others 2013). Since then it has been used extensively across East Asia; land readjustment was adopted by Japan and then the Republic of Korea and Taiwan, China. Typically, landowners pool their land for reconfiguring and upgrading and then receive a directly proportional amount (to their original contribution) of serviced land after the neighborhood is redeveloped (Sorensen 1999; Home 2007; Hong and Needham 2007; Lozano-Gracia and others 2013). During reconfiguring, a portion of land will be reserved for sale to private developers to raise funds to defray a portion of the redevelopment costs, capturing the benefits generated by the project.

In Taiwan, China, landowners contribute land according to a formula based on the expected appreciation in land value (Lozano-Gracia and others 2013). An important variation within that economy involves property owners contributing a combination of land and a share of development costs in return for rezoning their site to higher density (Zhao, Das, and Larson 2012).

Although one of the objectives of land readjustment is to self-finance land redevelopment, some projects still require public subsidies (Hong and Needham 2007). In Japan, for example, the government subsidized land readjustment projects that were related to urban regeneration and peri-urbanization if they could contribute to overall urban and regional development. In Japan land readjustment is also used to assemble lands for right of way for railways along with new town development (see chapter 4). The government of the Republic of Korea demanded land readjustment projects to be self-financing, thus pushing implementing agencies to increase the land contribution from owners. As building costs went up, some landowners who took part in land readjustment in the 1990s had to give up as much as 60 percent of their land, undermining their incentive to participate (Lee 2002).

The Indian Town Planning Schemes mandates landowners to give up as much as 50 percent of their land to the government during redevelopment—40 percent for infrastructure and 10 percent for social housing. The consolidated land is converted into new serviced plots and then returned to the original farmers who can then either sell to developers or retain for their own use. Landowners also pay half the infrastructure costs in the form of a betterment charge (Sanyal and Deuskar 2012).

Urban redevelopment scheme. This instrument is primarily used in Japan under the Urban Redevelopment Law (see chapter 4). Multiple property owners typically form an association to consolidate individual land parcels into a single developable site. Proposed redevelopment plans are sent to the local planning department, which then changes zoning codes and increases maximum floor area ratios in the target redevelopment district (typically around rail transit stations where the potential for commercial land use is high). The consolidated land is then used to build one or more high-rise buildings with new access roads and public open spaces. Through this process, the original owners and tenants are entitled to retain rights valued as equal to their original property; or, to speed up the redevelopment project for broader social purposes, a developer can temporarily assume all responsibility on behalf of all owners and tenants. The surplus floor area permitted is then sold to new property owners to partly cover the cost of land assembly and of public facilities within the district. This instrument is often used in redeveloping aging wooden-building districts that are vulnerable to fire hazards caused by earthquakes. The national government financially supports a third of the site survey, land assembly, and open-space-foundation costs using a national general fund and half of public infrastructure costs using a special roadway fund—if the redevelopment project meets the legal requirements.

The majority of literature on LVC concentrates on land value retention by governments; the importance of how to create value and then capture is thus implicit in the discussion. Land value creation is crucial because not only does it give government the legitimacy to recoup the increment, but it also brings the sustainability issues of this public finance approach into the picture (Hong 2013). Yet if the government keeps withdrawing revenue without simultaneously creating value, the resource will eventually be depleted. Thus, combining TOD with LVC will provide much-needed balance.

Other Land-Based Revenue-Generation Instruments

Non-LVC instruments include exaction or impact fees—incremental charges for new entrants to land markets that aim to cover the costs needed to expand infrastructure and services to accommodate new growth so as to maintain some predefined level of services. They focus on cost recovery, not value recoupment.

Such fees require developers to build public infrastructure or facilities (or to set aside land for these purposes) as a condition of getting development approval (Peterson 2009). It is fee-based because developers can also pay the government an equivalent amount of money for fulfilling the requirement (Altshuler, Gómez-Ibáñez, and Howitt 1993). The logic behind this approach is that as new development will increase demand for local infrastructure and social services, it must pay for the added capacity.

Exactions were introduced in the 1920s when suburban development outside U.S. cities resulted in the need for dedicated space for public facilities. Development of agricultural land into urban subdivisions required streets, sewers, water, electricity, schools, and parks. Developers were asked to contribute land to build these facilities inside subdivisions. In Brazil, developers of large-scale housing developments are required to build the corresponding community infrastructure.

In the 1970s, legal limits on property taxation and decreasing support from the U.S. federal government prompted municipalities to seek new tools (Frank and Rhodes 1987). In Portland, Oregon, and Austin and Fort Worth, Texas, developers were required to contribute, for the construction of public facilities, five acres of land per 1,000 additional residents (or pay $200,000–$1 million per 1,000 residents) brought into the city by their development. In Portland, the exaction was also known as a system development charge that allowed the city to issue bonds up front to buy land for parks and then use development fees to repay the debt. Despite their popularity, the main issue with exactions is accurately estimating the land contribution or an equivalent fee that matches infrastructure's future demands.

Conclusion

All LVC instruments share the common goal of capitalizing on land value increments generated by public and community actions to finance public goods. It is an attractive idea because of the perceived efficiency and fairness.

Although tax- and fee-based LVC instruments are common, they lack a clear cost-benefit link, and payers do not always know how their payments are used or whether the money will be spent on the type of public goods they desire. This generates public resistance to them, and realistically the amount collected is normally insufficient to cover the costs of major infrastructure development such as a metro. That said, these LVC instruments remain important to finance citywide local infrastructure and services such as local streets and roads, water and sewer systems, fire protection and crime prevention, public health, and education.

For financing major urban transit projects, development-based LVC instruments are useful. They rely on the sale of land or leasing of development rights in the hands of the state, including land assembled from that owned by private landholders. Having publicly owned land will not be enough to adopt development-based LVC instruments. The government needs to enhance land value before recapturing the increment for public investment, an approach that will help create public acceptance by establishing a clearer link between value creation and capture. With transit, the government or transit agencies can enhance land value in pursuing TOD principles. They can also capture benefits of the recurrent revenues from the property-related revenues in TOD areas, as well as the increased ridership.

More important, land value creation requires good urban governance and institutional capacities. Cities need open and efficient land management, technical knowledge and expertise, private sector investment, a well-designed master plan, and an effective monitoring mechanism. All are crucial for facilitating LVC through public-private partnerships in integrating transport investments with land development and management.

Opportunities for LVC are market driven. When the real estate market is in a downturn, the required motivation for private property investment may be absent. In the face of rapid urbanization, public infrastructure investment cannot wait for the market to recover. Thus, relying totally on the development-based LVC instruments to generate funds to finance public goods is nonviable. Local governments need to have alternative sources of financing, including other forms of public-private partnerships and transfers or subsidies from higher levels of government.

Local governments may also explore other LVC instruments to recoup part of the future land value increments or may create land value by assembling private lands whose value has not yet been fully explored due to the lack of public investment or outdated land use regulations (or both).

In short, well-designed development-based LVC can be a powerful strategic financing and planning apparatus for transit and TOD-related investments.

Notes

1. In this section, the terms *property value* and *land value* are used interchangeably because most empirical studies use property values based on real estate transactions, as it is hard to separate land values and building values.

2. Agglomeration economies, in general, address increases in economic productivity of workers, firms, and/or cities, as a result of higher density of economic and social activities, which can be explained by various locational advantages such as (1) sharing production inputs, (2) sharing infrastructure, (3) sharing consumer services and amenities, (4) matching labor pools to job opportunities, (5) matching firms in production processes, and (6) capturing knowledge spillovers through face-to-face communications (Cervero et al. 1998; Chatman and Noland 2011). Some of these explanations may be strongly related to accessibility benefits, while others may not. Thus the "net" external economic benefit of transportation investment alone is often questionable.

3. A few exceptions focus on middle-income countries, including Gu and Zheng (2008), Yankaya (2004), and Rodríguez and Mojica (2008).

4. To prevent operational inefficiencies among transit agencies, local governments should provide operating subsidies to their transit companies to compensate, primarily, for fiscal losses attributable to regulatory requirements, such as serving remote areas, ensuring late-night and early morning services, and ensuring affordable transit tariffs.

5. http://www.wmata.com/business/joint_development_opportunities/About.cfm, accessed June 25, 2014.

References

Altshuler, Alan A., José A. Gómez-Ibáñez, and Arnold M. Howitt. 1993. *Regulation for Revenue: The Political Economy of Land Use Exactions.* Washington, DC: Brookings Institution/Cambridge, MA: Lincoln Institute of Land Policy.

Anderson, John E. 2012. "Collecting Land Value through Public Land Leasing." In *Value Capture and Land Policies*, edited by Gregory K. Ingram and Yu-Hung Hong, 123–44. Cambridge, MA: Lincoln Institute of Land Policy.

Bahl, Roy. 2008. "Opportunities and Risks of Fiscal Decentralization: A Developing Country Perspective." In *Fiscal Decentralization and Land Policies*, edited by Gregory K. Ingram and Yu-Hung Hong. Cambridge, MA: Lincoln Institute of Land Policy.

Banister, David, and Joseph Berechman. 2000. *Transport Investment and Economic Development.* London: UCL Press.

Biderman, Ciro, Paulo H. Sandroni, and Martim O. Smolka. 2006. "Large-Scale Urban Interventions: The Case of Faria Lima in São Paulo." *Land Lines* 18 (2): 8–13.

Black, J. A., A. Paez, and P. A. Suthanaya. 2002. "Sustainable Urban Transportation: Performance Indicators and Some Analytical Approaches." *Journal of Urban Planning and Development* 128 (4): 184–209. doi:10.1061/(ASCE)0733-9488(2002)128:4(184).

Blanco, Fernando. 2006. "The Evolution of Brazilian Municipal Finances, 2000–2004." In *Brazil: Inputs for a Strategy for Cities: A Contribution with a Focus on Cities and Municipalities*, Volume 2, Background Papers Report. Washington, DC: World Bank.

Bourassa, Steven C., and Yu-Hung Hong. 2003. *Leasing Public Land: Policy Debates and International Experiences*. Cambridge, MA: Lincoln Institute of Land Policy.

Borrero, Oscar, Esperanza Durán, Jorge Hernández, and Magda Montaña. 2011. "Evaluating the Practice of Betterment Levies in Colombia: The Experience of Bogotá and Manizales." Working Paper, Lincoln Institute of Land Policy, Cambridge, MA.

Cervero, Robert. 1995. "Transit-Induced Accessibility and Agglomeration Benefits: A Land Market Evaluation." IURD Working Paper 691, University of California, Institute of Urban and Regional Development, Berkeley.

Cervero, Robert, David Aschauer, and Cambridge Systematic Inc. 1998. *Economic Impact Analysis of Transit Investments: Guidebook for Practitioners*. Washington, DC: National Academy Press.

Cervero, Robert, and Jin Murakami. 2009. "Rail and Property Development in Hong Kong: Experiences and Extensions." *Urban Studies* 46 (10): 2019–43.

Chatman, Daniel G., and Robert B. Noland. 2011. "Do Public Transport Improvements Increase Agglomeration Economies? A Review of Literature and an Agenda for Research." *Transport Reviews: Transdisciplinary Journal* 31 (6): 725–42. doi:10.1080/0144647.2011.587908.

Duncan, Michael. 2011. "The Synergistic Influence of Light Rail Stations and Zoning on Home Prices." *Environment and Planning A* 43 (9): 2125–42. doi:10.1068/a43406.

Dunphy, Robert T., Robert Cervero, Frederic C. Dock, Maureen McAvery, Douglas R. Porter, and Carol J. Swenson. 2004. *Developing Around Transit: Strategies and Solutions That Work*. Washington, DC: Urban Land Institute.

Dye, Richard F., and Richard W. England. 2011. *Land Value Taxation: Theory, Evidence, and Practice*. Cambridge, MA: Lincoln Institute of Land Policy.

England, Richard W. 2003. "State and Local Impacts of a Revenue-Neutral Shift from a Uniform Property to a Land Value Tax: Results of a Simulation Study." *Land Economics* 70 (1): 38–43.

Frank, James E., and Robert M. Rhodes. 1987. *Development Exactions*. Chicago: Planners Press.

Gatzlaff, Dean H., and Marc T, Smith. 1993. "The Impact of the Miami Metrorail on the Value of Residences near Station Location." *Land Economics* 69 (1): 54–66.

George, Henry. 1879. *Progress and Poverty: An Inquiry into the Cause of Industrial Depressions and of Increase of Want with Increase of Wealth: The Remedy*. Garden City, NY: Doubleday.

Giuliano, Genevieve. 2004. "Land Use Impacts of Transportation Investments: Highway and Transit." In *The Geography of Urban Transportation*, edited by Susan Hanson and Genevieve Giuliano, 237–73. New York: The Guilford Press.

Graham, Daniel J. 2007. "Agglomeration Economies and Transport Investment." Discussion Paper 2007-11, Joint Transport Research Centre, London.

Gu, Yizhen, and Siqi Zheng. 2008. *The Impacts of Rail Transit on Housing Prices and Land Development Intensity: The Case of No.13 Line of Beijing*. Technical report. Beijing Municipal Institute of City Planning and Design and Tsinghua University-Institute of Real Estate Studies.

Hansen, Walter G. 1959. "How Accessibility Shapes Land Use." *Journal of the American Institute of Planners* 25 (2): 73–76. doi: 10.1080/01944365908978307.

Home, Robert. 2007. "Land Readjustment as a Method of Development Land Assembly: A Comparative Overview." *The Town Planning Review* 78 (4): 459–83.

Hong, Yu-Hung. 2013. "The Symmetry of Land Value Creation and Capture." Working Paper 3, Land Governance Laboratory, Hudson, OH.

Hong, Yu-Hung, and Diana Brubaker. 2010. "Integrating the Proposed Property Tax with the Public Leasehold System." In *China's Local Public Finance in Transition*, edited by Joyce Y. Man and Yu-Hung Hong, 165–90. Cambridge, MA: Lincoln Institute of Land Policy.

Hong, Yu-Hung, and Barrie Needham, eds. 2007. *Analyzing Land Readjustment: Economics, Law, and Collective Action*. Cambridge, MA: Lincoln Institute of Land Policy.

Ingram, D. R. 1971. "The Concept of Accessibility: A Search for an Operational Form." *Regional Studies* 5 (2): 101–7. doi:10.1080/0959 5237100185131.

Knight, Robert L, and Lisa L. Trygg. 1977. "Land Use Impacts of Rapid Transit: Implications of Recent Experience." Office of the Secretary of Transportation, Washington, DC.

Lari, Adeel, David Matthew Levinson, Zhirong Zhao, Michael James Iacono, Sara Aultman, Kirti Vardhan Das, Jason Junge, Kerstin Larson, and Michael Scharenbroich. 2009. *Value Capture for Transportation Finance: Technical Research Report CTS 09-18*, Minneapolis, MN: Center for Transportation Studies, University of Minnesota. http://trid.trb.org/view.aspx?id=898454.

Lee, Tae-Il. 2002. "Land Readjustment in Korea." Paper presented to Lincoln Institute Workshop on Land Readjustment, Cambridge, MA, March 21–22.

Levine, Jonathan, Joe Grengs, Qingyun Shen, and Qing Shen. 2012. "Does Accessibility Require Density or Speed? A Comparison of *Fast* Versus *Close* in Getting Where You Want to Go in U.S. Metropolitan Regions." *Journal of the American Planning Association* 78 (2): 157–72. doi:10.10 80/01944363.2012.677119.

Lozano-Gracia, Nancy, Cheryl Young, Somik V. Lall, and Tara Vishwanath. 2013. "Leveraging Land to Enable Urban Transformation: Lessons from Global Experience." Policy Research Working Paper 6312, World Bank, Sustainable Development Network, Urban and Disaster Risk Management Department, Washington, DC. http://elibrary.worldbank.org/doi /pdf/10.1596/1813-9450-6312.

Medda, Francesca. 2011. "Land Value Finance: Resources for Public Transport." In *Innovative Land and Property Taxation*, edited by Remy Sietchiping, 42–52. Nairobi, Kenya: UN-HABITAT.

Misczynski, Dean J. 2012. "Special Assessments in California: 35 Years of Expansion and Restriction." In *Value Capture and Land Policies*, edited by Gregory K. Ingram and Yu-Hung Hong, 97–115. Cambridge, MA: Lincoln Institute of Land Policy.

Murakami, Jin. 2010. "The Transit-Oriented Global Centers for Competitiveness and Livability: State Strategies and Market Responses in Asia." Dissertation, University of California, Berkeley. www.escholarship.org /uc/item/19034785.

Peterson, George E. 2009. *Unlocking Land Values to Finance Urban Infrastructure*. Washington, DC: World Bank and Public-Private Infrastructure Advisory Facility.

Peterson, George E., and Olga Kaganova. 2010. "Integrating Land Financing Into Subnational Fiscal Management." Policy Research Working Paper 5409, World Bank, Washington, DC.

Ricardo, David. 1821. *On the Principles of Political Economy and Taxation*. 3rd ed. London: John Murray.

Rithmire, Meg. 2013. "Land Politics and Local State Capacities: The Political Economy of Urban Change in China." *The China Quarterly* 216: 872–895. doi:10.1017/S0305741013001033.

Rodríguez, Daniel A., and Carlos H. Mojica. 2008. *Land Value Impacts of Bus: The Case of Bogota's TransMilenio*. Land Lines report, April. Cambridge, MA: Lincoln Institute of Land Policy.

Sandroni, Paulo H. 2011. "Recent Experience with Land Value Capture in São Paulo, Brazil." *Land Lines* 23 (3): 14–19.

Sanyal, Bishwapriya, and Chandan Deuskar. 2012. "A Better Way to Grow? Town Planning Schemes as a Hybrid Land Readjustment Process in Ahmedabad, India." In *Value Capture and Land Policies*, edited by Gregory K. Ingram and Yu-Hung Hong, 149–82. Cambridge, MA: Lincoln Institute of Land Policy.

Smith, Jeffery J., and Thomas A. Gihring. 2006. "Financing Transit Systems through Value Capture: An Annotated Bibliography." *American Journal of Economics and Sociology* 65 (3): 751–86.

Smolka, Martim O. 2013. *Implementing Value Capture in Latin America Policy Focus Report*. Cambridge, MA: Lincoln Institute of Land Policy.

Smoke, Paul. 2008. "Local Revenues under Fiscal Decentralization in Developing Countries: Linking Policy Reform, Governance, and Capacity." In *Fiscal Decentralization and Land Policies*, edited by Gregory K. Ingram and Yu-Hung Hong. Cambridge, MA: Lincoln Institute of Land Policy.

Sorensen, Andre. 1999. "Land Readjustment, Urban Planning and Urban Sprawl in the Tokyo Metropolitan Area." *Urban Studies* 36 (13): 2333–60.

UK Department for Transport. 2005. "Transport, Wider Economic Benefits and Impacts on GDP." Discussion Paper, July, UK Department for Transport, London. http://webarchive.nationalarchives.gov.uk/+/http:/www.dft.gov.uk/pgr/economics/rdg/webia/webmethodology/sportwidereconomicbenefi3137.pdf.

UN (United Nations). 1976. *The Vancouver Action Plan-Recommendation D.3*. United Nations Conference on Human Settlement, Vancouver, Canada.

Wachs, Martin, and T. Gordon Kumagai. 1973. "Physical Accessibility as a Social Indicator." *Socio-Economic Planning Sciences* 7 (5): 437–56. doi: 10.1016/0038-0121(73)90041-4.

Weisbrod, Glen, and Burton Weisbrod. 1997. "Assessing the Economic Impact of Transportation Projects: How to Choose the Appropriate Technique for Your Project." *Transportation Research Circular* 477 (October).

Yankaya, Ugar. 2004. "Modeling the Impact of Izmir Subway on the Value of Residential Property Using Hedonic Price Model." Master's Thesis, Izmir Institute of Technology: City and Regional Planning.

Zhao, Zhirong Jerry, Kirti Vardhan Das, and Kerstin Larson. 2012. "Joint Development as a Value Capture Strategy in Transportation Finance." *Journal of Transport and Land Use* 5 (1): 5–17.

PART II

Lessons Learned from Global Development-Based Land Value Capture Practices

CHAPTER 3

Rail Plus Property Program, Hong Kong SAR, China

Hong Kong SAR, China, is one of the few Asian global cities whose rail transit generates a substantial operating profit. The transit also productively sustains the world's densest urban form. These successes are due to the Rail Plus Property program run by MTR Corporation Limited. This semiprivate railway entity applies the value capture mechanism to recoup the costs of transit investment, operation, and maintenance, using development rights of publicly owned land and leasing some sites (above/around the stations and depots of new railway lines) granted by the government, working with private developers. Consequently, more than half of all MTR Corporation's income comes from activities in large property development and long-term asset management. Globally, the story of the city's Rail Plus Property value capture model seems unique, combining a state leasehold system, extreme urban density, entrepreneurial city authorities and transit agency, a solid legal framework, and well-established operating procedures. Yet other entrepreneurial cities can apply the model, with adjustments, allowing their planning departments and transit agencies to manage land supply and site design—particularly those with a large amount of public land under strong planning controls and legal systems.

Urban Development Context

Hong Kong SAR, China, the "Pearl of Asia," has been a world-class finance, business services, and tourism hub of East and Southeast Asia since the oil crises of the 1970s. The laissez-faire British colony first developed during the 1950s and 1960s along its waterfronts and later with harbor reclamations and landfills, having extraordinary floor area ratios (FARs) of up to 20:1. The emergence of white-collar jobs and middle-income households called for drastic urban renewal and massive new town development programs during the 1980s (Bristow 1984). Yet the 1984 Joint Declaration between the governments of the United Kingdom and China limited the supply of new land up to 50 hectares a year, while the city's urban development in the 1980s and 1990s was subject to the speculative pressures of private developers along with mega-scale infrastructure works, such as rail transit development and international airport relocation projects (Dimitriou and Cook 1998).

Once sovereignty was returned to China in 1997, some socio-spatial integration between Hong Kong SAR, China, and mainland China was likely. Given its unique geographic advantage for increasing cross-border business, the city now has more than 7.1 million residents and continues to attract Chinese and other Asian immigrants to the limited areas of Hong Kong Island, the Kowloon Peninsula, and the New Territories and Islands.

The population is projected to reach 8.6 million by 2026, growing slightly faster than the roughly 0.5 percent a year of the past decade (figure 3.1), though the rising trend in moving to or from the rest of the country will increase uncertainties in projecting population growth and urbanization patterns (HKSAR Census and Statistics Department 2012).

Despite the increased pressures on land development, built-up areas are still less than 25 percent of the entire territory. The "Garden City" concept was introduced by the Abercrombie Report in postwar 1948, which fed into a series of Territorial Development Strategies for using scarce land resources to meet competing demands: housing, commercial, transport, recreation, nature conservation, heritage preservation, and other community needs. Its careful urban planning and land management have allowed the city to be one of the most densely populated in the world, with 16,020

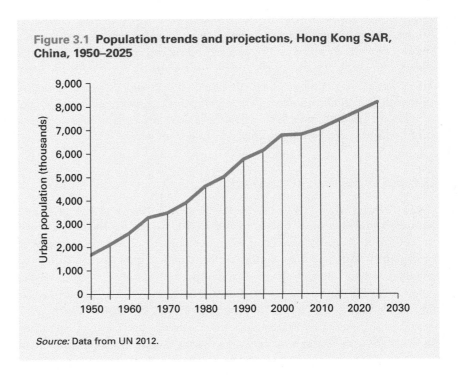

Figure 3.1 Population trends and projections, Hong Kong SAR, China, 1950–2025

Source: Data from UN 2012.

people per square kilometer in Hong Kong Island and 45,730 per square kilometer in Kowloon (HKSAR Census and Statistics Department 2013) (map 3.1). These are extremely favorable conditions in which to profitably run combined railway and property projects.

Hong Kong SAR, China's, policymakers and town planners have consistently embraced the symbiotic relationship between mass transit railway investments and urban development throughout a series of Territorial Development Strategies (HKSAR Planning Department 2013). Early mass transit railway lines were sited in the dense, built-up parts of the city, since this was where the majority of passengers resided. As residential development spread outwards into the New Territories, mass transit railway investments were viewed as a way of forming a "backbone" of the territorial development that channels key commercial centers, the Hong Kong International Airport, recreational areas, and new towns. In more recent years, railways have also served as critical catalysts for urban regeneration and regional integration, public housing, open spaces, and community facilities on former brownfield and cross-border sites.

Map 3.1 Urban population density along mass railway transit lines, Hong Kong SAR, China, 2011

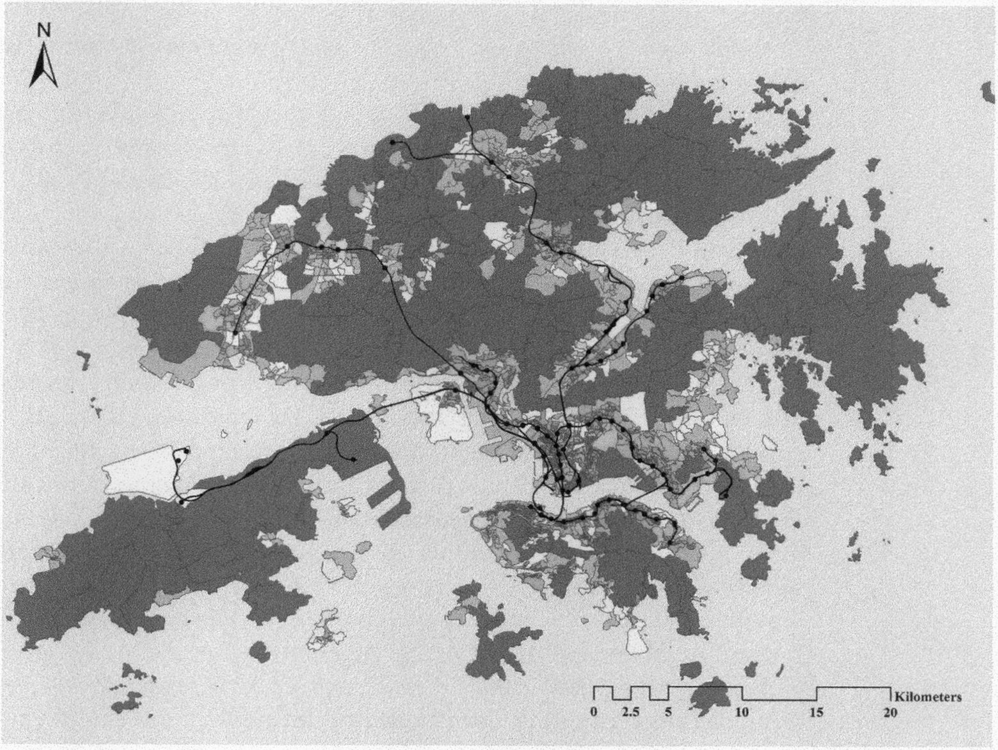

Source: Data from Murakami 2010, 2014.

About 12 million passenger journeys are made every day on the city's public transport system, including railways, trams, buses, minibuses, taxis, and ferries. Mass Transit Railway is expected to become the major passenger mode, handling up to 50 percent of total public transport patronage by 2016. In contrast, there are only about 443,000 licensed private cars, or 62 vehicles per 1,000 residents—much fewer than in cities in the developed world, due in large part to the high costs of owning a private car (HKSAR Transport Department 2013; Dimitriou and Cook 1998). The urban geography also makes it increasingly difficult to supply additional road capacity in the built-up areas, whereas demand for cross-harbor and cross-border movements has increased in recent years.

Regulatory and Institutional Framework

Urban Planning System

The statutory planning system in Hong Kong SAR, China, is mainly concerned with two types of detailed plans: outline zoning plans and development permission area plans, as a temporary measure for certain nonurban areas. Both types are prepared by the Planning Department for the Town Planning Board to decide whether to approve applications. The legal duty of the board and its members is to act in the most beneficial way for the health, safety, convenience, and general welfare of the community by representing diverse professions, expertise, and community interests (Civic Exchange 2006).

There are also special categories. Development scheme plans prepared by the Urban Renewal Authority are for redeveloping old areas. In contrast, comprehensive development area (CDA) zones are introduced by the Town Planning Board when it wants to encourage a comprehensive approach to the urban design and development of an area, typically involving multiple land parcels and property owners, and including public open space and local community facilities. (They are applied, for example, to mixed-use property developments around many Mass Transit Railway stations.)

The Planning Department has created Hong Kong Planning Standards and Guidelines to ensure that land use will facilitate social and economic development and provide public facilities. They stipulate measures relating to, for instance, residential densities, community facilities, recreational facilities, open and green space, industrial land, retail facilities, utility services, internal transport facilities, environmental planning, conservation, and urban design guidelines. A range of FARs guides development density in public and private residential areas (table 3.1). The highest density zone for residential development, "R1," is designated to key districts well served by high-capacity public transport facilities, such as mass railway transit stations and other major bus interchanges (see map 3.1).

Table 3.1 Maximum domestic floor area ratios for Metroplan area and new towns

Territorial category	Zone	Area	Location	Maximum FAR
Metroplan area	R1	Existing development areas	Hong Kong Island	8.0/9.0/10.0
			Kowloon and New Kowloon	7.5
			Tsuen Wan, Kwai Chung, and Tsing Yi	8.0
		New development areas and CDAs		6.5
	R2			5.0
	R3			3.0
New towns	R1			8.0
	R2			5.0
	R3			3.0
	R4			0.4

Source: HKSAR Planning Department 2011.
Note: CDA = comprehensive development area; FAR = floor area ratio.

Land Administration System

The city's land law is unique largely due to its colonial heritage. The leasehold system inherited many aspects of English land law. Technically, the king or queen of England holds all land, and as this philosophy was extended to the colonies, the only tenure in Hong Kong was leasehold, except for the site of St. John's Cathedral in Central, the only freehold land in Hong Kong (Goo 2009). This land tenure concept continued even after the return of sovereignty to China—which has its own "state lease-hold system"—meaning that all lands within the territories of Hong Kong SAR, China, are now state property. The government of Hong Kong SAR, China, is responsible for their management, use, and development and for their lease or grant to individuals, legal persons, or organizations for use or development under the Basic Law passed by China in 1990.

In accord with current land administrative law, land parcels are generally leased for 50 years at a premium and subject to an annual rent payment equivalent to 3 percent of the ratable value of the property starting from the date of the land grant, adjusted in step with any changes in the ratable value. Leases not containing a right of renewal are extended for 50 years without payment of an additional premium, though an annual rent is charged from the date of extension equivalent to 3 percent of the property's ratable value, adjusted in step with any change in the ratable value thereafter. However, when land that is not efficiently used is needed for public purposes, it is reasonable to expect that the government of Hong Kong SAR, China, will not renew the lease.

The Lands Department is in a strong negotiating position in land transactions and related development activities across all territories. The department auctions off or tenders out public land to private developers. Developers, in turn, bid to lease land so as to obtain the right to develop and sell to end-users. However, the highest bidder is not guaranteed the lease; developers must comply with the conditions of sale before acquiring the right to develop. Land leases stipulate the obligations and duties of the owner as well as the requirements related to town planning, civil engineering, and urban development (Nissim 2012; Hui 2004). Lease conditions typically include the following: lease term; permitted uses; maximum building heights; minimum and maximum gross floor area; maximum permitted site coverage; building covenant; deeds of mutual covenant; master layout plan requirements; design, disposition, and height limitations; car parking, loading, and unloading requirements; restrictions on vehicle ingress and egress; landscaping and environmental requirements; recreational facilities; and other site-specific conditions.

Two types of covenant—building covenant and deeds of mutual covenant—are important safeguards against speculative land investment and inappropriate asset management. A building covenant is set up to ensure that the site is developed with an acceptable amount of floor space within a reasonable time. The volume of floor space generally required to fulfill this condition is 60 percent of the maximum floor space permitted to be built; the time frame is usually 48 months. If at the end of the building covenant period there has been no progress, the government can exercise its right to reclaim the site without making any compensation. A deed of mutual covenant is placed to ensure a fair balance between the interests of all public and private parties, including future purchasers, over the responsibilities and costs for the long-term management of properties. This action is most common for complex mixed-use developments with commercial floors in the podium and residential or office floors above.

Funding sources for public infrastructure and services have been revenue from land leasing practices, accounting for nearly 20 percent of the income of the government of Hong Kong SAR, China. The state leasehold system has essentially four value capture mechanisms: initial land auctioning, contract modification, lease renewal, and collection of land rent. The government has relied heavily on initial auctioning to capture increased land value (accounting for about 75 percent of total lease revenues) because the costs of delineating, negotiating, and enforcing the parties' rights to benefit from land at the auctions (the transaction costs of land leasing expected) are the lowest among the four value capture mechanisms (Hong 1998).

Rapid disposition of low-value land parcels cannot generate strong public revenues, as regulating developable land supply would escalate land prices. When property market prices in the city become too high, the government requires purchasers to pay stamp duty on property transactions to prevent speculation (Hui, Ho, and Ho 2004). The ad valorem stamp duty rates announced on February 22, 2013, range from 1.5 percent to 8.5 percent based on the property value (HKSAR Inland Revenue Department 2013).

MTR Corporation

The Mass Transit Railway (MTR) Corporation was established in 1975 as a government-owned enterprise to build, operate, and maintain a mass transit railway system for Hong Kong SAR, China's public transport needs and to conduct its business according to prudent commercial principles (Dimitriou and Cook 1998). Through the 1980s and 1990s, the government was its sole owner. In 2000, it was succeeded by the MTR Corporation Limited and about 23 percent of its shares were offered to private investors on the Hong Kong Stock Exchange. The presence of private shareholders has exerted a strong market discipline on MTR Corporation, prompting company managers to become more business-minded (Cervero and Murakami 2009).

MTR Corporation was one of two rail agencies that served the city, the other being the Kowloon-Canton Railway Corporation (KCRC) fully owned by the government of Hong Kong SAR, China. In December 2007, the company began to operate KCRC's railway system under a concession agreement with the government, generally called the "Rail Merger." The merged 218.2-kilometer rail network consists of 10 railway lines with 84 stations serving Hong Kong Island, Kowloon, and the New Territories. A light rail network with 68 stops covers the districts of Tuen Mun and Yuen Long in the New Territories. The MTR Corporation network also includes the Airport Express, which runs between the Hong Kong International Airport and AsiaWorld-Expo in Chek Lap Kok Island, the International Commerce Centre in Kowloon, and the International Finance Centre in Central (map 3.2).

MTR Corporation's chief mission is to construct, operate, and maintain a modern, safe, reliable, and efficient mass transit railway system. Supplemented by a competitive service performance of buses and private vehicles, the integrated network carried about 4.12 million passenger trips a day in 2012 (HKSAR Transport and Housing Bureau 2012b). MTR Corporation's share of the franchised public transport market in Hong Kong SAR, China, was 46.4 percent that year. Its share of cross-harbor traffic was 66.7 percent and of cross-boundary traffic 54.2 percent. It kept its share to and from the international airport at 21.8 percent. As a result of the high ridership and efficient operations, the company generated a net operating profit of HK$6.694 billion (US$869 million) from its transit operation and achieved farebox recovery of 185.5 percent for 2012 (MTR Corporation 2013). These are outstanding figures when compared to other world-class metro systems' operating performance.

Relations with the Government of Hong Kong SAR, China

The government is the majority owner of about 77 percent of the issued MTR Corporation shares under the control of the financial secretary, permitting it to pass special resolutions (which require at least 75 percent of the shares) at MTR Corporation's general meetings, while it can pass ordinary resolutions on its own with a majority (at least 50 percent of the shares) under the law. MTR Corporation has the power to appoint persons to the board by ordinary resolution—in other words, the government can

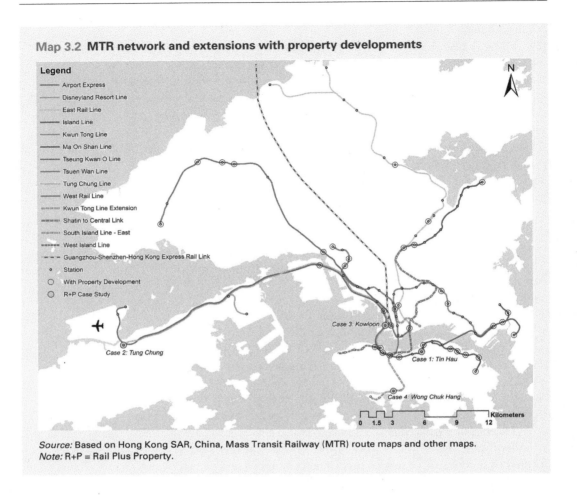

Map 3.2 MTR network and extensions with property developments

Source: Based on Hong Kong SAR, China, Mass Transit Railway (MTR) route maps and other maps.
Note: R+P = Rail Plus Property.

determine board members on its own. The government can appoint the chairman of MTR Corporation with the majority of the votes, while the chief executive of Hong Kong SAR, China, may appoint and remove additional directors of the company under the MTR Ordinance (MTR Corporation 2007).

Due to the public-private nature of its railway and related businesses, the interests of MTR Corporation and its subsidiaries may conflict with those of the government on, for example, railway construction or public land grants and leases. For this reason, the Hong Kong Stock Exchange granted the company a special waiver not to be strictly in compliance with the rules applicable to commercial entities for those transactions involving the government (MTR Corporation 2007).

Before the Rail Merger of 2007, the Legislative Council Panel on Transport formed a subcommittee to oversee matters on integrated railways. One of the most important issues is whether the proposed funding arrangements for new railway projects are appropriate and whether passengers can enjoy a reasonably priced and efficient transit service. The subcommittee has examined forms of funding for railway construction projects in detail, as now discussed.

Land Value Capture (LVC)

Funding Arrangements for MTR Corporation

Just like many other metro projects, MTR line construction in the 1970s and 1980s was capital intensive and required substantial funding. With high-grade ratings in the international capital markets, MTR Corporation attracted private financiers. Yet it was still important for the government to cover and even cut some of the company's project costs without raising fares by arranging government land grants for rail and property development. The basic rule applied in Hong Kong SAR, China, is that the government grants MTR Corporation a "running line lease" at a nominal charge for use of the land to develop railway infrastructure, such as stations and track. Railway depot sites are granted to the company as a normal land grant, and land premium is charged on the basis of industrial use, as railway maintenance is regarded as an industrial activity. When the railway depot site is also used for property development, an extra land premium is paid for property development rights. Indeed it was the government, with an equity holding of HK$800 million, that granted the assembled rights of way for lines, stations, and depots and sold the development rights of sites above the new stations and depots to MTR Corporation to build the Kwun Tong line within the original financial limit of HK$5 billion (Dimitriou and Cook 1998).

By 1983, however, MTR Corporation's capital costs had already reached HK$10 billion for 26 kilometers of both the Kwun Tong and Tsuen Wan lines, with 25 stations. Additionally, it had submitted the new Island Line proposals (previously approved in 1980), at an estimated cost of HK$7.1 billion. While the construction was successful, it had accumulated debts of HK$18.7 billion by 1985. Nevertheless, from 1986 it turned back into an efficient borrower in the capital markets due to its low interest rates, increasing fare revenue, and property development earnings (Dimitriou and Cook 1998; Strandberg 1989).

In the early 1990s the Hong Kong Airport Core Program was set out as a series of infrastructure projects (at a total cost of HK$160.2 billion) along with the relocation of the airport from Kai Tak to North Lantau. Beginning in the late 1990s when MTR Corporation began pursuing 15 property development packages along the Airport Express Line, the net yields provided crucial income in achieving commercial returns on this new line and in financing the subsequent Tseung Kwan O extension. It took about 10 years to pay off the debt for the Airport Express project. From 2007, property development earnings have produced capital funds that no longer go to paying off this debt, allowing them to be used to cover the project costs of Tseung Kwan O and other extensions (Cervero and Murakami 2009).

After the rail merger, new rail construction projects could be categorized into two: natural extension and non-natural extension of mass transit railway. The government of Hong Kong SAR, China, usually arranges new projects for natural extension based on the ownership approach and for non-natural extension on the ownership or the concession approach. Under the ownership approach, MTR Corporation is responsible for design, finance, construction, operation, and maintenance of the rail project and ultimately owns the line. Under the concession approach, the government (or KCRC) is responsible for funding the new railway's infrastructure while MTR Corporation pays service concession fees for the right to operate the railway (HKSAR Legislative Council 2008).

The government initially discusses the appropriateness of providing capital grants or property development rights to MTR Corporation—a profit-oriented organization undertaking a nongovernment project—on the basis of the ownership approach. The granting of property development rights is a way to fill the funding gap of new rail construction that could not be recovered by future operating revenues. When a new rail project with property development rights is financially nonviable (due in large part to the lack of developable sites along the lines), the government considers providing capital grants to MTR Corporation, given the expected large social and economic benefits (HKSAR Legislative Council 2008).

In 2013, five new railway projects were under construction: South Island Line–East (SIL-E), Kwun Tong Line Extension (KTE), West Island Line (WIL), the Hong Kong Section of Guangzhou-Shenzhen-Hong Kong Express Rail Link (XRL), and the Shatin to Central Link (SCL) (HKSAR Transport and Housing Bureau 2012b). The form of funding for each project is assessed case by case (table 3.2).

A railway project is considered not financially viable if its net present value for a 50-year period falls short of the expected return on capital,

Table 3.2 Funding arrangements for five new railway projects, Hong Kong SAR, China

Project	Route length (km)	Number of stations	Capital cost (HK$ billion)	Funding gap (HK$ billion)	Funding arrangement
SIL-E	7	5	12.4	9.9	Development rights
KTE	2.6	2	5.3	3.3	Development rights
WIL	3	3	15.4	12.7	Capital grant
XRL	26	1	66.9	N/A	Service concession
SCL	17	10	79.8	N/A	Service concession

Sources: HKSAR Legislative Council 2008; HKSAR Transport and Housing Bureau 2011; MTR Corporation 2013.
Note: KTE = Kwun Tong Line Extension; N/A = not applicable, because all capital cost was financed by the government under service concession; SCL = Shatin to Central Link; SIL-E = South Island Line–East; WIL = West Island Line; XRL = Express Rail Link.

which is the weighted average cost of capital plus 1–3 percent with MTR Corporation. This shortfall is the funding gap. Independent consultants usually review the estimated cost and revenue for new railway projects prepared by MTR Corporation. The company has proposed current project contingencies to be 13 percent of the estimated capital costs based on unforeseen additional expenditures on past railway projects in Hong Kong SAR, China, which ranged from 12 percent to 25 percent of the tendered prices. To safeguard the public interest from project risks, any excessive capital grant will be reimbursed to the government, with interest (the clawback mechanism) (HKSAR Legislative Council 2009).

Rail Plus Property

Rail Plus Property (R+P) development is a core part of MTR Corporation's business model, capturing real estate income to finance the capital and running costs of new railway lines as well as higher rail transit patronage from the high-quality catchment areas created and managed by the company.

The basic mechanism for capturing MTR Corporation's added (land) value is through public-private transactions and partnerships. Originally, because the government owns all land in the territory, private developers usually bought 50-year leases that granted property development rights through public auctions/tenders. Under the R+P program, however, the government exclusively grants to MTR Corporation development rights over the land above and around new stations and depots at the full market value "without the presence" of the new rail line (the "before-rail" market price). With several land lease conditions, MTR Corporation uses these rights to partner with developers (selected from a list of qualified bidders) based on the full market value "with the presence" of the new rail line (the "after-rail" market price). The difference of MTR Corporation's share of development profits between the before- and after-rail prices needs to be enough to bridge the funding gaps estimated by the company and by external project assessors (figure 3.2). It does not sell development rights to other private developers but instead partners with property developers. It remains in full control of the land and sells the completed units. This mechanism is fundamentally different from other LVC models, which sell off development rights of public land to private developers and subsequently lose control over the land, as has happened to some rail companies elsewhere in the world.

Although entitled to capture the land value added by R+P,[1] MTR Corporation has never been the sole beneficiary of R+P. Society has also reaped substantial rewards through this financial approach: from 1980 to 2005, the government received an estimated HK$140 billion in net financial returns (nominal value). This is based on the difference between earned income (HK$171.8 billion from land premiums, market capitalization, shareholder cash dividends, and initial public offer proceeds) and the value of injected equity capital (HK$32.2 billion).

From 2000 to 2012, property developments produced more than 38 percent of MTR Corporation's net income, transit operations 34 percent,

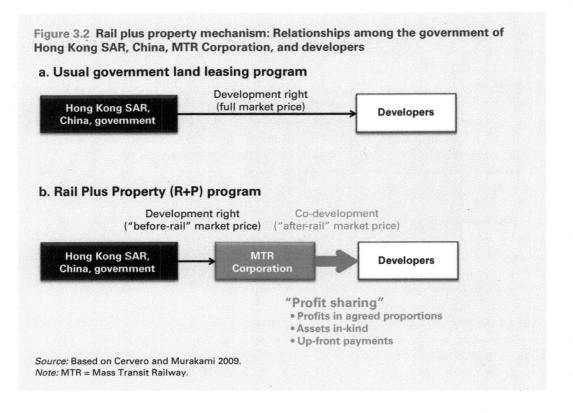

Figure 3.2 **Rail plus property mechanism: Relationships among the government of Hong Kong SAR, China, MTR Corporation, and developers**

a. Usual government land leasing program

b. Rail Plus Property (R+P) program

Source: Based on Cervero and Murakami 2009.
Note: MTR = Mass Transit Railway.

and station commercial and property management businesses about 28 percent (figure 3.3). Property-related recurring income needs to grow to keep up with the increasing costs of long-term rail-related infrastructure maintenance.

MTR Corporation's formula for property business is based on minimizing direct risks in property development projects, reducing the company's exposure to the real estate market and its related risks. For their part, developers must cover all development costs (such as land premiums, construction and enabling work costs, marketing and sales expenses, professional fees, finance charges, and others) and cope with all project risks.

MTR Corporation negotiates with developers to derive benefits from the property developments through sharing profits in agreed proportions from the sale or lease of the properties (after deducting development costs), sharing assets in kind, or receiving up-front payments from the developers, taken case by case.

In the R+P model, MTR Corporation is the "master planner and designer" to align the interests of multiple stakeholders in different project phases. It prepares a development layout plan, resolves all interfaces with rail stations, takes care of tendering land parcels, acts as a liaison between the government and developers, monitors development quality and the sale of completed properties, and manages properties after completion. For

Figure 3.3 Shares of MTR Corporation net income, 2000–12

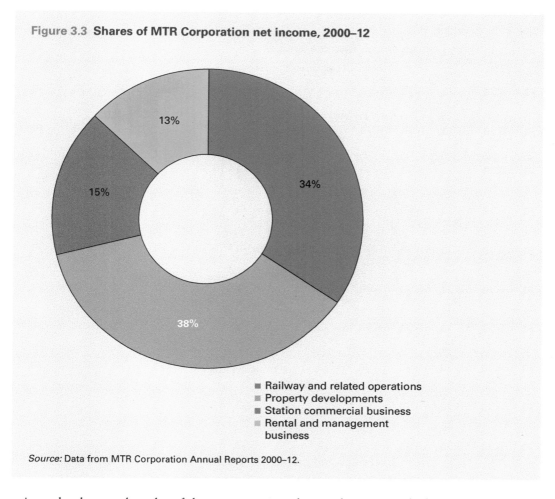

- Railway and related operations
- Property developments
- Station commercial business
- Rental and management business

Source: Data from MTR Corporation Annual Reports 2000–12.

private developers, the rules of the game are very clear at the outset, which eases uncertainties.

While many properties are high-rise towers above MTR station podiums, the R+P model is not a "cookie-cutter" approach to making the cityscape transit supportive. Indeed, the development parameters of R+P (such as area size, building densities, floor uses, and site designs) vary from place to place, essentially depending on the city's urban planning and market demands. FARs of at least 4.0 (as observed in recent MTR Corporation projects) are generally viewed as necessary if R+P is to be financially viable; however, MTR Corporation's actual site coordination remains flexible by covering large R+P sites with the CDA zone. In addition, the design principle of R+P has changed by generations: newer development packages since the late 1990s have practiced the design concepts of transit-oriented development—high-density, mixed-use, and pedestrian-friendly—in a more physically comprehensive manner than seen in the 1980s (figure 3.4).

The evolution of the physical typology and R+P practices highlights how MTR Corporation's objective of LVC has shifted from supplemental

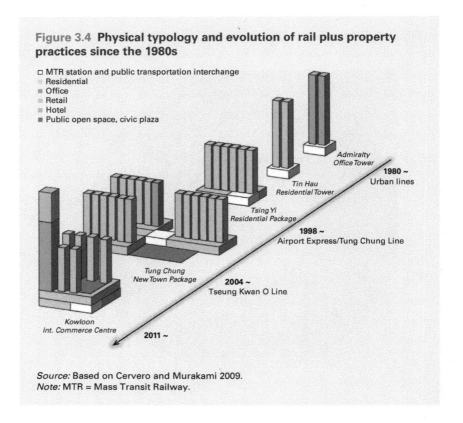

Figure 3.4 Physical typology and evolution of rail plus property practices since the 1980s

□ MTR station and public transportation interchange
▨ Residential
▪ Office
▨ Retail
▪ Hotel
▪ Public open space, civic plaza

Admiralty
Office Tower

1980 ~
Urban lines

Tin Hau
Residential Tower

Tsing Yi
Residential Package

1998 ~
Airport Express/Tung Chung Line

Tung Chung
New Town Package

2004 ~
Tseung Kwan O Line

Kowloon
Int. Commerce Centre

2011 ~

Source: Based on Cervero and Murakami 2009.
Note: MTR = Mass Transit Railway.

finance on small and simple towers in limited land plots toward sustainable finance and urbanism with large and complex packages, as seen in the next section. These later practices have greater synergistic impacts on the transit ridership bonus as well as on property price premiums throughout extensive station catchment areas (Cervero and Murakami 2009).

Development Cases

To show the above practices as applied to R+P projects since the 1980s, this section discusses four cases. Each presents its own financial, ownership, and responsibility arrangements between public and private entities.

Case 1: Tin Hau Station, Island Line

High-rise residential towers on small sites loom over Island Line, built in the 1980s. The Tin Hau station's R+P practice is a typical case, producing a FAR above 14:1 on a smaller than 0.6 hectare site in the built-up area (table 3.3). Completed in 1989, this property development is among MTR Corporation's earliest R+P project portfolios. It has ample provision for car parking and bus connections, though the somewhat imposing scale of these

Table 3.3 Tin Hau Station's rail plus property parameters

Completion	1989
Distance to central business district	4.6 km (Hong Kong Island)
Site area	0.58 ha
FAR	14.4
Floor area use	Residential: 61,000 sq. m. (72.9%) Retail: 3,700 sq. m. (4.4%) Other: 19,000 sq. m. (22.7%)
Car parking	650 spaces
Cost and profit sharing	Developer paid land premium and development cost; investment return split by end-profit sharing

Note: FAR = floor area ratio; km = kilometer; ha = hectare; sq. m. = square meter.

intermodal facilities detracts from the pedestrian environment. The surrounding neighborhood consists mainly of residential towers and an aging retail district, though the two towers on the top of the Tin Hau Station are a little isolated in the old streetscape (photo 3.1). In sum, Tin Hau's R+P was designed for a small site, mainly for financial objectives and with modest attention to the station catchment area's quality.

Photo 3.1 Tin Hau's rail plus property residential towers in the urban neighborhood of Hong Kong Island

Source: © Jin Murakami, 2007. Used with permission. Further permission required for reuse.

Case 2: Tung Chung Station, Tung Chung Line

This station, a core part of Tung Chung New Town, is the gateway community to nearby Hong Kong International Airport, constructed with the rail lines in the 1990s. The station's R+P project was arranged at a fundamentally different scale than most of its predecessors designed in the 1980s. Occupying a 21.7-hectare parcel, Tung Chung was conceptualized around the design principles of transit-oriented development and built along the lines of a master-planned new town, comprising predominantly residential housing intermixed with retail shops, offices, and a hotel next to the station. Several hundred meters from the station is an arc of residential towers with 30-plus stories, connected to the town center and amenity podiums by a network of elevated walkways and footbridges separated from car traffic. On exiting the station, MTR users are greeted by a spacious civic square dotted with public amenities (table 3.4, map 3.3, and photo 3.2), rather than being overwhelmed by high-rise towers, as so often happens in the denser parts of Hong Kong Island and Kowloon. Due to its site scale, the project was divided into three packages among 11 developers.

Case 3: Kowloon Station, Airport Express

Opened as a key intermediate terminus of the Airport Express in 1998, the Kowloon Station case shows that R+P with the principles of transit-oriented development need not be limited to greenfield projects. On reclaimed land in West Kowloon, the distinctive R+P packages that integrate the 118-story International Commerce Centre with residential and retail complexes on the

Table 3.4 Tung Chung Station's rail plus property parameters

Completion	1998–2011
Distance to central business district	35.1 km (Lantau Island)
Site area	21.7 ha
FAR	4.7
Floor area use	Residential: 935,910 sq. m. (90.8%) Office: 14,999 sq. m. (1.5%) Retail: 55,862 sq. m. (5.4%) Hotel: 22,000 sq. m. (2.1%) Other: 2,063 sq. m. (0.2%)
Car parking	3,869 spaces
Project phase	3 packages
Developers	11 developers
Cost and profit sharing	Developers paid land premium and development cost; investment return split by both up-front profit and end-profit sharing

Note: FAR = floor area ratio; ha = hectares; km = kilometers; sq. m. = square meter.

Map 3.3 Tung Chung's master layout plan: Integrating MTR station, properties, pedestrian network, and amenity podiums in the comprehensive development area

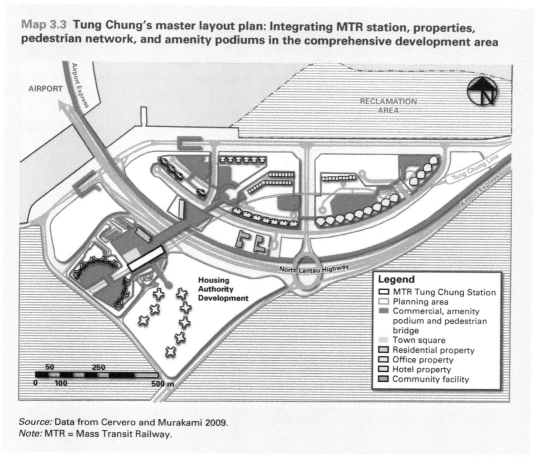

Source: Data from Cervero and Murakami 2009.
Note: MTR = Mass Transit Railway.

Photo 3.2 Pleasant public place of Tung Chung Station

Source: © Jin Murakami, 2014. Used with permission. Further permission required for reuse.

Kowloon Station net out at a moderate FAR of 8.1 within a 13.5-hectare CDA zone (table 3.5). Built as part of a city-led waterfront redevelopment initiative, the station area plan contains a generous amount of public open space and cultural and entertainment facilities, coordinated with the government and private developers. The intermodal vehicle facilities and pedestrian circulation systems are well integrated within the podium development, offering seamless travel services (figure 3.5). However, this podium design has disengaged station area activities from the surrounding context with a high blank-wall ratio (about 89 percent) and has limited ground-level integration and interaction with neighboring districts in West Kowloon. Due to its vertical multiplicity, engineering complexity, and market conditions, this R+P project was divided into seven components and completed with 13 developers phase by phase from 1998 to 2010.

Case 4: Wong Chuk Hang Station, South Island Line–East (SIL-E)

The latest R+P concept can be seen at the ongoing SIL-E project, a new rail corridor running from north to south of Hong Kong Island through the Wong Chuk Hang area. Under the ownership approach, MTR Corporation is responsible for the finance, design, construction, operation, and maintenance of the new line, though a development right grant was required to bridge the funding gap of HK$9.9 billion. In May 2011, the Chief Executive of Hong Kong SAR, China, ordered that approval should be given to

Table 3.5 Kowloon Station's rail plus property station parameters

Completion	1998–2010
Distance to central business district	2.6 km (Kowloon Peninsula)
Site area	13.5 ha
FAR	8.1
Floor area use	Residential: 608,026 sq. m. (55.5%) Hotel/serviced apartments: 231,778 sq. m. (21.1%) Retail: 82,750 sq. m. (7.5%) Hotel: 167,472 sq. m. (15.3%) Other: 6,163 sq. m. (0.6%)
Car parking	5,621 spaces
Project phase	7 packages
Developers	13
Cost and profit sharing	• Developers paid land premium and development cost • Investment return split by both upfront profit and end-profit sharing • In-kind profit sharing (MTR owns 81% of the shopping mall)

Note: FAR = floor area ratio; ha = hectares; km = kilometers; sq. m. = square meter.

grant MTR Corporation development rights to the ex-Wong Chuk Hang
Estate site (HKSAR Transport and Housing Bureau 2011).

Figure 3.5 Rail plus property development layers atop Kowloon

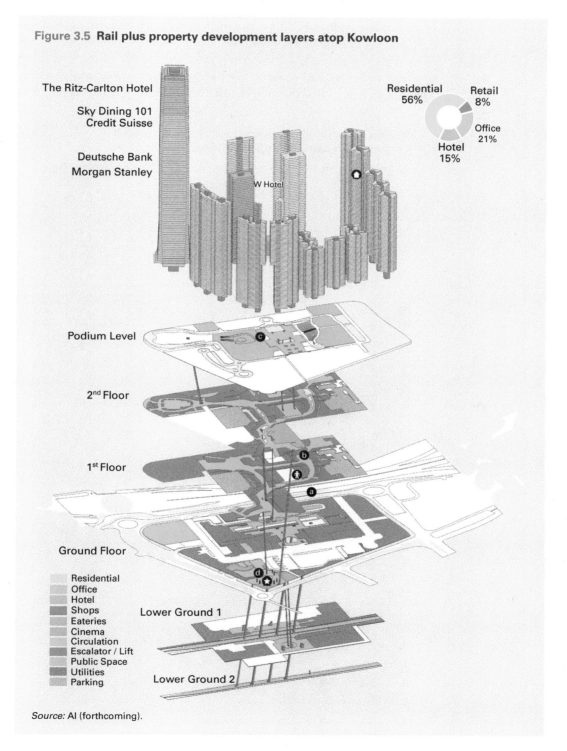

Source: AI (forthcoming).

That site has been reserved for the new rail line's depot plus joint property development, which had become technically feasible through past development experiences in Hong Kong SAR, China, such as the residential towers constructed above MTR Corporation's depot at Fo Tan Station (photo 3.3). Having directly worked with the district council and local community in the past few years, MTR Corporation has responded to requests raised by affected owners and residents for the design and provision of facilities. This has, in turn, raised the project cost. Yet generally the local community

Photo 3.3 Residential towers developed above MTR Corporation's depot at Fo Tan Station

Source: © Jin Murakami, 2014. Used with permission. Further permission required for reuse.

and other stakeholders who strongly wanted a new public transport inter-change, retail services, and social welfare facilities have welcomed redevelop-ment of the Southern District. MTR Corporation has proposed developing the roughly 7.2-hectare site with 14 towers of over 350,000 square meters of residential floor area (table 3.6). In particular, this R+P plan includes a specified amount of floor space for social enterprises and social welfare entities in the CDA depot site, which is predominantly surrounded by gov-ernment, institutional, or community zones (map 3.4).

While three independent consultants have estimated that the profit gen-erated from the depot site alone might not be enough to fully bridge the funding gap of SIL-E under a range of optimistic and pessimistic scenarios, the R+P plan is expected to act as a key catalyst to rejuvenate the South-ern District's industrial area, increasing economic growth and employment opportunities and providing a labor force. MTR Corporation plans to com-plete this R+P project in three phases over about nine years, depending on Hong Kong SAR, China's, market conditions (HKSAR Transport and Housing Bureau 2011).

Debate over Land Value Capture and Housing Affordability

There has long been public concern about housing affordability in Hong Kong SAR, China, due to the government's limited land supply through the R+P development or other land lease schemes. Certainly, land scarcity could increase the financial viability of property development in general, yet the relationship between public land supply and property prices is unclear in the city (Tse 1998; Peng and Wheaton 1994).

Table 3.6 Wong Chuk Hang Station's rail plus property parameters (approved by Town Planning Board in February 2013)

Completion	2024 (tendering: 2015–20)
Distance to central busi-ness district	7.9 km (Hong Kong Island)
Site area	7.2 ha
FAR	6.5
Floor area use	Residential: 357,500 sq. m. (76.9%) Retail: 47,000 sq. m. (10.1%) Social welfare: 2,615 sq. m. (0.6%) Transport: 58,000 (12.5%)
Car parking	931 spaces
Project phase	3–6 packages

Note: FAR = floor area ratio; ha = hectare; km = kilometer; sq. m. = square meter.

Map 3.4 Planning Department's outline zoning plans around future Wong Chuk Hang Station: CDA and government, institutional, or community zones

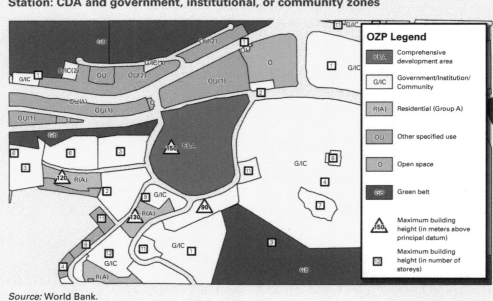

Source: World Bank.

Several macroeconomic and institutional factors influence private property investment and rents in Hong Kong SAR, China, complicating matters. Indeed, adequate housing supply can be achieved by increasing the density of development in target areas along with adequate transit infrastructure and services. Whereas the R+P practices in recent years (such as Wong Chuk Hang Station) have become increasingly attuned to striking a balance between financial and social welfare objectives, the provision of affordable dwelling units for all residents is beyond the scope of MTR Corporation's property business. Hong Kong SAR, China, has a Housing Authority, another statutory body, which is responsible for implementing most public housing programs, and more than 2 million people (or about 30 percent of the population) are living in public rental housing flats (HKSAR Transport and Housing Bureau 2012a).

Some may argue that the R+P approach has exacerbated the issue of housing unaffordability and socioeconomic segregation in the past few decades, but in fact the high-end development concept of R+P does not apply to all MTR stations, and a number of public housing and subsidized flats are within 500 meters of many MTR stations. While inefficiency in providing social housing units has long been an issue, sales of development rights under carefully limited land supply, instead of charging a high income tax and other tax rates to all residents, have enabled the government of Hong Kong SAR, China, to fund a wide range of high-quality local infrastructure and social welfare programs without accumulating too much public debt.

Conclusion

The R+P development run by MTR Corporation in Hong Kong SAR, China, is internationally recognized as an innovative model of transit finance and urban development for the 21st century. Yet despite its great potential for emerging economies, it seems that policymakers and practitioners in other cities in the developing world do not yet fully understand its possibilities. Key mechanisms and steps to implement the R+P program are summarized below, from upstream visionary planning to downstream project management:

- Master plans and policy documents consistently state the importance of a mass transit railway network and stations as a "backbone" of urban and regional development, particularly during rapid growth period.
- A public leasehold system is prudently designed and applied to control urban land supply, attract private resources, and ensure public interest in new rail corridors.
- Zoning plans, through CDA zoning, set up special FARs around key stations to incentivize private investment in strategic locations, while maintaining comprehensiveness and providing flexibility for private developers to negotiate and design.
- Property development rights are exclusively granted at a pre-rail market price for a business-oriented rail corporation to cover the capital and running costs of a rail project and to master multiple functions and phases of rail and property development at lower transaction costs.
- The grant of development rights starts with small parcels above stations/depots primarily for generating project revenue and later evolves into large, high-quality new towns, iconic business centers, and local community hubs to benefit society more widely.
- Private developers cover land premiums and bear project risks for higher financial returns, whereas the government and MTR Corporation (to some degree) are protected from market and development risks.
- The rule of cost and profit sharing between public agencies, MTR Corporation, and private developers is clear and sound, which can ease project uncertainties and public opposition.
- Development parameters around rail stations vary by location in a city and do not always strictly follow on urban design principles and standards but work flexibly reflecting market demands and socioeconomic conditions.
- After project completion, MTR Corporation stays on as an asset manager not only to capture up-front profits of property development but also to maximize management-related recurrent revenues in the long-term business portfolio.

Note

1. Which could be accessibility and agglomeration benefits plus amenity benefits of pedestrian circulation design and "synergetic" effects of transit-built environment coordination.

References

Al, Stefan, ed. Forthcoming. *Mall City: A Catalog of Hong Kong*. Honolulu: University of Hawai'i Press.

Bristow, M. Roger. 1984. *Land Use Planning in Hong Kong: History, Policies, and Procedures*. New York: Oxford University Press.

Cervero, Robert, and Jin Murakami. 2009. "Rail and Property Development in Hong Kong: Experiences and Extensions." *Urban Studies* 46 (10): 2019–43. doi:10.1177/0042098009339431.

Civic Exchange. 2006. *The User's Guide to the Town Planning Process: How the Public Can Participate in the Hong Kong Planning System*. Hong Kong SAR, China.

Dimitriou, Harry T., and Alison Cook, eds. 1998. *Land-Use/Transport Planning in Hong Kong: The End of an Era: A Review of Principles and Practices*. Aldershot, UK: Ashgate.

Goo, S. H. 2009. *Land Law in Hong Kong*. 3rd ed. Hong Kong SAR, China: LexisNexis.

HKSAR (Hong Kong Special Administrative Region) Census and Statistics Department. 2012. "Trends in Population and Domestic Households in Hong Kong." *Hong Kong Monthly Digest of Statistics*. Hong Kong SAR, China, April.

———. 2013. *Hong Kong in Figures 2013 Edition*. Hong Kong, February.

HKSAR Inland Revenue Department. 2013. "Ad Valorem Stamp Duty (AVD)." March. www.ird.gov.hk/eng/faq/avd.htm.

HKSAR Legislative Council. 2008. *Report of the Subcommittee on Matters to Railways for Submission to the Panel on Transport*. Hong Kong SAR, China, June 24.

———. 2009. *Item for Public Works Subcommittee of Finance Committee*. Hong Kong SAR, China June 10.

HKSAR Planning Department. 2011. *Hong Kong Planning Standards and Guidelines*. Hong Kong SAR, China, August. www.pland.gov.hk/pland_en/tech_doc/hkpsg/full/index.htm.

———. 2013. *Hong Kong The Facts: Town Planning*. Hong Kong SAR, China: HKSAR Information Services Department, June.

HKSAR Transport and Housing Bureau. 2011. "South Island Line (East) Funding Arrangement." Legislative Council Brief, Hong Kong SAR, China, May.

———. 2012a. *Hong Kong The Facts: Housing*. Hong Kong SAR, China: HKSAR Information Services Department, September.

———. 2012b. *Hong Kong The Facts: Railway Network*. Hong Kong SAR, China: HKSAR Information Services Department, September.

HKSAR Transport Department. 2013. *Hong Kong The Facts: Transport*. Hong Kong SAR, China: HKSAR Information Services Department, June.

Hong, Yu-Hung. 1998. "Transaction Costs of Allocating Increased Land Value under Public Leasehold Systems: Hong Kong." *Urban Studies* 35 (9): 1577–95. doi:10.1080/0042098984295.

Hui, Eddie Chi-man. 2004. "An Empirical Study of the Effects of Land Supply and Lease Conditions on the Housing Market: A Case of Hong Kong." *Property Management* 22 (2): 127–54. doi:10.1108/026 37470410532402.

Hui, Eddie Chi-man, Vivian Sze-Mun Ho, and David Kim-Hin Ho. 2004. "Land Value Capture Mechanisms in Hong Kong and Singapore: A Comparative Analysis." *Journal of Property Investment & Finance* 22 (1): 76–100. doi:10.1108/14635780410525153.

MTR Corporation. 2007. "Rail Merger." MTR Corporation Limited Circular, Hong Kong SAR, China, September 3, 2007.

———. 2013. *MTR Corporation Annual Report 2013: Creating Value, Driving Growth*. Hong Kong SAR, China. www.mtr.com.hk/eng /investrelation/2013frpt.htm.

———. 2000–12. Annual Report. Hong Kong SAR, China, 2000–2012. www.mtr.com.hk/eng/investrelation/financialinfo.php.

Murakami, Jin. 2010. "The Transit-Oriented Global Centers for Competitiveness and Livability: State Strategies and Market Responses in Asia." Dissertation Research Paper Prepared for the University of California Transportation Center, Berkeley.

———. 2014. "Inter-city Access and Intra-city Agglomeration: An Empirical Analysis of the Spatial Impacts of High-Speed Rail (HSR) Terminal Development in Hong Kong." HKSAR ECS Research, City University of Hong Kong, Kong SAR, China.

Nissim, Roger. 2012. *Land Administration and Practice in Hong Kong*. Hong Kong SAR, China: Hong Kong University Press.

Peng, Ruijue, and C. William Wheaton. 1994. "Effects of Restrictive Land Supply on Housing in Hong Kong: A Econometric Analysis." *Journal of Housing Research* 5 (2): 263–91.

Strandberg, Keith W. 1989. "Hong Kong's Mass Transit Railway: Leaving a Legacy for Hong Kong's Future." *Mass Transit* 16 (1/2): 22–26.

Tse, Raymond. 1998. "Housing Price, Land Supply and Revenue from Land Sales." *Urban Studies* 35 (8): 1377–92. doi:10.1080/0042098984411.

UN (United Nations). 2012. World Urbanization Prospects: The 2011 Revision, CD-ROM Edition. New York: Department of Economic and Social Affairs, Population Division.

CHAPTER 4

Inclusive Land Value Capture Schemes, Integrating and Regenerating the World's Largest Metropolis: Tokyo, Japan

Tokyo is well served by the world's most extensive railway network. Yet no single entity could have developed and managed such a huge, "seamless" structure without a clear national capital region plan and strong partnerships. Its rail transit system consists of multiple public, semiprivate, and private passenger lines, along with large real estate developments around key stations and former rail yards. The land value capture (LVC) models vary by development generation, location, and stakeholder, but usually call for moves to incentivize land readjustment and to maximize rail's value added. These efforts are under the market freehold system, coordinating zoning codes, floor area ratios (FARs), local infrastructure and social facilities, feeder service plans, urban design, and asset management guidelines between public and private entities. Techniques and lessons drawn from Tokyo's rich rail-oriented culture over the last five decades apply to both traditional capital cities and newly emerging megacities of the developing world, where policymakers need to overcome institutional barriers and integrate multiple policy objectives and urban functions of station area development.

Urban Development Context

Tokyo is the world's largest metropolis; Asia's global business, entertainment, and cultural center; and Japan's capital city. Its roughly 14,000 square kilometers of conurbation added more than 21 million people from 1950 to 2010, accounting for more than those living in most megacities in the world today. And despite slowing population growth, Tokyo will stay the planet's largest metropolis with a population projected to exceed 38.6 million in 2025 (figure 4.1).

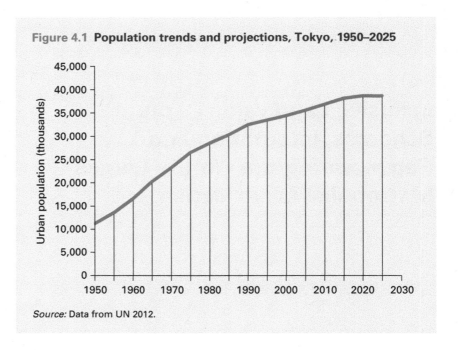

Figure 4.1 Population trends and projections, Tokyo, 1950–2025

Source: Data from UN 2012.

The metropolitan area stretches over multiple jurisdictions, including the Tokyo metropolitan government; 23 wards; Kanagawa, Chiba, and Saitama prefectures; and numerous cities, towns, and villages. Each entity draws up its own master plan, taking into account both upper-level strategies and local specifics, while the national government presents a regional development vision as well as transport infrastructure development strategies that guide the local master plans (Sorensen, Okata, and Fujii 2009). The first National Capital Region Master Plan (NCRMP) was written in 1958, addressing the target population, green belt, and satellite cities to manage urban growth. While the green belt setup was not effectively working due to strong housing demand and opposition from farmers in the surrounding areas, satellite cities were successively adopted in the NCRMPs of the 1960s, 1970s, and 1980s to overcome excessive commuting and congestion caused by Tokyo's monocentrism. By the 5th NCRMP of 1999, about nine satellite business centers had been identified. Connecting them by intercity transport networks, the NCRMP attempts to form both highly self-contained but also mutually supportive subregions to accommodate a diverse range of residents in the suburbs (map 4.1).

A series of the NCRMPs' spatial strategies tried to guide long-term regional development in a polycentric direction by encouraging public and private investments in new town line extensions given the strong economy, but Tokyo's real estate markets were too "hot" for local governments to control rapid growth and motorization. Property prices peaked between the mid-1980s and early 1990s due to inflated demand for developable sites and speculative investments in Tokyo's suburban and extra-urban areas.

Map 4.1 Population density and polycentric development structure, 5th National Capital Region Master Plan, 1999

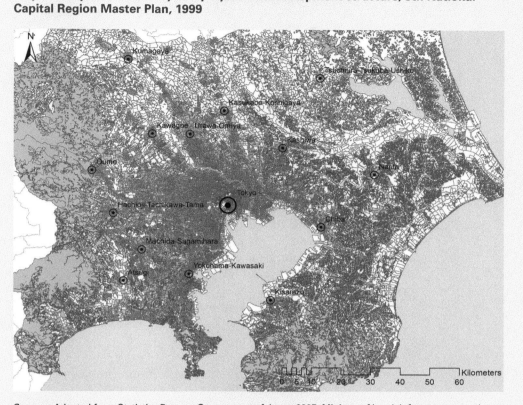

Sources: Adapted from Statistics Bureau, Government of Japan 2005; Ministry of Land, Infrastructure, and Transport 2006; and Murakami 2010.

Rapid price increases were the driving force for the original owners to trade land at inflated prices and for public agencies and private developers to assemble small lots to generate capital gains. With accelerating money supply and inadequate credit assessment, the land price bubble crashed in 1991, leading to Japan's decade-long economic stagnation (Saxonhouse and Stern 2003; Oizumi 1994).

Over the last decade or so, Tokyo's spatial transformation has largely reflected urban revitalization, a shrinking and aging society, inflated public debts, municipal budget constraints, and sustainable energy uses (Ministry of Land, Infrastructure, and Transport 2006; Sorensen 2006). Its urban regeneration projects were initiated chiefly by the national government's land liberalization policy, which aimed to enhance Tokyo's global competitiveness and its quality of urban living in the central areas, offering greater location advantages with high accessibility and agglomeration economies.

In accord with the Urban Regeneration Special Act of 2001, eight districts and 2,514 hectares were designated in the central area of Tokyo, especially where publicly owned land and former rail yards were available for large redevelopment projects (map 4.2). In these special districts, Japanese City Planning Law permits exceptionally relaxed site use, FARs, building height and area, and wall clearance while taking into account the redevelopment impact on local infrastructure and services, built environments, and social activities. Such land deregulation makes it possible for transit agencies and private developers to propose design parameters case by case and for governments to concentrate public-private investments around key railway stations (Ministry of Land, Infrastructure, Transport, and Tourism 2013a).

Regulatory and Institutional Framework

Development Instruments

Under Japan's market freehold system, the philosophy of urban planning is minimum intervention. Yet local governments, public housing and redevelopment agencies, private developers, property and business owners, and railway corporations can all access key land development instruments to apply LVC to transit investment and to promote transit-oriented development.

Among these instruments, land readjustment has been the most important in preventing urban sprawl and forming rail-supportive landscapes

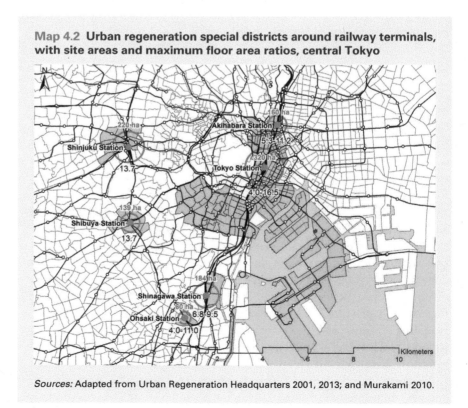

Map 4.2 Urban regeneration special districts around railway terminals, with site areas and maximum floor area ratios, central Tokyo

Sources: Adapted from Urban Regeneration Headquarters 2001, 2013; and Murakami 2010.

over the past few decades (Sorensen 1999, 2000; Cervero 1998). Tradition-ally, development entities—including public housing agencies, local plan-ning and road departments, and private railway corporations—acquired low-priced agricultural land for real estate development with full public services before new rail lines came to suburban areas. But based on the land readjustment approach, multiple landowners can organize a cooperative body that consolidates irregularly shaped agricultural parcels, returning smaller but fully serviced and regularly shaped residential and commer-cial parcels with higher property value to the original landowners. Roads, utilities, parks, sidewalk networks, station plazas, open spaces, and other infrastructure are funded partly by the sale of the land reserved from the original owners for new private development and public services. Land readjustment is often administered alongside the national government's Road Program or Urban Street Program. These programs essentially subsi-dize transit-oriented infrastructure and facilities, such as bus lanes, station plazas and transport terminuses, pedestrian access and circulation systems, bicycle parking, urban green space, and street amenities on the basis of the former Roadway Special Fund.[1]

Land readjustment is harder to carry out in already built-up areas, as development regulations there are inadequate for landowners to reassemble their properties and regenerate large capital gains from their land parcels. Thus, a stronger incentive mechanism is needed to endorse the profitability of second- or third-generation development activities and to ensure another development project is available for local governments and private stake-holders. Under the Urban Redevelopment Law, the national government pays for a third of the costs of site survey, land assembly, and open space foundation using the national general fund, and half of public infrastruc-ture costs using the (former) Roadway Special Fund. Districts with aging wooden buildings are particularly targeted, in view of earthquake and fire hazards (Ministry of Land, Infrastructure, Transport, and Tourism 2013b).

Multiple property owners usually establish one cooperative entity to receive government subsidies, consolidate separate land parcels into one developable site, and build one or more high-rise buildings with new access roads and public open spaces. The local planning department then reviews the proposed plan for redevelopment, changes zoning codes, and increases maximum FARs in the target redevelopment district (typically around rail transit stations where the potential of commercial land use is high). Through this process, the original owners and tenants are entitled to keep the property rights of floor spaces in the new building(s), which are valued as equal to their original property, or one developer can take up all property rights to speed the redevelopment project for broader social purposes. The "surplus" floor area permitted by the local government is sold to new prop-erty owners to partly cover the costs of land assembly and public facilities within the district (figure 4.2).

The instruments used for land development in Japan are mainly inclu-sive through stakeholders' consensus building. However, government

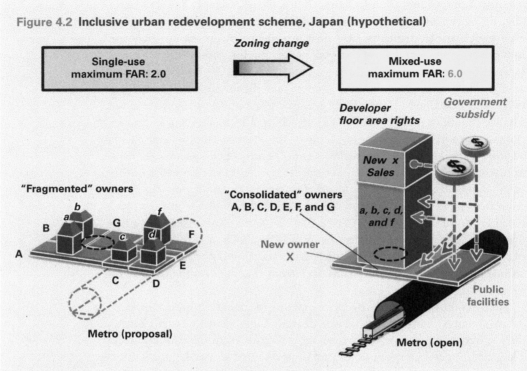

Figure 4.2 Inclusive urban redevelopment scheme, Japan (hypothetical)

Source: Adapted from Ministry of Land, Infrastructure, Transport, and Tourism 2013b.
Note: FAR = floor area ratio. Under the Urban Redevelopment Law, landholders (A, B, C, D, E, F, and G) and tenants (a, b, c, d, and f), and developers can create development opportunities in built-up areas, typically where a metro station exists or has newly opened. To capture the potential accessibility benefits conferred by the metro station, the local government first converts zoning codes from single use to mixed use with higher FAR. The figure presents stakeholders' contributions to land values before urban redevelopment (left) and their benefits after the redevelopment (right).

authorities under the Eminent Domain Law can compulsorily take over private property for public projects, with compensation but without land-owners' consent, and this power is sometimes controversial, as with the Narita International Airport dispute (Tokyo Metropolitan Government Expropriation Commission 2013; Bowen 1975). In recent years, the more inclusive strategic planning approach—"Public Involvement"—has been progressively adopted to keep government policymaking and development criteria more accountable; discourage individual landholders' selfish, short-sighted, and speculative actions; and deliver public-private partnership projects smoothly for long-run individual and societal interests (Ministry of Land, Infrastructure, Transport, and Tourism 2008).

Multiple Railway Agencies

The metropolitan area is covered by the world's largest urban railway net-work, with many public, semiprivate, private, and privatized passenger lines. Over the past century policymakers have nationalized, corporatized, and then privatized railway agencies repeatedly as they and markets react to changes in public and private entities' finances, and to social demands for regional and local transport services.

The railway agencies fall into three categories (table 4.1). The metropolitan area has about 48 rail transit operators, including monorail, new fixed-guideway transit, classic mountain-ride, and ocean-side tram lines. Encircling Tokyo's core area is the Yamanote line of the East Japan Railway Company (JR East), which was privatized from the former Japanese National Railways (JNR), with major terminal stations and high-rise office developments at or near the Tokyo, Shibuya, Shinjuku, Shinagawa, Ikebukuro, and Ueno stations. Within the Yamanote loop is a dense underground network of both the publicly owned Tokyo Metro and Toei Subway lines. Also crisscrossing central Tokyo are JR East's multiple services. Radiating outward from the Yamanote loop are major private commuter lines, plus the JR group's intercity and high-speed rail lines. The private suburban lines stop at major terminuses on the Yamanote loop, allowing passengers to directly switch onto the Tokyo Metro and other municipal subway lines without transfers by integrating terminal functions and sharing train services across multiple lines (map 4.3).

Railway agencies are licensed to develop and operate new lines listed in the national government's regional network plan. Under the general development model, public and private sector agencies built, owned, and operated rail lines over the past few decades. The Railway Business Law, along with the privatization of JNR in 1987 (box 4.1), allows railway agencies to separate ownership and operation in order to cope with the growing costs and risks of new projects; settle a financial balance over multiple rail lines; and improve passenger services through open access to multiple operating

Table 4.1 Classification of Japanese railway agencies

Category	Agency	Ownership
Special-purpose enterprise	Japan Railway Construction, Transport, and Technology Agency (former Japan Railway Construction Agency and former JNR Settlement Corporation)	National government
	Tokyo Metro (former Teito Rapid Transit Authority)	National and metropolitan governments
	Seven Japan Railway Companies (former Japanese National Railways)	Fully or partially privatized
Private corporation	Private railway corporations	Private
	Third sector	Private, national, metropolitan, and municipal governments
Metropolitan/ municipal government	Public transport bureaus	Metropolitan/municipal government

Source: Adapted and updated from Japan Society of Civil Engineering 1991.
Note: JNR = Japanese National Railways.

Map 4.3 Tokyo metropolitan area railway network built, operated, and owned by multiple public-private agencies

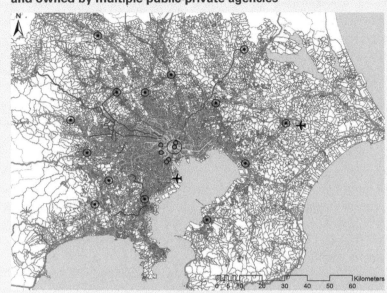

Sources: Adapted from Murakami 2010; Ministry of Land, Infrastructure, Transport, and Tourism 2013a.

businesses on the same track, which enables multiple transit agencies to provide "seamless" passenger services over the metropolitan area.

Relations with the National Government

The long-term development of Tokyo's railway network is discussed at the national government level. The Ministry of Land, Infrastructure, Transport, and Tourism of Japan periodically holds external committee meetings

---

Box 4.1 JNR privatized

In 1987, Japanese National Railways (JNR) was privatized in one of the biggest institutional reforms in decades—not only because it changed ownership, management, and operations of railway systems, but also because it influenced the geographic division of regional rail services and disposed of large areas of public land (often former rail yards) for private redevelopment near terminal stations.

Based on the JNR Reform Law of 1986, JNR was divided into private railway companies by regions and into public agencies for other special purposes. This move was the cumulative result of huge financial debts of about ¥37 trillion ($256 billion) due to inefficient fare price and real estate business regulations, rapid motorization in Japan's suburban and rural areas, very expensive capital investments in *Shinkansen* ("high-speed rail" in Japanese), and growing labor costs by the mid-1980s. In particular, the new JNR Settlement Corporation took over many of the former JNR's assets (such as rail yards) and prepared developable land parcels with local governments for auction from 1987 to 1998, which led to the recent regeneration boom in Tokyo's central areas.

where rail experts recommend extension projects for the next decade, based on changing economic and social needs. The latest Railway Network Master Plan of 2000 stresses five strategies: responses to urban restructuring; corridor capacity increases; terminal and transfer improvements; high speed rail and airport access investments; and seamless feeder bus and nonmotorized travel services (Transport Policy Committee 2000).

To start a new railway business, agencies go through a series of legal procedures, such as license application, approval of construction plan, inspection of completed infrastructure and rolling stock, approval of facility transfer and use, approval of fare proposals, submission of operational plans, and agreements. The national government, in comparison, issues a railway business license based on certain criteria, such as travel demand, supplied capacity, master plan, ability of applicants, and the public interest gained by the railway project. Generally, Tokyo's railway business is presumed to recover the operation and maintenance costs of railways from fare revenue, so the tariff across the entire railway network needs to be appropriate for protecting railway users and stabilizing railway business. Thus, the Ministry of Land, Infrastructure, Transport, and Tourism gives approval to fare proposals submitted by agencies based on four criteria: business efficiency, public equity, travel affordability, and fairness in market competition.

The government has long selected new projects proposed by railway agencies based on their business profitability, and self-evidently the profitability of railway investment is heavily affected by land development around stations. Historically, railway businesses in Tokyo were attractive enough for entrepreneurs to generate large capital gains during the rapid growth period. In recent years, however, this has become harder to do, largely due to escalating construction costs; lengthening construction periods; increasing market competition among multiple rail lines, private automobiles, and air services; and weakening real estate markets along new town corridors. All these factors require innovative financing, including development-based LVC.

LVC

Funding Arrangements

New railway projects require Tokyo's public and private agencies to raise huge capital funds from various sources including fare revenues, public investments, bonds, subsidies, zero-interest loans, long-term debt, and LVC.

Funds for such projects come principally from users. Most railway agencies reserve a portion of their fare revenues to finance future extensions. The Special Urban Railway Reserve Fund, based on the Urban Rail Development Promotion Special Measure Act of 1986, also makes it possible for railway agencies to collect extra money from their current services to support future improvement projects that may be necessary but may not generate much additional demand or revenue (such as quadruple-track line and station-function upgrade programs). This approach has certain advantages for private railway agencies—including tax-exempted resources, lower interest rates, moderate fare increases, and user-linked or corridor-specific funds—yet it is applied mainly to relatively short-term capital improvement projects that do not call for too much land acquisition or assembling (within 10 years).

Private railway corporations generally fund about 10–20 percent of urban lines' construction costs by selling equity in the stock market, but national and local governments invest in the essential urban lines that do not fit private projects through the Japan Development Bank, the public subway agency, and joint public-private companies. In addition, publicly owned subway and new town railway lines are eligible for a range of local bond issues (for instance, the Subway Project Special Bond, Capital Cost Relief Bond, Transport Bond, Corporate Debt Payment Bond, and Japan Railway Construction Agency Bond), though growing metropolitan and municipal debts for large infrastructure projects have become more contentious for taxpayers.

As profits from railway development have fallen since the 1960s and 1970s, the national government has steadily raised its financial assistance to cover railway agencies' construction costs by setting up project-based subsidy programs. More recently, its funding arrangements have shifted toward existing stock improvement and airport access development in response to sweeping changes in Tokyo's demographic patterns, travel demands, and economic development strategies. Private railway corporations with local governments have adopted other funding mechanisms as well, such as quadruple- and elevated-track project subsidies using the Roadway Special Fund (which usually accounts for a third of bridge or underpass construction costs) and land readjustment projects that save land acquisition costs and promote real estate developments simultaneously.

Types of LVC

Japan's transit agencies have long applied an LVC mechanism to finance their railway development, alongside other funding arrangements. LVC techniques vary by location and stakeholder. The metropolitan area has six main LVC types (strictly speaking, not limited to development-based LVC), as listed under "Mechanism" in table 4.2.

One of the most popular mechanisms in Tokyo is to internalize accessibility and agglomeration benefits from private railway investment. Typically, private railway agencies collectively carry out land readjustment projects around stations by receiving the land reserved for new town development and internalizing the capital gains from real estate businesses (for example, the Tokyu Corporation Tama Denentoshi Line).

The national government's new town development program, along with other subsidy mechanisms, can require developers to pay half of the construction costs of new town lines (connecting sub-business centers and new towns) and provide the rights of way for new town lines to metropolitan, municipal, and private railway bodies at a base land price. Yet such schemes made land acquisition pricey and increased the new town line's fare levels (Hokusou Line).

The latest suburban extension model in the metropolitan area is integrating housing development and railway investment. In accord with the Housing-Railway Integration Law of 1989, several local governments with public housing agencies can designate station districts and catchment areas in their master and district plans and simultaneously assemble the developable land parcels for new housing units as well as the rights of way for new railway lines through land readjustment projects. With the Tsukuba Express, the Railway Construction Agency incrementally purchased rights-of-way segments from local governments and housing agencies at an assessment price and then built or transferred infrastructure (including land) to the new railway corporation jointly owned by the multiple local governments at a "with-rail" price. But local governments and housing agencies could only make a capital gain from selling land parcels reserved for housing development around new stations if demand for suburban housing was very strong.

Local towns and rural villages that the national railway line passes can submit a petition to the Japan Railway Companies (the former JNR) to add a full-service station to the line by paying the full construction costs of new station facilities, providing the rights of way for free, and creating station plazas and local access roads through land readjustment projects. Local stakeholders—residents, landholders, business owners—usually need to demonstrate enough ridership to justify the extra station, especially when the Japan Railway Companies are hesitant to increase service frequency and coverage as the stop would reduce trains' operating speeds.

Railway agencies (or local governments) sometimes attempt to make an agreement case by case with private developers and building owners in order to share construction costs or development benefits (for example, Yokohama MM21 Line). With the Tokyo Metro, building owners near new subway stations usually pay the construction costs of pedestrian access pathways to and from their properties (which may be called "building connection fees" in other countries).

Another significant practice is the sale of former rail yard sites in Tokyo's central areas. The JNR Settlement Corporation took over much of JNR's real estate to reduce the debt accumulated by the mid-1980s and sold it via public auction of large land parcels around the Japan Railway Companies' terminal stations for private redevelopment (which can be seen as one type of LVC). This LVC model usually involves local planning departments, developers, and future building owners in public-private infrastructure and service provision, land readjustment projects, and inclusive urban redevelopment schemes, but they have extraordinary FAR bonuses for profitable regeneration (such as Tokyo-Marunouchi, Shinagawa, and Shiodome).

Table 4.2 Summary of main land value capture types in the Tokyo metropolitan area

Type	Major location	Key stakeholder	Mechanism	Example
Internalization	Urban–suburban	Private railway corporations	Carrying out land readjustment projects along rail lines, receiving the land reserved for property development, and allocating the capital gains from real estate to railways internally ("internalizing" external businesses in private railway companies)	Tokyu Corporation Denentoshi Line
Requirement	Suburban	New town developers	Paying half of the construction costs of new town lines and providing the rights of way at a base price	Hokuso Line
Integration	Suburban	Local governments with developers	Reserving the rights of way for new rail lines and increasing developable parcels for housing sales jointly through land readjustment projects	Tsukuba Express
Petition	Suburban–rural	Local communities with developers	Paying the construction costs of new station facilities, providing the rights of way for free, and creating station plazas and access roads through land readjustment projects	JR Lines
Agreement	Urban–suburban	Developers, landholders, and building owners	Sharing the construction costs or development benefits of new rail projects (and pedestrian access pathways)	Yokohama MM21 Line (and Tokyo Metro)
Auction	Urban	JNR Settlement Corporation with developers	Selling former rail yard sites for private redevelopment around JR's terminal stations to reduce the former JNR's debt	JR Shinagawa Station

Source: Updated from Japan Society of Civil Engineering 1991.
Note: JNR = Japanese National Railways; JR = Japan Railway Company.

Private Business Practices

For major railway corporations, development-based LVC is an important business practice not only to fund capital-intensive railway projects but also to offer value-added lifestyles along railway corridors through their real estate and other service businesses (Murakami 2012). The private railway corporations in Tokyo have played multiple roles, such as transport engineers, land brokers, and town planners in broader urban contexts. To explain their actual practices, the revenue proportions of seven major private railway corporations in the metropolitan area are presented (figure 4.3). Annual revenue from real estate and other businesses ranged between 18.2 percent and 40.5 percent in fiscal year (FY) 2011, which was much lower than in the 1980s and 1990s (Association of Japanese Private Railways 2013; Cervero 1998). The largest is Tokyu Corporation, with annual revenue of about ¥96 billion ($1.2 billion) from real estate and non-railway business.

Among many railway agencies, Tokyu Corporation is internationally well known for its development-based LVC practices over past decades. Nonetheless, its development strategy in recent years has evolved to tackle the huge demographic and business changes along railway corridors (Murakami 2012). Its net income shares from multiple business practices for FY2003–12 are shown in figure 4.4. Real estate accounted for about 34 percent of net income, and transport—railway and feeder bus services—about 41 percent. It raises about 25 percent of total income from residential, business, and leisure services, which indicates the growing importance of providing multiple services with railway investment and real estate development, helping support the railway's long-term operation and maintenance costs.

In addition, the Japan Railway Companies have also acquired real estate and retail service expertise since the 1987 privatization and have seized LVC opportunities in their own properties in and around stations. In particular,

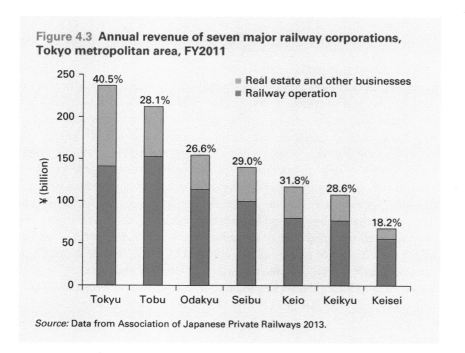

Figure 4.3 Annual revenue of seven major railway corporations, Tokyo metropolitan area, FY2011

Source: Data from Association of Japanese Private Railways 2013.

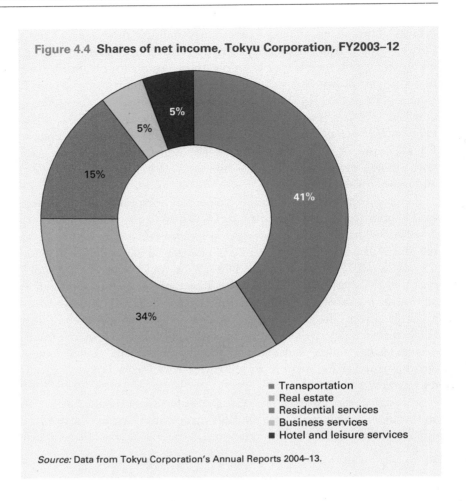

Figure 4.4 **Shares of net income, Tokyu Corporation, FY2003–12**

- Transportation
- Real estate
- Residential services
- Business services
- Hotel and leisure services

Source: Data from Tokyu Corporation's Annual Reports 2004–13.

JR East's station space utilization and shopping center and office building business practices have become substantial revenue sources, accounting for about 23 percent of corporate income over the last decade (figure 4.5). The concentrations of retail service and property business activities are observed within JR East's terminal buildings and station concourses, where the railway company enjoys the government's large property tax reduction that aims to support railway operations and public space uses. While JR East's "in-station" business model (*Ekinaka* in Japanese) has gained wider commercial popularity across other private railway corporations, there was public criticism that such in-station business practices with the government's tax reduction redistributed sales transactions from other retailers and undermined the viability of traditional street-level businesses outside railway stations. In 2007, the Tokyo Metropolitan Government responded by levying a surcharge of ¥2.2 billion ($21 million) on the private railway companies' properties across 83 stations (Tokyo Metropolitan Government 2007).

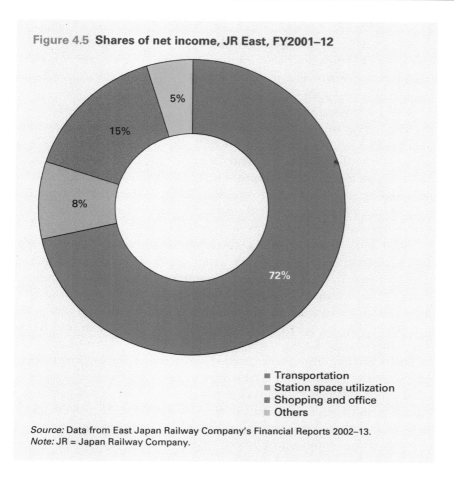

Figure 4.5 Shares of net income, JR East, FY2001–12

- Transportation
- Station space utilization
- Shopping and office
- Others

Source: Data from East Japan Railway Company's Financial Reports 2002–13.
Note: JR = Japan Railway Company.

Four Development Cases

Four development cases stand out among those in the metropolitan area, selected from different LVC types, stakeholders, locations, and periods. Each case attempts to provide detail on local contexts and needs, innovative LVC mechanisms, key instruments, development parameters, stakeholder relationships, successful implementation, and challenges.

Case 1: Futakotamagawa Station, Tokyu Denentoshi Line— Internalization by Private Railway Corporations

Tokyu Corporation practiced the garden city concept along its Denentoshi Line extensions between 1966 and 1984. The business territories defined by the corporation are about 490 square kilometers across the 17 jurisdictions, with some 5 million residents in 2.5 million households whose income is 50 percent higher than the national average. Of all the territories, the garden city districts account for about 50 square kilometers with 600,000 residents along the Denentoshi Line (Tokyu Corporation 2013).

The garden city development is high-quality and self-sufficient and supports a well-mixed variety of businesses within a suburban setting: offices, banks, universities and private schools, medical and community centers, public service branches, department stores and supermarkets, hotels, and recreational facilities (Cervero 1998).

With a shrinking and aging society, demography is a critical factor for the corporation to update and sustain its development model in the coming decades. Over the last decade, for example, its business territories have gained about 400,000 residents, and the proportion of adults older than 65 has increased from 15 to 19 percent—an aging trend set to continue for the next two decades, reaching 29 percent by 2035. Such changes have called for a range of large-scale redevelopment projects and unconventional service facilities in recent years (Tokyu Corporation 2013).

The redevelopment around Futakotamagawa Station reflects the corporation's new strategy and key approaches to recent and projected market trends (table 4.3). About 19 kilometers southwest from the central business district (Tokyo Station), the five redevelopment packages attempt to form a new center for commercial, residential, and leisure activities, with urban accessibility around Tokyu's railway station and suburban amenities by the Tama River (figure 4.6).

The inner-city office spaces included in this mixed-use development target innovative industries and creative workers, distinguishing itself from other office buildings for conventional white-collar businesses in Tokyo's central areas. The corporation has also differentiated the new shopping facilities for younger consumers from existing retail stores for elderly residents around the station, intending to generate commercial synergies rather than redistributive effects in the same station area.

The project has provided a generous amount of new public facilities, such as a transit plaza, local roads, and parks, through an urban redevelopment scheme that has raised public subsidies (¥36.6 billion/$355 million) and substantial floor area sales (¥100.1 billion/$971 million). Nonetheless, the redevelopment has taken nearly 15 years, involving more than 200 landowners and tenants in inclusive and complex floor area reallocation procedures (figure 4.7). Owning more than 95 percent of the property rights around the station, the corporation has made a real effort to integrate multiple objectives and functions into one redevelopment, so as to generate recurrent benefits through synergistic area management activities rather than temporary profits from speculation (Murakami 2012).

Case 2: Kashiwanoha Campus Station, Tsukuba Express— Integration of Housing Development and Railway Investment

Tsukuba Express is the latest large-scale suburban railway development in the metropolitan area, opening with 20 stations in 2005. The 58.4-kilometer

Table 4.3 Futakotamagawa Station redevelopment project

Project period	2000–15 (15 years)
Distance to central business district	18.8 km
Daily ridership	77,422 passengers (2011)
Site area	11.2 ha
FAR	3.8 (2.1–6.5)
Floor area use	District I-a: 17,200 sq. m. (retail) District I-b: 106,700 sq. m. (retail and office) District II-a: 156,400 sq. m. (retail, office, and hotel) District II-b: 9,400 sq. m. (retail and residential) District III: 133,300 sq. m. (residential and retail)
Public facilities	Trunk road: 1,820 meters District road: 260 meters Transit plaza: 5,800 sq. m. Park: 2,520 sq. m.
Car parking	2,258 spaces
Project phase	2 phases (5 packages)
Instrument	Urban redevelopment scheme
Key stakeholders	Tokyu Corporation (owning over 95% of total area); 211 local landholders and tenants
Project costs	Phase I: ¥102.9 billion ($999 million) Phase II: ¥39.1 billion ($379 million)
Funding arrangements	Subsidies: ¥36.6 billion ($355 million) Floor area sales: ¥100.1 billion ($971 million) Others: ¥5.4 billion ($52 million)

Source: Adapted from Futakotamagawa East District II Urban Redevelopment Association 2013a.
Note: FAR = floor area ratio; ha = hectare; km = kilometer; sq. m. = square meter.

line, which offers 130 kilometer an hour passenger services between the central areas of Tokyo (Akihabara) and multiple satellite towns (like Kashiwanoha Campus Town and Tsukuba Science City), is the only case implemented in accord with the Housing-Railway Integration Law of 1989. The Metropolitan Intercity Railway Company was established in 1991 jointly by the multiple local governments along the railway corridor with private shareholders. While other new town line projects in the 1980s and 1990s suffered from high land acquisition costs and interest payments (such as the Hokuso Line), Tsukuba Express in recent years has more innovatively adapted land readjustment projects with zero-interest loans, as well as public assistance programs to finance the roughly ¥808 billion ($7.5 billion) cost of construction.

Figure 4.6 Redevelopment layout around Futakotamagawa Station

Source: Futakotamagawa East District II Urban Redevelopment Association 2013a with data from Tokyu Corporation and Setagaya Ward.

There were 18 land readjustment districts, accounting for about 2,903 hectares around 13 stations. Across the 18 districts, the prefectural government, Urban Renaissance Agency (former Housing and Urban Development Public Corporation), and municipal governments reserved rights of way for development through their land readjustment practices. They then transferred the assembled land parcels to the Railway Construction Agency at an assessment price, significantly economizing on painstaking land acquisition tasks (figure 4.8). The local governments and public housing agency simultaneously promoted transit-oriented townships with original landholders and new residents by coordinating land parcels reserved for sale or public facilities around the new stations.

Kashiwanoha Campus Station, 32 kilometers northeast from Tokyo center, presents further information for practitioners considering future suburban developments (table 4.4). The Chiba prefectural government's land readjustment project began in 2000 when it designated a 272.9-hectare district occupied mainly by a golf course, fields, forested hills, and small factories. Through readjustment, the large area has been converted into developable land parcels for residential, commercial, industrial, educational,

Figure 4.7 Futakotamagawa redevelopment floor area reallocation, phase I

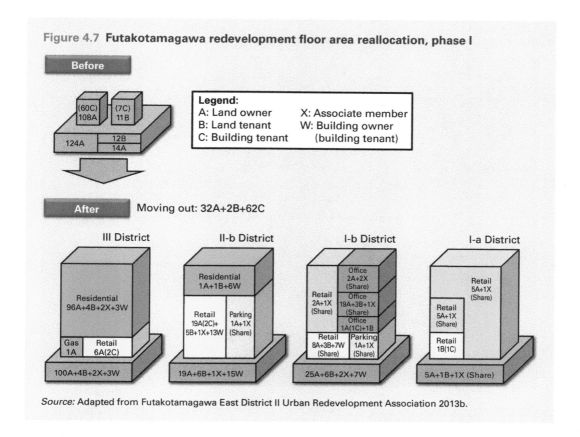

Before

(60C) 108A   (7C) 11B

124A   12B 14A

Legend:
A: Land owner   X: Associate member
B: Land tenant   W: Building owner
C: Building tenant   (building tenant)

After   Moving out: 32A+2B+62C

III District

Residential 96A+4B+2X+3W

Gas 1A | Retail 6A(2C)

100A+4B+2X+3W

II-b District

Residential 1A+1B+6W

Retail 19A(2C)+ 5B+1X+13W | Parking 1A+1X (Share)

19A+6B+1X+15W

I-b District

Office 2A+2X (Share)

Retail 2A+1X (Share) | Office 19A+3B+1X (Share)

Office 1A(1C)+1B

Retail 8A+3B+7W (Share) | Parking 1A+1X (Share)

25A+6B+2X+7W

I-a District

Retail 5A+1X (Share)

Retail 5A+1X (Share)

Retail 1B(1C)

5A+1B+1X (Share)

Source: Adapted from Futakotamagawa East District II Urban Redevelopment Association 2013b.

and social service uses served by roads, utilities, parks, green spaces, and a new railway station. With the provision of full-service public facilities and changes in maximum FARs (2.0–4.0), the total asset price is estimated to increase from ¥232.6 billion ($2.2 billion) to ¥330.1 billion ($3.1 billion), or 41.9 percent before and after land readjustment. The project costs of ¥96.3 billion ($891 million) have largely been recovered from sales of reserved land parcels—about ¥60.9 billion ($563 million, 63.2 percent)— and other sources, though Tokyo's demand for suburban housing has been unfavorable in the last decade.

Local efforts in the new suburban township development involved key landholders and research institutes around the railway station. Mitsui Fudosan Corporation, an original owner of the former golf course, is of particular importance as the largest landholder and developer in the district. With its real estate expertise and resources to maximize the value of its assets, the corporation has invested in a new shopping mall and residential tower package under the Smart City concept (information technology applications, electric vehicle stations, and renewable energy systems) that target young households with children (photo 4.1). Having large satellite campuses near the new station, two universities have together held urban design workshops with the developer, city government, railway company,

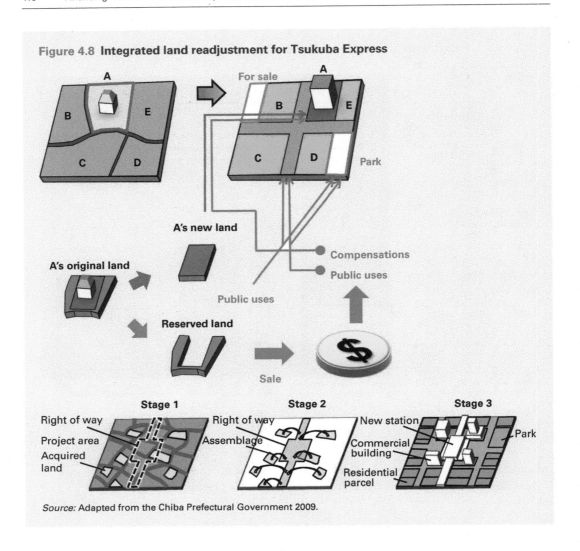

Figure 4.8 Integrated land readjustment for Tsukuba Express

Source: Adapted from the Chiba Prefectural Government 2009.

commercial associations, and nonprofit organizations, which may add further value to the district in the long run.

Case 3: Yokohama MM21 Line—Agreement with Land Developers and Building Owners

For several decades, the city of Yokohama has been recognized internationally as a pioneering developer. Notably, the MM21 district, about 30 kilometers southwest of Tokyo center, is an icon of modern waterfront development, and one that aimed to form a regional business cluster of about 160,000 workers. The city's project team, with the Urban Renaissance Agency, set up a land readjustment district over the 100-hectare way front area, including the Mitsubishi group's large shipyard, in the early

Table 4.4 Land readjustment project around Kashiwanoha Campus Station on Tsukuba Express

Project period	2000–23 (23 years)
Distance to central business district	32.0 km
Daily ridership	12,744 passengers (2012)
Population	26,000 (projection)
Site area	272.9 ha
FAR	2.0–4.0
Land use	Residential: 110.5 ha (40.5%)
	Commercial: 20.9 ha (7.7%)
	Industrial: 31.6 ha (11.6%)
	Educational: 7.7 ha (2.8%)
	Social service: 12.4 ha (4.5%)
	Railway: 2.3 ha (0.8%)
Public facilities	Road: 66.6 ha (24.4%)
	Park and green space: 10.3 ha (3.8%)
	Water: 10.6 ha (3.9%)
Project	1 district
Instrument	Land readjustment project
	(Reduction rate: 40%: 13.55% for reserved land and 26.45% for public use)
Key stakeholders	Chiba prefectural government; Mitsui Fudosan Corporation; universities; 900 landholders and tenants
Project costs	¥96.3 billion ($891 million)
Funding arrangements	Subsidies: ¥32.5 billion ($301 million)
	Land Sales: ¥60.9 billion ($564 million)
	Others: ¥2.9 billion ($27 million)

Sources: Chiba Prefectural Government 2013; Tsukuba Express 2013.
Note: FAR = floor area ratio; ha = hectare; km = kilometer.

1980s (table 4.5). In this development, the high-rise commercial towers, given the maximum FAR of 8.0, are directly served by the new MM21 subway line, connecting the existing Yokohama Station and 4.1 kilometers of the Bay Shore commercial and recreational districts, with five distinctively designed stations (map 4.4). Acquisition of the 1.3-hectare rights of way for the MM21 line was incorporated into the land readjustment scheme.

Photo 4.1 Shopping mall and residential tower package under the Smart City concept around Kashiwanoha Campus Station

Source: © Mitsui Fudosan Corporation. Used with permission. Further permission required for reuse.

Table 4.5 MM21 waterfront development project

Project period	1983–2006 (23 years)
Distance to central business district	30.5 km
Daily ridership	33,067 passengers (2012)
Employment	160,000 (projection)
Site area	101.8 ha
FAR	4.0–8.0
Land use	Commercial: 66.1 ha (64.9%)
Public facilities	Road: 24.4 ha (24.0%)
	Highway: 1.5 ha (1.5%)
	Park and green space: 5.0 ha (4.9%)
	Water: 2.4 ha (2.3%)
	Station plaza: 1.1 ha (1.1%)
	Railway: 1.3 ha (1.3%)
Project	1 district
Instrument	Land readjustment project
	(Reduction rate: 36.5%)
Key stakeholders	Mitsubishi Real Estate; City of Yokohama; Urban Renaissance Agency; Yokohama MM Railway Company

(continued next page)

Table 4.5 MM21 waterfront development project *(continued)*

MM21 Line	
Project period	1992–2004 (12 years)
Length	4.1 km (6 stations)
Project costs	¥257 billion ($2 billion)
Funding arrangements	Benefit sharing: ¥74.0 billion ($578 million)
	Contribution: ¥27.0 billion ($211 million)
	Public loan: ¥129.0 billion ($1 billion)
	Bank loan: ¥27.0 billion ($211 million)

Source: Urban Renaissance Agency 2006.
Note: FAR = floor area ratio; ha = hectare; km = kilometer.

The Yokohama MM Railway Company, which operates the MM21 line, is the third sector body, jointly owned by the city of Yokohama, prefectural government, private railway corporations, Mitsubishi Real Estate, and bankers. Subway line development cost about ¥257 billion ($2 billion), due in large part to the difficulty of underground construction in reclamation districts. To finance such a megaproject, the city made negotiation-based agreements with major developers and landowners, including Mitsubishi Real Estate, which was an original landholder of the former shipyard and an owner of the new commercial towers, for sharing accessibility benefits from the MM21 line investment. The land premiums to be shared were estimated at ¥74 billion ($578 million), accounting for nearly 29 percent of project costs (City of Yokohama 2009).

Although Yokohama's benefit-sharing arrangement worked in practice, similar projects often raise the question of how to decide on the allocation of vertical space between underground structure constraints and FAR bonuses. The following case finds some possible solutions.

Case 4: Shinagawa Station, JR Yamanote Line—Settlement of Former JNR Debt

The former JNR's yard site sales for debt settlement has had major impacts on Tokyo's landscape over the past few decades, as had the recent urban regeneration boom. The high-rise commercial tower redevelopment around JR Shinagawa Station illustrates how the JNR Settlement Corporation arranged large sales of former yard sites in Tokyo's central area, and during the "post-bubble" period of Japan created highly value-added business environments with multiple developers, property owners, and local governments (photo 4.2). Through the 1987 privatization, about 10 hectares of the Shinagawa rail yard was transferred to the JNR Settlement Corporation not only to pay off the huge debt but also to increase asset values by

Map 4.4 MM21 land readjustment scheme with the rights of way for the new subway line

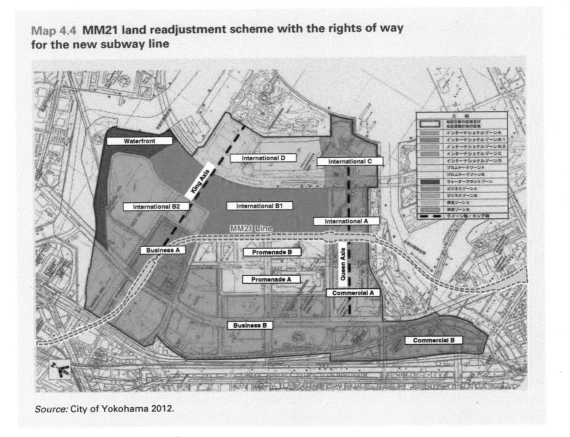

Source: City of Yokohama 2012.

promoting more comprehensive area planning and development around the station. The initial yard's function was gradually relocated to another site in Tokyo, costing about ¥42 billion ($382 million) over 18 years.

The redevelopment methods for this site were rather advanced in several respects (table 4.6). The JNR Settlement Corporation, bringing in JR East, private developers, new property owners, and local governments, designated the land readjustment district over the 13.7 hectares that encompassed the 10-hectare yard site, as well as surrounding public-private blocks. This extensive approach generated greater road access to the station and a better connected pedestrian network in and around the project district without much public assistance. This urban regeneration package was comprehensively adapted to convert both the land readjustment and private property redevelopment districts (totaling 16.2 hectares) into six hyper-blocks that incorporated "human-scale" circulation systems within the six large parcels (map 4.5).

Photo 4.2 Before and after rail yard redevelopment around JR Shinagawa Station, 1981 and 2008

1. Before

2. After

Source: ©Japan Railway Construction, Transport and Technology Agency, 1981 and 2008. Used with permission. Further permission required for reuse.

Table 4.6 Former rail yard redevelopment project around JR Shinagawa Station

Project period	1992–2006 (14 years)
Distance to central business district	6.8 km
Daily ridership	329,679 passengers (2012)
Employment	40,000 (projection)
Site area	16.2 ha
FAR	6.8–9.5
Floor area use	A-1: 337,119 sq. m. (commercial) A-2: 7,381 sq. m. (commercial) B-1: 469,770 sq. m. (commercial) B-1: 114,586 sq. m. (residential) B-2: 62,740 ha (commercial) B-3: 70,307 ha (commercial) B-4: 39,961 ha (commercial)
Public facilities	Road: 3.9 ha (28.2%) Park: 0.5 ha (3.4%) Transit plaza: 1.0 ha (7.0%)
Car parking	3,188 spaces
Project	1 district (6 superblocks)
Instrument	Government land sales Land readjustment project (Reduction rate: 40.78%) Urban redevelopment scheme
Key stakeholders	JNR Settlement Corporation; JR East; Central Japan Railway Company; Tokyo Metropolitan Government; two ward governments; 20 private corporations; nine individual landholders
Project costs	Yard relocation: ¥42 billion (US$382 million) Land readjustment: ¥33 billion (US$300 million) Roads, bridges, and so on: ¥50 billion (US$455 million) Private buildings: ¥360 billion (est.) (US$3.3 billion)
Land valuation	Land sales: ¥30 billion (US$272 million) Before: ¥1.9 million per sq. m. (1996) (US$17,000/sq. m.) After: ¥3.3 million per sq. m. (2007) (US$30,000/sq. m.)

Source: Japan Railway Construction, Transport and Technology Agency 2006.
Note: FAR = floor area ratio; ha = hectare; JNR = Japanese National Railways; JR = Japan Railway Company; km = kilometer; sq. m. = square meter.

To incentivize the provision of residential, pedestrian, and public amenity spaces within the private commercial redevelopments, substantial FAR bonuses were given to the new property owners. For instance, the B-1 commercial district (base FAR 7.0) achieved the maximum FAR of 9.5 by including 35,433 square meters of collective housing floor area for a bonus FAR of 0.6 and by creating public open and green spaces as well as a pedestrian skyway network for a bonus FAR of 1.9. This attracted amenity-conscious business entities and increased property prices. Land values of the station area soared by over 73.6 percent, but such a jump was also likely due to intercity accessibility benefits produced by JR Central's new Shinkansen stop, which opened in 2003. The construction costs of the wide bridge with the new Shinkansen terminus were paid for from the developer-building owner side through a petition process, largely because JR Central had taken a passive position since the early stages of the regeneration plan.

Map 4.5 Access roads, pedestrian facilities, and green spaces provided by private property owners within the superblocks for floor area ratio bonuses

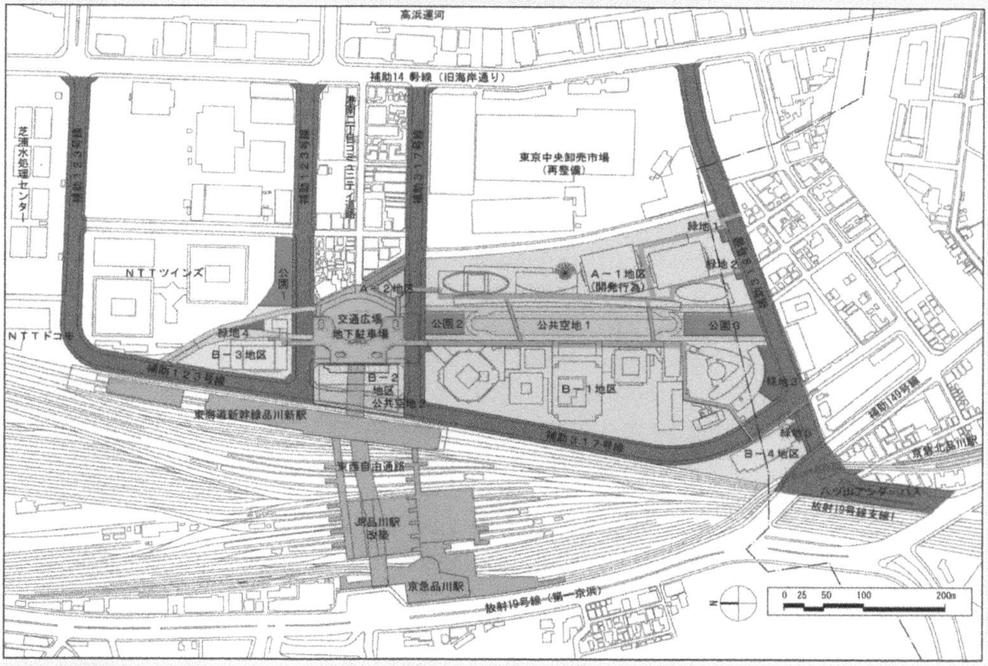

■ Planned access road	■ Public open space
■ District road	■ Underground car access
■ Park	■ Pedestrian deck
■ Skywalk	■ Underground car parking

Source: Japan Railway Construction, Transport and Technology Agency 2004.

Conclusion

Tokyo metropolitan area has adopted a draft of LVC railway practices related to stakeholders, location, period, and scale. Key procedures may be analyzed and lessons drawn from its transit-oriented experiences for traditional capital city-regions and newly emerging megacities of developing countries:

- The national-, provincial-, or metropolitan-scale government's master plan principally leads to polycentric regional development and railway extension strategies, though multiple public, private, and semiprivate entities use different development approaches and LVC techniques in the same metropolitan area. All stakeholders need to share a clear vision and take collective actions, so as to face the macroeconomic and demographic trends of the future.

- Under market freehold systems, the land readjustment and urban redevelopment schemes are two main instruments to apply LVC to transit finance and develop transit-oriented systems in built-up areas and urban fringes. Both instruments, however, essentially require inclusive decision making, which is often time-consuming, and smooth implementation relies on traditional social ties or economic incentives. Eminent domain may help practitioners speed up land assembly; however, careless application is likely to generate long-lasting social tensions and mistrust.

- Some degree of railway privatization is necessary to progressively apply the development-based LVC concept through property developments and related transactions around stations. Entrepreneurial railway agencies should acquire expertise not only in conventional system engineering but also in real estate investment, town planning, and marketing to set up appropriate development parameters, analyze market profiles, offer multiple services, and maximize value increments in their station properties and wider catchment areas. Essentially, railway agencies need to be entitled to keep the long-term ownership and stewardship of properties to generate recurrent revenues from both development and service activities around stations.

- A variety of LVC techniques can be adapted by stakeholder, location, period, and scale across a single city-region. Policymakers have to understand the characteristics of each approach and design combinations of techniques in their local context. There is no single development-based LVC model that can solve all financial and spatial concerns.

- The rights of way for a new railway line can be assembled cost-effectively by transit agencies and local governments through land readjustment projects, especially where local residents are waiting for railway access. This can promote property development along the new line at the same time, which would achieve target ridership and fare revenues in the following years.

* Major landholders/developers in a designated district can help in land readjustment. With enough real estate knowledge and resources, they are more likely to invest in local infrastructure, take initiatives in planning, and maximize the value of their land around a new station.

* To create high-quality built environments around a station, substantial density bonuses should be provided. This incentivizes private transit agencies and developers to supply social infrastructure and services, maximize synergistic effects, and mitigate redistributive impacts through inclusiveness. This technique can also be used to provide human-scale built environments within the superblocks already constructed in many developing countries.

Note

1. A fuel tax and vehicle registration fee earmarked for road-related projects.

References

Association of Japanese Private Railways. 2013. "Major Private Railways: Databook." Tokyo. www.mintetsu.or.jp/activity/databook/.

Bowen, Roger Wilson. 1975. "The Narita Conflict." *Asian Survey* 15 (7): 598–615.

Cervero, Robert. 1998. *The Transit Metropolis: A Global Inquiry.* Washington, DC: Island Press.

Chiba Prefectural Government. 2009. "Human- and Environment-Friendly Town Planning: Kashiwa North Central District." Chiba City, Japan.

———. 2013. "Kashiwa North Central District Town Planning." Chiba City, Japan. http://www.pref.chiba.lg.jp/tosei/tsukuba/ensenseibi/kashiwa hokubu/.

City of Yokohama. 2009. "8th City of Yokohama Committee Meeting for the Third-sector Entities' Business Performance Improvement: Material Number 2." Yokohama, Japan.

———. 2012. "Minato Mirai 21 Central District, District Plan, Planning Map." Yokohama, Japan. www.city.yokohama.lg.jp/toshi/tikukeikaku/c-010m.html.

East Japan Railway Company. 2002–13. "East Japan Railway Company Financial Report." Shibuya, Japan. http://www.jreast.co.jp/investor/.

Futakotamagawa East District II Urban Redevelopment Association. 2013a. "Summary of Building Projects." Tokyo. www.futakotamagawa -rise.com/future02.html.

———. 2013b. "Summary of Building Projects." Tokyo. www.futakota magawa-rise.com/future03.html.

Japan Railway Construction, Transport and Technology Agency. 2004. "Shinagawa Station East Gate Town Planning and Land Readjustment Project Report: Record of Shinagawa Station East Gate Town Land Readjustment Project." Yokohama, Japan.

———. 2006. "Shinagawa Station East Gate Land Readjustment Project: Commemorative Booklet to Remark Completion." Yokohama, Japan.

Japan Society of Civil Engineering, ed. 1991. *Transportation Development Framework: Mechanism and Challenge*. Tokyo: Japan Society of Civil Engineering.

Ministry of Land, Infrastructure, and Transport. 2006. "National Capital Region Master Plan." Tokyo, September. www.mlit.go.jp/kokudokei kaku/vision/s-plan/s-planhonbun.pdf.

Ministry of Land, Infrastructure, Transport, and Tourism. 2008. "Knowledge Sharing About Public Involvement." Tokyo. www.nilim.go.jp/lab /gbg/pi/pi.html.

———. 2013a. "Geographic Information System Download Service – Railway." Tokyo. http://nlftp.mlit.go.jp/ksj/gml/datalist/KsjTmplt-N02-v2_2 .html.

———. 2013b. "Urban Redevelopment Project." Tokyo. www.mlit.go.jp /crd/city/sigaiti/shuhou/saikaihatsu/saikaihatsu.htm.

———. 2013c. "Urban Regeneration Special Districts: Regulation and Inducement." Tokyo. www.mlit.go.jp/jutakukentiku/house/seido/kisei /60-2toshisaisei.html.

Murakami, Jin. 2010. "The Transit-Oriented Global Centers for Competitiveness and Livability: State Strategies and Market Responses in Asia." Dissertation, University of California, Berkeley. www.escholarship.org /uc/item/19034785.

———. 2012. "Transit Value Capture: New Town Codevelopment Models and Land Market Updates in Tokyo and Hong Kong." In *Value Capture and Land Policies*, edited by Gregory K. Ingram and Yu-Hung Hong, 285–320. Cambridge, MA: Lincoln Institute of Land Policy. www.lincoln inst.edu/pubs/2026_Value-Capture-and-Land-Policies.

Oizumi, E. 1994. "Property Finance in Japan: Expansion and Collapse of the Bubble Economy." *Environment and Planning A* 26 (2): 199–213. doi:10.1068/a260199.

Saxonhouse, Gary R., and Robert M. Stern. 2003. "The Bubble and the Lost Decade." *The World Economy* 26 (3): 267–81. doi:10.1111/1467 -9701.00522.

Sorensen, André. 1999. "Land Readjustment, Urban Planning and Urban Sprawl in the Tokyo Metropolitan Area." *Urban Studies* 36 (13): 2333–60. doi:10.1080/0042098992458.

————. 2000. "Land Readjustment and Metropolitan Growth: An Examination of Suburban Land Development and Urban Sprawl in the Tokyo Metropolitan Area." *Progress in Planning* 53 (4): 217–330. doi:10.1016/S0305-9006(00)00002-7.

————. 2006. "Livable Cities in Japan: Population Ageing and Decline as Vectors of Change." *International Planning Studies* 11 (3–4): 225–42. doi:10.1080/13563470701231703.

Sorensen, André, Junichiro Okata, and Sayaka Fujii. 2009. "Urban Renaissance as Intensification: Building Regulation and the Rescaling of Place Governance in Tokyo's High-Rise Manshon Boom." *Urban Studies* 47 (3): 556–83. doi:10.1177/0042098009349775.

Statistics Bureau, Government of Japan. 2005. "Population Census of Japan." Tokyo. www.stat.go.jp/data/kokusei/2005/.

Tokyo Metropolitan Government. 2007. "Press Release Document." Tokyo. www.metro.tokyo.jp/INET/OSHIRASE/2007/10/20ha2200.htm.

Tokyo Metropolitan Government Expropriation Commission. 2013. "Eminent Domain." Tokyo. www.shuyou.metro.tokyo.jp/07syuyouseidotoha/07syuyouseidotoha.html.

Tokyu Corporation. 2013. "Fact Sheet." Tokyo. www.tokyu.co.jp/ir/english/library/library_06.html.

————. 2004–13. "Tokyu Corporation Annual Report." Tokyo. www.tokyu.co.jp/ir/library/library_09.html.

Transport Policy Committee. 2000. *Railway-Centered Transportation Network Development Master Plan in the Tokyo Metropolitan Area.* Transport Policy Committee Response. Tokyo: Ministry of Land, Infrastructure and Transport. www.mlit.go.jp/kisha/oldmot/kisha00/koho00/tosin/kotumo/mokuji_.htm.

Tsukuba Express. 2013. "Tsukuba Express Summary." Metropolitan Intercity Railway Company, Tokyo. www.mir.co.jp/feature/about_tx/.

UN (United Nations). 2012. World Urbanization Prospects: The 2011 Revision, CD-ROM Edition. New York: Department of Economic and Social Affairs, Population Division.

Urban Regeneration Headquarters. 2001. "Activity Report: Promoting Private Investment in Urban Development." Tokyo. www.kantei.go.jp/jp/singi/tosisaisei/sanko/kadai4.pdf.

————. 2013. "Urban Regeneration Project: Program Map." Tokyo. www.kantei.go.jp/jp/singi/tiiki/toshisaisei/05suisin/map02.html.

Urban Renaissance Agency. 2006. "Minato Mirai 21 Central District Land Readjustment: Projects Review." Yokohama, Japan. www.ur-net.go.jp/toshisaisei/urbanr/pdf2/mm21.pdf.

CHAPTER 5

Development-Based LVC Practices in North America and Europe: New York City and Washington, DC, United States; and London, United Kingdom

Some cities in North America and Europe have also used development-based land value capture (LVC). Urban railways have helped improve urban dwellers' mobility and accessibility and develop world-class service- and knowledge-based business clusters by enhancing economic competitiveness, environmental sustainability, and social equity.

Three cities in particular have intensified property development and the financing of local infrastructure and services around their key terminals. New York City has a long history of programs with transferable development rights (TDRs) for preserving landmarks and densifying commercial activity on and around Grand Central Terminal. The Washington Metropolitan Area Transit Authority (WMATA) has extensively used joint development (JD) programs to achieve transit-oriented development (TOD) by sharing the benefits and costs of planning and development with local governments and private developers. In London, local governments and private developers, redeveloping the King's Cross rail yard, stress the importance of sharing the benefits conferred mainly around the newly integrated transit terminus. The three cases—though less so than Hong Kong SAR, China, and Tokyo—provide analogies and lessons for practitioners in developing countries.

Context: The United States

The funding sources for fixed-guideway transit projects in the United States can be roughly categorized into four types: funds directly generated by transit agencies, federal government financial assistance, local government financial assistance, and state government financial assistance. In 2011, directly generated funds accounted for 44.0 percent of all operating expenditure and 24.4 percent of all capital expenditure, and federal funds 9.8 percent of operating expenditure and 44.0 percent of capital expenditure. Local government funds are usually generated from taxes or fees assessed within a jurisdiction and in 2011 covered roughly 22.0 percent of operating expenditure and 18.5 percent of capital expenditure. The capital funds for transit "directly generated by transit agencies and local government sources" jumped from 1995 to 2011 by about 160 percent (APTA 2013).

Despite increasing dependency on transit agent and local government sources, these financial figures indicate that fixed-guideway transit ridership has not been high enough to recover capital costs and operation and maintenance costs. Indeed, farebox recovery from all such transit systems in U.S. transit metropolises was far below 100 percent, though the numbers of transit passengers grew by 36 percent from 1995 to 2012. Certainly, high project costs and low passenger volumes contribute to the low-cost-recovery rate of these transit projects in the country. Realistically, their financial viability depends on the degree of transit-supportive urban development patterns in each project. Higher density areas tend to have higher transit capital expenses as well as higher transit passenger volumes, based on data from 59 transit projects in 19 U.S. metropolitan areas (Guerra and Cervero 2011).

Given severe municipal fiscal constraints, increased market demand for new and existing fixed-guideway transit projects with TOD infrastructure that could support cost-effective operation requires innovative approaches. A report from the U.S. Environmental Protection Agency on how to fund TOD infrastructure highlights a range of financing options and cases that fall into six broad categories: direct fees, debt, credit assistance, equity, grants and other philanthropic sources, and LVC (U.S. EPA 2013). The report expands on the sixth category, indicating that LVC typically takes the form of one or more of the following: creation of a new assessment, tax, or fee (a special tax or development impact fee); diversion of new revenue generated by an existing tax (tax-increment financing); or a revenue-sharing agreement that allows a government agency to share some of the revenue generated by developing publicly owned land (through the JD programs).

Here we attempt to analyze the use of development-based LVC in the United States—specifically TDRs and JD programs—as financing and planning tools to promote TOD in global financial and business centers like New York City and Washington, DC.

New York City: Evolution of Transfer of Development Rights in Manhattan

The TDR concept was initially adopted by New York City along with the first American Zoning Ordinance of 1916, in response to urban neighborhood opposition to skyscrapers. It allowed landholders to sell their unused

densities or "air rights" to adjacent land parcels, and developers to realize further densification in already well-developed Manhattan by exceeding New York City's existing zoning code, such as floor area ratio (FAR),
building height and setback limits, with the air rights transferred. The modern application of TDR as a land use (regulation) technique to preserve
historically important buildings, public open spaces, and valuable natural
resources began from the enactment of the New York City Landmarks
Preservation Law in 1968. The U.S. Supreme Court case—*Penn Central
Transportation Co. v. New York City*, in 1978—further acknowledged the
TDR concept to mitigate the economic impact of the city's land use regulation on and around historic landmarks (New York State 2011).

Theoretically, TDR could achieve local planning goals without causing
an economic disbenefit to private landowners or spending a lot of municipal funds to acquire land, yet court cases long ago raised the question of the
uncertain demand for development rights mandatorily transferred within
the designated marketplace. Generally, a TDR program fails if market
demand for air rights does not exist, development opportunities are already
oversupplied in target districts, or market values of TDRs are insufficient
with high transaction costs between districts. Thus, TDR programs should
be accompanied by an amendment to city- or regionwide comprehensive
zoning plans that designates sending districts and receiving districts in a
strategic way (Nelson, Pruetz, and Woodruff 2012; New York State 2011).[1]

Yet how and where New York City's TDR programs are best suited in
modern property markets are still research issues. The Furman Center for
Real Estate and Urban Policy at New York University (2013) sheds light
on the TDR market in New York City using data on actual transactions
between 2003 and 2011. New York City's zoning code, or the Zoning Resolution, allows landholders to transfer unused development rights, mainly
in three ways: the Landmark Program helps compensate owners of designated landmarks for the (financial) burden of preserving old buildings by
allowing them to transfer unused development rights not only to adjacent
lots, but also across streets; the Zoning Lot Merger groups properties into
one large lot, allowing transfer of development rights through contiguous
lots; and the Special Purpose District allows zoning codes to be customized
so as to promote densification in very specific areas, which include redevelopment districts around Grand Central Terminal and Hudson Yards. The
study found that 385 of all 421 TDR transactions (91.4 percent) occurred
through the Zoning Lot Merger, of which 328 were arm's-length transactions between unaffiliated parties. The vast majority of the TDR deals
were in Manhattan, especially Midtown, where generous zoning codes
allow for further densification of developable parcels, and there is strong
market demand for commercial redevelopment around Grand Central,
with an average transaction price of $203 per square foot during 2003–11
(map 5.1).

Map 5.1 Lots transferring development rights, New York City, 2003–11

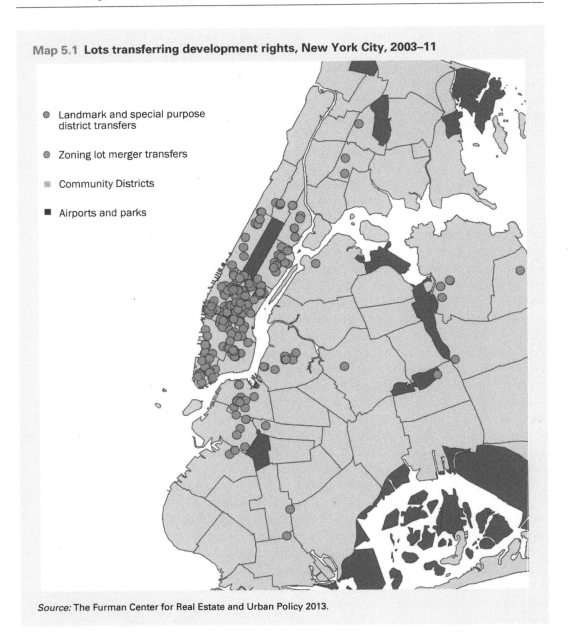

- Landmark and special purpose district transfers
- Zoning lot merger transfers
- Community Districts
- Airports and parks

Source: The Furman Center for Real Estate and Urban Policy 2013.

Reinvestment in and around Grand Central

Grand Central Terminal is at 42nd Street and Park Avenue in Midtown Manhattan, covering 48 acres. Built by the New York Central Railroad in the heyday of American long-distance passenger railway markets in the early 20th century, it was the largest and busiest station in the world, with 44 platforms serving 67 tracks. Among its many firsts, Grand Central Station electrified its tracks, eliminating dangers from steam-powered trains and allowing the entire train system to develop underground. This subterranean system also allowed for expansion above and around the station. In 1913, the *New York Times* reported that the "new" land created above the tracks was worth $2 million–$3 million per block. That land was among the most valuable on the continent, where the area taken up by one Pullman car was valued at $30,000. The newspaper called the development of real estate and the use of air rights as an "adequate return on the entire investment" (*New York Times* 1913). Park Avenue's transformation into one of the most iconic areas in Manhattan was largely due to the sale of air rights once the rail yards were moved underground (Morris 1969).

In 2013, Grand Central celebrated its 100th birthday and has been on the National Register of Historic Places since the mid-1970s. It now contains retail and office functions and is served by both multiple subway and commuter rail lines. Much of the area surrounding the terminal is built above the rail shed; the track network extends between Madison and Lexington Avenues but then narrows to about the width of Park Avenue going north. The area immediately surrounding it is one of the most densely developed areas in New York City. Many of the avenues and cross streets surrounding Grand Central are dominated by restaurants and other retail uses, some of which are built on large lots or take over entire blocks. The Park Avenue area north of Grand Central is marked by high-rise corporate headquarters, whereas the mixed-commercial/residential areas lie to the east of Lexington Avenue (Parsons Brinckerhoff 2013).

The area around the station allows for a FAR up to 21.6 through a special permit established in 1992. This was created to facilitate the transfer of development rights from landmarks—mainly from Grand Central—to new developments, while providing for improvements to the existing (mostly below-grade) pedestrian network surrounding them. However, due to the full public review required, as well as myriad other requirements, only one project (completed in 2001) has used this permit. Grand Central Terminal still has more than 1 million square feet of unused development rights.

There are four other ways to increase the FAR. A 1.0 FAR transfer is permitted through a certification process in the core area, which includes the western side of Madison Avenue and the eastern side of Lexington Avenue; it has only been used three times. Sites directly adjacent to subway entrances are eligible for subway station improvement bonuses of up to 20 percent more than the permitted base via a City Planning Commission special permit. Extensive development rights are available via transfer from the New York City Landmarks Preservation Committee—Designated Landmarks, but receiving properties must be adjacent or across the street and must get a City Planning Commission special permit. Finally, a 1.0 FAR bonus is permitted in areas outside the Grand Central subdistrict if a public plaza is provided (Parsons Brinckerhoff 2013).

Surrounded by Manhattan's major commercial activities, Grand Central Terminal is the second busiest subway station as a transfer point for the S, 4, 5, 6, and 7 lines, carrying almost 43 million passengers in 2012. East Side Access (ESA)—Long Island Rail Road (LIRR)'s new connection to Grand Central and scheduled to open in 2019—aims to provide direct access to East Midtown for LIRR commuters and to reduce train congestion, especially at Penn Station (map 5.2). A study by the Regional Plan Association (2013) shows that most time-saving benefits from the ESA project will accrue to the East Side nearest Grand Central in Manhattan, where 560,000 jobs are predicted to locate closer to the new ESA terminal (under Grand Central) than to Penn Station, since travel times could drop by 18 minutes a day on average and up to 42 minutes a day at best (map 5.3). These estimates may well understate as the study does not consider pedestrian access, egress, and amenity improvements around the new LIRR terminal promoted by New York City.

The ESA project has required capital improvement plans in and around Grand Central. As of December 19, 2012, the Capital Program budget of the Metropolitan Transportation Authority (MTA) totaled more than $29 billion for 2010–14 (including some amendments in the last few years), of which all LIRR capital projects account for about $2.3 billion. In particular, the ESA terminal at Grand Central costs $16.5 million under the Station and Buildings budget category, while the existing Grand Central elements require $93.8 million for tunnel constructions and facility renewals under the Metro-North Railroad budget category (MTA 2013).

Partly to finance the MTA's capital reinvestments in Grand Central, the New York City administration intended to adapt a TDR-based District Improvement Fund mechanism as part of the proposed East Midtown Rezoning project (box 5.1). However, the former Bloomberg administration had to withdraw the proposal as the City Council failed to support it. City Council members opposing it recognized the need for rezoning but had

Map 5.2. Long Island Rail Road's projected East Side Access—direct commuter connection into Grand Central

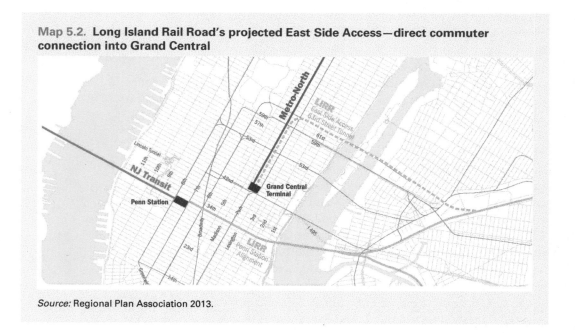

Source: Regional Plan Association 2013.

Map 5.3 Time savings by East Side Access and concentration of employment around Grand Central

1. Average travel time saving

Average Travel Time-Index Savings From
LIRR Stations, Post-ESA (minutes)

- 0 to -2.4
- -2.5 to -4.0
- -5.0 to -9.9
- -19.0 to -14.9
- -15.0 to -20.5

2. Employment density

Concentration of Employment, 2009
(Jobs per acre)

- < 100
- 100 – 500
- 500 – 1000
- 1000 – 1500
- 1500 – 2500

Source: Regional Plan Association 2013.
Note: ESA = East Side Access

several concerns including "the price, methodology and timing of the air rights to be sold by the City for the District Improvement Bonus as well as the certainty and funding level of the needed infrastructure improvements" (Council of the City of New York 2013). These issues would be revisited under the administration of Mayor Bill de Blasio.

Box 5.1 Proposed East Midtown rezoning and transferable development rights scheme

The zoning code of East Midtown's subdistrict (a 73-block area surrounding Grand Central) is a key deterrent to reinvestment in the area. Commercial zoning is typically 15 floor area ratio (FAR) along the avenues and 12 on some mid-blocks. This area contains about 400 buildings, with the average age over 70 years. In April 2013, the city's Planning Commissioner announced the beginning of a review on rezoning, provision of higher FAR, and projected revenue of up to $750 million for improving pedestrian access to transit and for maintaining the transit infrastructure.

The purpose of the rezoning is to ensure the economic competitiveness of East Midtown as a world-class business center and job generator for New York City. The plan provides zoning incentives to promote development of a handful of new, state-of-the-art commercial buildings so that East Midtown's premium office stocks remain attractive to a broad range of high-profile business entities. The rezoning redefines the Grand Central Subdistrict as a Grand Central Subarea. It would allow the owners of lots in the designated subarea that meet certain site criteria to add further densities above the maximum FAR 15 or 12, through the following three mechanisms (figure B5.1.1):

- *District Improvement Fund.* Owners of qualifying sites can obtain an additionally permitted FAR of 1.2–3.0 in exchange for making contributions to this fund, which will finance transit and pedestrian network improvements in the subarea.
- *Landmark Transfer.* After contributing to the District Improvement Fund, owners of qualifying sites in the new subarea can gain a further FAR of 1.2–6.6 by making further contributions to the fund, purchasing unused development rights from Grand Central Terminal, or directly improving transit infrastructure and pedestrian environments without special permit review. (Grand Central Core would be allowed up to 24.0 FAR under this zoning.)
- *Superior Development Special Permit.* Owners of qualifying sites in the new subarea will be permitted to build skyline-piercing towers by offering the "Superior Development" that provides substantial public benefits to the city through a special permission review process. (Grand Central Core would be allowed up to 30.0 FAR under this framework.)

(continued next page)

Conclusion

TDR was introduced to promote efficient land use without much public spending in land acquisition, typically when the municipal tax or fee base is weak. TDR has good potential to achieve multiple objectives with TOD, including financial viability of transit, economic competitiveness, environmental sustainability, and social equity. But although TDR has a long history of market transactions—from many court cases across U.S. cities—it is still hard to see how TDR can contribute to urban densification in an efficient way while protecting the public interest. Notably, use of TDR programs in assuring TOD is limited to a few commercial redevelopment cases in New York City, specifically Manhattan, accompanied by heavy capital reinvestment and rehabilitation in existing subway stations and pedestrian networks. In other words, from the case of New York City, we cannot conclude that TDR programs will lead extensively to pedestrian-friendly, high-density, mixed-income residences or mixed-use development along new transit extensions in suburban property markets.

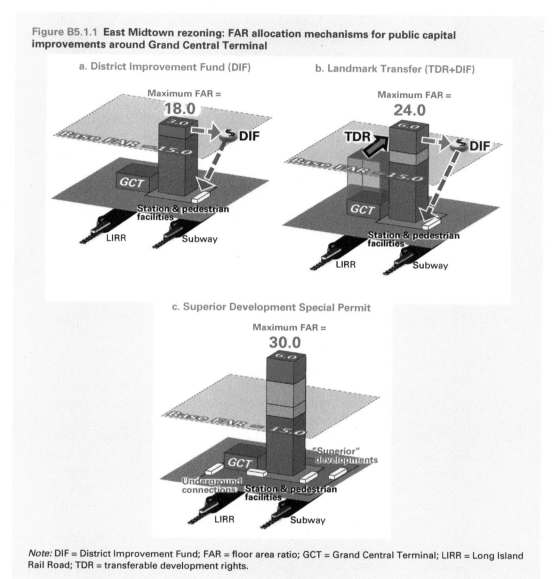

Figure B5.1.1 **East Midtown rezoning: FAR allocation mechanisms for public capital improvements around Grand Central Terminal**

Note: DIF = District Improvement Fund; FAR = floor area ratio; GCT = Grand Central Terminal; LIRR = Long Island Rail Road; TDR = transferable development rights.

Obviously, Manhattan is the world's most recognized agglomeration of finance and business activities. This reputation has attracted many domestic and international workers to seek creative jobs and open-minded lifestyles, which has required further commercial floor area along with social space—also supported by Manhattan's geographic and building constraints. Thus, in Manhattan, TDR programs could be lucrative for developers, as they clearly cannot build outward but can build upward within well-configured central business districts. Additionally, New York City's urban mobility options are critical. The transport component of the draft Environmental Impact Statement prepared for the proposed rezoning identified several areas where vehicular and pedestrian traffic would be adversely affected by such commercial densification. Certainly, the TDR-based District Improvement Fund seems rational as it incorporates private developers' financial contribution and density allocation mechanisms into funding TOD infrastructure.

On the contribution rates for bonus FAR in the proposed East Midtown Rezoning, the Furman Center's study (2013) points out that the uniformly designated contribution rates (at $250 per square foot for commercial use and $360 per square foot for residential use) would mitigate administrative costs and market unpredictability, but any single rate is very unlikely to reflect the actual market value of the bonus FAR granted to many of the respective development sites within the rezoned districts. This pricing inflexibility might diminish the funding capability to support public capital improvements and lead to unintended spatial consequences in East Midtown, especially if the District Improvement Fund's contribution rates for East Midtown are inconsistent with the redevelopment costs of competing office space being built in other parts of Manhattan. One alternative entails auctions to better reflect the market value of additional FAR based on site conditions, which have recently been introduced and implemented as the Certificate of Additional Construction Potential, sold within the Urban Operations of São Paulo, Brazil (see chapter 8).

To mitigate issues of pricing inflexibility, it is essential for New York City to establish information systems to make the TDR market more transparent on the attributes of market transactions. By doing so for landowners, private developers, local stakeholders, and transit agencies, the resultant transparency could improve the efficiency and fairness of TDR programs. More specifically, a "Development Rights Bank," founded by multiple municipalities beyond their jurisdictional boundaries, could play a pivotal role in consolidating unused or floating air rights around stations and along corridors. Such a system could acquire and retain development certificates as marketable products to ensure accurate pricing and promote TDR transactions dynamically and flexibly.

The local affordability gap is another major concern with TDRs in New York City. Raising public capital funding for improving local infrastructure out of TDR-transaction and FAR-distribution mechanisms should free municipal resources for other welfare purposes. However, this type of commercial densification has historically paid little attention to ensuring the interest of local communities, which would suffer from rising costs, and increasingly unaffordable living options. Additionally, rents for such areas would become further and further out of the grasp of small business owners, which would in turn dramatically alter the business and social landscape inside and outside designated areas.

Washington, DC: WMATA's Entrepreneurial Joint Development Program

Development-based LVC programs have increasingly been adopted by local governments for fixed-guideway transit projects in the United States, most of them in New York City and Washington, DC (Landis, Cervero, and Hall 1991), in the form of JD programs between transit companies and private landholders or developers. Most JD programs around New York City's subway stations are small and do not directly finance railway infrastructure via incentive agreements or cost sharing. In contrast, those undertaken by WMATA (Washington, DC) have been relatively capital intensive and large. WMATA has adopted development-based LVC instruments with developers, project by project. WMATA's JD program is the most advanced development-based LVC model in the United States for financial impact and project scale.

The concept of modern JD was introduced by federal agencies to financially support their highway and airport projects during the 1950s. The application of JD projects for fixed-guideway transit investment came later, recognized in the Urban Mass Transportation Act (UMTA) of 1964. Locally, WMATA also embarked on its own railway-related real estate business in the early 1960s. Its 1969 guideline, "Commercial Tie-Ins with Metro Stations," stipulated a partnership model between WMATA and landholders who would realize capital gains on property through tie-ins with Metro investments. A major amendment to UMTA in 1974 and the Surface Transportation Act of 1978 further made discretionary funds available for JD projects, including land acquisition. More critically, President Reagan's administration in the 1980s deeply cut federal financial assistance to local governments as part of the Republican Party's move toward privatization. Accordingly, local transit agencies needed to increase revenues from JD projects. Since the early 1990s, the focus of JD projects has moved toward the incorporation of public-private initiatives in developing and operating fixed-guideway transit systems by making efforts to eliminate legal and regulatory barriers against transit-supportive development activities in real estate markets (Landis, Cervero, and Hall 1991). Such public-private initiatives have prevailed in WMATA's JD program.

Construction of WMATA's first Metro line began in 1969, took in four regional bus services in 1973, and opened the first phase of Metrorail in 1976. The system now serves 86 stations over 106 miles (170 kilometers) of track in the metropolitan area (map 5.4). Both Metrorail and Metro bus systems serve about 5 million within a 1,500–square mile (3,885–square kilometer) jurisdiction across the District of Columbia, Maryland, and Virginia. This means that WMATA is an interstate transit company undertaking a tri-jurisdictional operation collectively funded and managed by three states and governed by a board of directors. Specific oversight is through three entities: a Tri-State Oversight Committee, the Office of the Inspector General, and the Federal Transit Administration. Multiple jurisdictions with joint development interests in WMATA transit zones include the District of Columbia; the counties of Arlington, Fairfax, Montgomery, and Prince George's; and the cities of Alexandria, Falls Church, Fairfax, and Rockville. In its 30-plus year history, WMATA has participated in more than 65 JD projects within its service territories (WMATA Office of Property Development and Management 2008) and

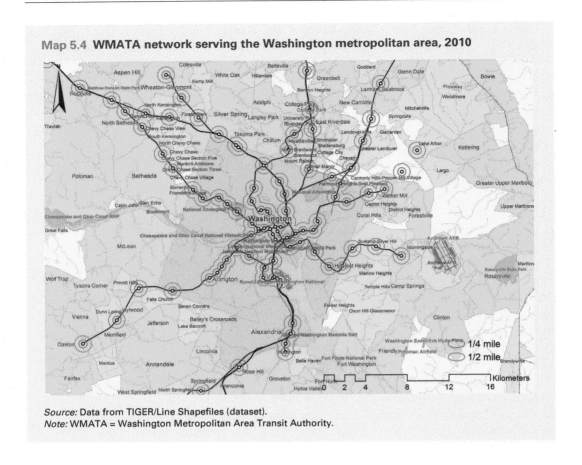

Map 5.4 WMATA network serving the Washington metropolitan area, 2010

Source: Data from TIGER/Line Shapefiles (dataset).
Note: WMATA = Washington Metropolitan Area Transit Authority.

has spurred more than $235 billion in economic development at or next to Metro property (WMATA 2012).

Such economic development benefits around Metro stations can be translated into local tax revenues. According to a 2011 WMATA report, proximity within a half mile of the station adds 6.8 percent property tax revenues to single-family houses, 8.9 percent to commercial office properties, and 9.4 percent to multifamily buildings. Development within a half mile of Metro stations generated around $3.1 billion and within a quarter mile generated $1.8 billion in property tax revenues in 2010 across multiple jurisdictions (figure 5.1). A total of 27.9 percent of the tax base of the area served by WMATA is from the value of real estate within a half mile of Metro stations. And of the more than 800 million in assessed property values in the area served by WMATA, about 15 percent is within a quarter-mile buffer of Metro stations and 28 percent within a half-mile buffer (AECOM 2011). In the same year, commercial properties within a half mile of Metro stations generated $189 million in property tax, of which $115 million came from commercial properties within a quarter mile.

Special assessment taxes (surtaxes levied on real estate in the designated area that benefits from public investment) have been applied around

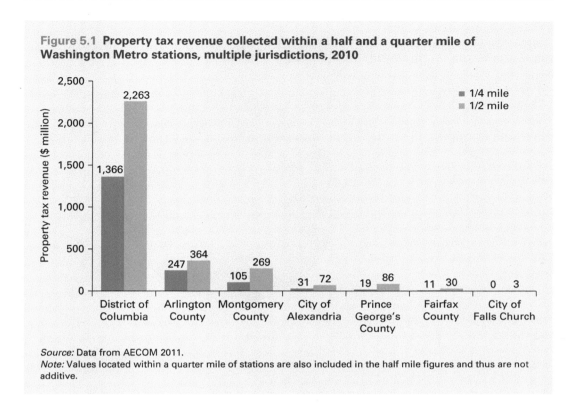

Figure 5.1 Property tax revenue collected within a half and a quarter mile of Washington Metro stations, multiple jurisdictions, 2010

Source: Data from AECOM 2011.
Note: Values located within a quarter mile of stations are also included in the half mile figures and thus are not additive.

WMATA's Red Line. The New York Avenue–Florida Avenue–Gallaudet University station is the first Metro infill project. The District of Columbia, the federal government, and area businesses funded the more than $100 million construction project. As the first public-private partnership (PPP) Metro project, a 30-year special assessment was placed on commercial properties within 2,500 feet (762 meters) of station entrances (Parsons Brinckerhoff 2010). In 2001, the assessed value of the 35-block area was about $535 million and in 2007 roughly $2.3 billion.

Local governments have seen steep hikes in revenue from property taxes and special assessment taxes around Metro stations; WMATA has also raised property-related revenues by adapting four development-based LVC instruments: air rights sale, site leasing, long-term development agreements of WMATA-owned land on and around Metro stations, and connection payments from private developers on non-WMATA-owned sites (McNeal and Doggett 1999). Yet the revenues generated from JD businesses contributed only a trivial amount of WMATA's annual operating revenues—0.74–1.33 percent—in FY2004–12 (figure 5.2). Revenues from parking—4.66–6.38 percent over the same period—were larger. WMATA receives sizable operating subsidies from its owners, the local governments, in that it indirectly receives benefits from property taxes or special assessment taxes collected by local governments. In addition, both joint development and parking businesses may have contributed to the increase in

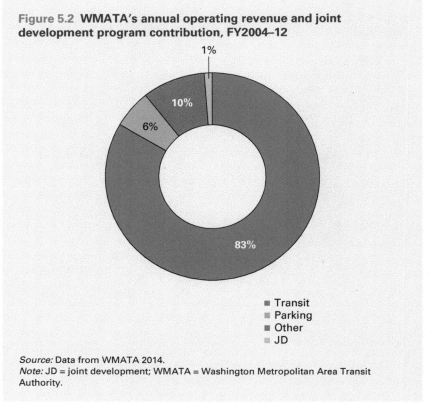

Figure 5.2 WMATA's annual operating revenue and joint development program contribution, FY2004–12

- Transit
- Parking
- Other
- JD

Source: Data from WMATA 2014.
Note: JD = joint development; WMATA = Washington Metropolitan Area Transit Authority.

WMATA's transit passenger revenues from $419.6 million in FY2004 to $752.6 million in FY2012 by enhancing built environments and access functions around Metro stations, based on TOD principles.

JD Programs and TOD Policies

The majority of projects under WMATA's JD program involve converting surface parking lots to structures, freeing adjacent land for private residential, commercial, or office development (Goldin 2010; McNeal and Doggett 1999). As defined by WMATA's guideline on JD projects, the property business attempts to promote TOD principles, providing affordable housing, improving access to stations, attracting new transit riders, and increasing transit fare revenue to support WMATA's operation and maintenance expenses. WMATA's JD program must also meet the following Federal Transit Agency's requirements: enhance economic development or incorporate private investment; enhance the effectiveness of a public transport project and relate physically or functionally to that project, or establish new or enhanced coordination between public transport and other transport; and provide a fair share of revenue for public transport. Private investment need not be monetary and can take the form of properties or other user or social benefits to be generated either initially or over the development lifecycle (WMATA Office of Property Development and Management 2008).

As WMATA's passenger service coverage is so extensive, JD projects must cooperate with local zoning codes and other planning and design regulations of each jurisdiction. Local jurisdictions in turn review proposals and evaluate them against local policies, land use plans, zoning, and other development-related capital-improvement proposals (WMATA Office of Property Development and Management 2008). In this way, proposals can be evaluated both on their local and regional impact.

Arlington County, as one progressive example, adopted a corridor-wide General Land Use Plan (GLUP) in accord with agreed-on development goals. The GLUP allows for flexibility to rezone areas for higher densities than originally specified. Project review involves revised zoning as allowed by the GLUP, a special exception, a full site plan, and county board approval. In planning for the Metro projects, 11 percent of the county was rezoned to encourage mixed-use, high-density development. This is in contrast to the remaining 89 percent of the county area that is generally low density (Arlington County Department of Community Planning, Housing and Development, Planning Division 2012). The targeted spatial layout was based on the bull's eye concept—concentrating high- and mid-density redevelopment around transit stations and tapering density[2] toward existing neighborhoods. Each of the sector plans sought to create urban villages, spanning around a quarter to a half mile from the Metro station (map 5.5).

The required site plan allows flexibility by allowing up to six times the allowable FAR and height, while reducing parking requirements. However, it is still ultimately tied to the GLUP and sector plans on uses, including specified mixes, density, height, design, and public improvements. In contrast, in 2008 Maryland incorporated the term TOD into its state laws and funding mechanisms, which has allowed the state department of transportation to use departmental resources—including land, funds, and personnel—to support the public-private TOD projects "designated" for economic development, housing, and environmental improvement. The 2008 TOD law also helps offset some of the political and up-front costs generated by local infrastructure as well as land acquisition by allowing the state to be a major player in prioritizing TOD projects for government support, by promoting greater ability to apply tax incremental financing and special assessment districts,[3] and by making local funding programs more flexible for revitalization activities and small businesses around Metro stations (Maryland Department of Transportation 2012).

Conclusion

WMATA's JD program is generally seen as one of the better development-based LVC successes that is entrepreneurial in raising local transit funds. Still, WMATA's annual reports in recent years explicitly state that the financial contributions from JD projects have not been significant. As in other U.S. cities, parking fees around WMATA Metro stations generate larger receipts. Recent figures on WMATA's annual revenue structure may discourage other transit agencies from converting parking lots into

Map 5.5 Higher-density corridor surrounded by lower-density zones

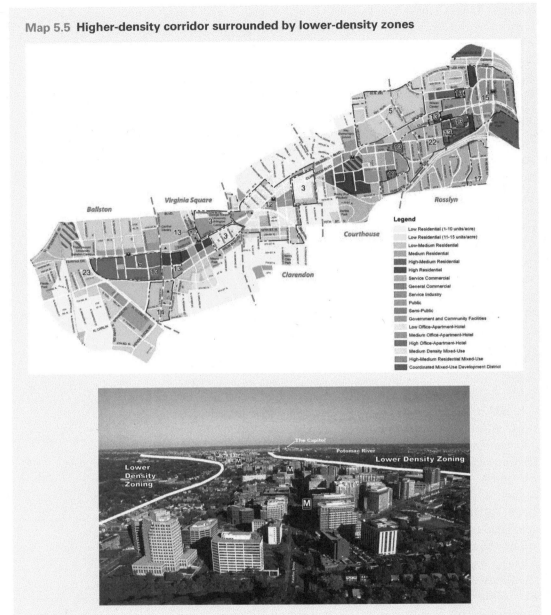

Source: Arlington County Department of Community Planning, Housing and Development, Planning Division 2012. Photo © Arlington County Department of Community Planning, Housing and Development, Planning Division. Used with permission. Further permission required for reuse.

commercial and residential use properties on the basis of TOD principles as practiced in the United States. However, WMATA's annual reports also imply that its JD projects have indirectly led to steady increases in transit ridership and fare revenue, accompanied by state and local TOD initiatives.

In fact, however, the multibillion-dollar development benefits generated by the transit-supportive land policies near Metro stations have been generated largely by related local jurisdictions through property taxation and special assessment levies, which are more popular LVC techniques than JD programs throughout the United States. Thus, WMATA indirectly benefits from the tax revenue increase of the real estate precinct of its Metro stations, as it receives sizable operating subsidies from the local governments, which are also its owners. This benefit distribution pattern also explains why so many JD projects in the United States have applied cost sharing with private developers rather than benefit sharing.

State and local governments play critical roles in promoting the transit businesses themselves and TOD. Although WMATA cannot generate large revenues from joint development, local governments annually provide an operating subsidy, indirectly using property tax revenues, but because these go to the general treasury, local governments need to establish clear policies to allocate a portion of the tax revenues to support transit and TOD, given the positive economic, environmental, and social externalities.

For example, through its 2008 TOD law the Maryland state government has prioritized several development projects, making transport-related resources more flexible and helping set up small business activities around Metro stations. In recent years, WMATA's JD program has also been expected not only to increase financial returns on commercial property investments but also to promote cultural activities and community services by enhancing pedestrian-friendly built environments around Metro stations. Ideally, local governments will play a fundamental role in removing legal and regulatory impediments to TOD projects running smoothly, offer economic incentives to landowners and private developers, create a collaborative business climate, and establish fair rules to share long-term mutual development benefits beyond immediate capital costs around transit stations.

Both the financial contribution and physical scale of WMATA's JD projects are much smaller than those of the global best development-based LVC practices in Hong Kong SAR, China, and Tokyo. This is due to the differences in roles of local governments, degree of railway privatization, experience with private developers, and maturity of transit-supportive property markets. However, installing strong entrepreneurialism into transit agencies is key to successful adaptation of any development-based LVC scheme.

Context: Europe

In Europe, private investors in unregulated business conditions built rail transit in the early 19th century. When competition from road transport increased, private transit operations became financially less viable with most taking on different forms of public ownership. The recessions triggered by the oil shocks of the 1970s, however, greatly eroded governments' fiscal capacity to make railway investments and to provide operating subsidies. Yet politicians and others with vested interests lobbied to preserve or extend systems without adequately addressing the structural financial problem—the need to increase fares or taxes. Due to such soft budget constraints, most European railways had accumulated large deficits by the 1990s in proportions unsustainable to gross domestic product, forcing the major countries to take often unique approaches. In the United Kingdom, for example, the government attempted to offset some of its debt with receipts from privatizing the railways. Germany opted to pay it off directly. The overall policies of the European Union have emphasized the importance of making government contributions to railway activities more transparent on the basis of corporate accounting standards (Perkins 2005).

PPPs still account for a small share of railway investment in Europe, except in the United Kingdom, where the London Underground's tracks were privatized by the government to two private consortiums for £15.7 billion ($26.1 billion) under 30-year concessions in 2003. Another large PPP (also known as a private finance initiative, or PFI) was applied to the High Speed Channel Tunnel Rail Link between London and the Channel Tunnel. In 1996, the winning consortium—the London and Continental Railways (LCR)—estimated the total costs of the project at about £6 billion ($10 billion), including £1.8 billion ($3.0 billion) of government subsidies. Since LCR failed to raise enough revenue to cover operating expenses, direct subsidies increased to £2 billion ($3.3 billion). The government agreed to underwrite a £3.8 billion ($6.3 billion) bond issue to reduce LCR's debt service, and LCR agreed to pay back 35 percent of any profits after 2020 to the government. Further, the concession period was heavily cut from 999 to 99 years, with the line reverting to public ownership in 2086 at the same time as the Channel Tunnel (Perkins 2005). This suggests that while PPP/PFI schemes may be adopted to finance mega railway projects, European governments have sought more innovative and competitive ways to ensure sufficient revenue with private partners as well as local entities.

The redevelopment of railway station areas has become a major economic catalyst for many European cities since the early and mid-1990s (Bertolini and Split 1998). Entrepreneurial cities in Europe have embarked on urban regeneration projects around major intercity and intracity railway interchanges, promoting local economic development and environmentally sustainable transport and land use integration by restructuring the cities' economic geography and social relations. In particular, recent expansions of high-speed rail (HSR) links across Europe have provided opportunities for global-center or regional capital cities to make their central business districts internationally accessible and economically competitive. Essentially, they have been able to recapture substantial accessibility and agglomeration benefits through development-based LVC schemes. For example, railway interchange reinvestments were financed with revenues from redeveloping former train yards and adjacent brownfield sites. However, such urban redevelopment or "gentrification" highlights important socioeconomic issues of spatial division of classes, income disparities, and housing unaffordability alongside low population growth, international migration, and real estate booms. Most of these aspects are seen in the case of King's Cross land redevelopment in London.

London: Regeneration of King's Cross Lands

King's Cross Terminus—with the stations of St. Pancras and Euston—is expected to function as the principal transit center for London. The 2004 London Plan anticipated King's Cross to become the best accessibility location in Greater London with the completion of the Channel Tunnel Rail Link - High-Speed 1 (HS1), Thameslink 2000, and the Cross River Tram. King's Cross is also the biggest inner-city transit interchange in London, linking six metro lines at one venue (map 5.6).

In the Victorian era King's Cross was part of a large industrial area of the city, but by the late 20th century it had deteriorated into disused buildings, railway sidings, warehouses, and contaminated land. Regeneration

Map 5.6 Location of King's Cross Station and High Speed 1 on Greater London's Railway Network, 2011

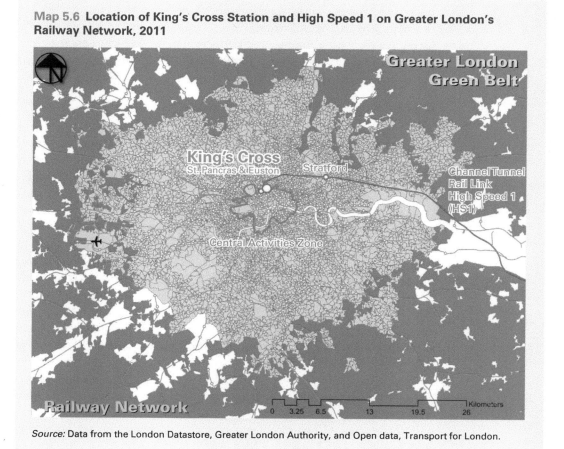

Source: Data from the London Datastore, Greater London Authority, and Open data, Transport for London.

had been debated since the mid-1980s, but due to weak market conditions and the uncertainty of delivering the HS1 and related development projects at the time, private developers could not embark on it. It was not until the site became an integral part of HS1 development that plans went ahead in the late 1990s.

Construction of the Channel Tunnel Rail Link made about 20 hectares of the underused land available for high-density commercial development as well as housing provision around King's Cross–St. Pancras (Mayor of London 2004). "Opportunity areas" were identified, and regeneration proceeded after the local authority approved the plans in 2006, with a target completion date of 2016. The first phase of the regeneration project, the University of the Arts London, opened its new campus in autumn 2011. About 27 hectares of the land is planned to contain more than 1,900 homes, 23 new and refurbished office buildings, 500,000 square feet (about 47,000 square meters) of shops and restaurants, 20 new streets, and 10 major new public spaces for a projected 45,000 people (figure 5.3). While the majority of private floor space will be allocated to produce business profits, more than 40 percent of the redeveloped former brownfield site will be used for public purposes, and across from the redevelopment site 20 historic buildings will be restored for modern use (King's Cross 2014). According to an assessment by LCR in 2009, the incremental economic impacts of HS1 through the King's Cross regeneration are estimated to be steep, with about 22,100 permanent jobs and 2,000 dwellings in the area (LCR 2009).

LVC Scheme and Section 106 Agreements around King's Cross

The construction cost of the HS1 project was £5.7 billion ($8.82 billion), of which Section 1 between the Channel Tunnel and North Kent cost £1.92 billion ($2.96 billion) and Section 2 between North Kent and St. Pancras cost £3.78 billion ($5.86 billion). The Department for Transport's (DfT) financial assistance of £8.16 billion ($13.5 billion) covers construction costs, the project's debts, and the operations of LCR and its subsidiaries. Originally, HS1 was planned to be privately financed, owned, and operated, yet there was significant doubt about the project's financial viability. Consequently, besides the additional cash grant of about £2 billion ($3.3 billion), LCR was also granted property development rights around King's Cross and Stratford Stations. This arrangement was to continue until the concession contract expired in 2086, at which point the assets would return to the government (Omega Centre 2008; Butcher 2011; U.K. Parliament n.d.). Accordingly, LCR was restructured into a property development entity in 2011. Based on the 1996 arrangement between the government and LCR, DfT will receive a 50 percent share of LCR's net profit after deducting the costs for the King's Cross development scheme (Comptroller and Auditor General 2005). As the King's Cross project is in progress, LCR expects to start earning new income from its core property holdings at King's Cross and Stratford between 2015 and 2020 (Comptroller and Auditor General 2012).

Figure 5.3 Redevelopment schemes of the King's Cross opportunity area

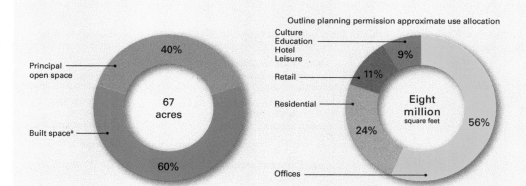

Source: © 2014 Argent (Property Development) Services LLP. Used with permission; further permission required for reuse.
a. Built space includes associated public spaces such as court yards and gardens.

Although the United Kingdom's properties are largely transacted under a market freehold system, many development-based LVC cases are on publicly owned sites, including DfT's. DfT-related agencies hold 87,944 assets across the United Kingdom. In addition, the local governments of Greater London, LCR, and other related agencies manage their own properties next to railway facilities. Under the supervision of DfT, LCR has been mandated to maximize its long-term asset value, and its development strategy has been to use its major sites as equity to participate in joint-venture development companies that can make long-term profits through urban regeneration around HS1 stations—chiefly King's Cross and Stratford. For King's Cross, the developer—Argent—was selected as a private partner in 2001. The London Borough of Camden granted outline planning permission for regeneration in 2006, and LCR, Argent, and another landholder—DHL— jointly formed the King's Cross Central Limited Partnership in 2008. And so LCR owns a 73 percent share of the 27-hectare land parcel and a 36 percent share of the new entity, though the partnership officially became the single landowner around King's Cross. Since 2008, the Partnership has invested more than £300 million ($498 million), and core sitewide infrastructure is in place.

One key LVC technique adopted by local governments in England and Wales is their use of Section 106 of the Town and Country Planning Act of 1990. This section provides a means for local authorities to negotiate agreements or planning obligations with a landowner or developer in association with the granting of planning permissions. Section 106 agreements can be financial in that landowners or developers are required to make some sort of financial commitment (lump sum or recurring) in exchange for development permission; or can be in kind that assure local interest, such as affordable housing or community facilities (figure 5.4). Once a Section 106 agreement is signed and planning permission is granted, developers have three years to exercise their property development rights, or the permission lapses (London Borough of Newham Strategic Development Committee

Figure 5.4 Stakeholders in the land value capture scheme and Section 106 agreements around King's Cross

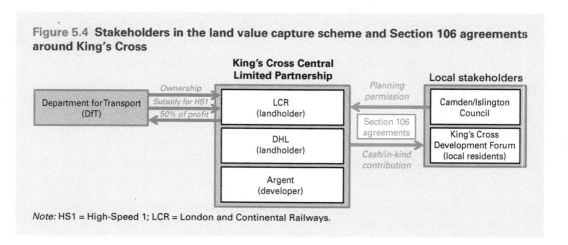

Note: HS1 = High-Speed 1; LCR = London and Continental Railways.

2011). The annual benefits to Londoners, through the financial contributions from developers who attain planning permissions, are estimated to be worth £100 million–£200 million ($155 million–$309 million) a year (London Assembly Planning and Special Development Committee 2008).

Section 106 Agreements and Spatial Coordination around King's Cross

The mixed-use redevelopment of the King's Cross site has involved a long process of spatial coordination with three local authorities: Camden Council, adjoining Islington Council, and the Greater London Authority. There has also been close consultation with related statutory bodies (such as English Heritage over buildings to be preserved) and with local community groups through the King's Cross Development Forum (Gossop 2007; King's Cross Railway Lands Group n.d.). In 2006 the Camden Borough Development Control Committee gave planning permission for redeveloping the King's Cross brownfield site via a Section 106 agreement, reflecting the consultation process of spatial coordination with local stakeholders (Camden Council 2006). The agreement contains the broad principles of the redevelopment scheme with "floor space maxima" to guarantee diverse site use (table 5.1). Yet these allocation figures allow for some flexibility as redevelopment is likely to take 10–15 years to complete. Thus, floor space of one use could, to a limited extent, be traded against another, depending on market conditions (Gossop 2007).

The Section 106 agreement package around King's Cross includes cash and in-kind contributions to the provision of local infrastructure and community services by the joint developer for the Camden council, including £2.1 million to create 24,000–27,000 local jobs through a Construction Training Centre and Skills and Recruitment Centre; 1,900 homes, more than 40 percent of which will be affordable housing; cash and in-kind contributions for community, sports, and leisure facilities; new green

Table 5.1 Floor space maxima by site use provided through Section 106 agreements around King's Cross Central

Use	Floor space (sq. m.)
Mixed-use development—total permissible	739,690
Offices	Up to 455,510
Retail	Up to 45,925
Hotels/served apartments	Up to 47,225
D1 (nonresidential institutions)	Up to 74,830
D2 (assembly and leisure)	Up to 31,730
1,900 homes	Up to 194,575

Source: Gossop 2007.
Note: sq. m. = square meter.

public spaces, plus new landscaped squares and well-designed and accessible streets, accounting for about 40 percent of the entire site; a new visitor center, education facilities, and a bridge across the canal to link streets; and cash contributions to improve adjacent streets, transit stops, and bus services (Camden Council 2006).

Conclusion

A series of HSR network expansions across Europe since the 1990s has provided opportunities for entrepreneurial governments to promote regeneration projects along with intercity and intracity transit terminus investments through various PPP/PFI schemes, including development-based LVC instruments. In recent years, this HSR investment–economic development scenario has been commonly adopted in Japan, the United States, China, India, and Brazil, for example. But in the United Kingdom PPP/PFI schemes to finance HSR projects have not always been successful, relying heavily on government contributions or resulting in (re-)nationalization of railway ownership and management. To ease the public-private debts accumulated by the HSR-related projects, the sales of development rights on former railway yards and train depots have been used in major global cities' financial and business locations, where regional accessibility and urban development potential is extremely high. King's Cross is a typical case. Essentially, as the HS1 project moved forward and opened new development opportunities in London, LCR was restructured from a mere railway construction company into an entrepreneurial property development and asset management agency.

To fully capture potential economic benefits, entrepreneurial railway agencies should pursue development opportunities on their lands and create capital gains with other private developers. Ideally, corporate profits will attract other multinational headquarters and business services to these locations with new interregional passenger services. However, the sizable intercity accessibility and development benefits conferred by HSR-related megaprojects should not be dominated by global corporate entities at the expense of local public interest around regional transit centers. Development-based LVC should not be merely adopted as a money-making tool. In the case of King's Cross, Section 106 agreements have been crucial in incorporating desirable planning principles into public-private funding and property development. Joint public-private developers are required to sustain multiple interaction and consultation opportunities with local authorities and residents to gain planning permission, yet such local interventions should not weaken the developers' market competitiveness and financial viability. As a case in point, the Section 106 agreements for King's Cross set out very flexible allocations of property floor uses, allowing the joint developers to respond to changes in market and other conditions.

In summary, the use of Section 106 agreements around King's Cross underlines the importance of balancing interregional business marketability

Annex table 5A.1 Data on case study cities in developed countries

City	Hong Kong SAR, China	Tokyo	New York	Washington, DC	London
Country	China	Japan	United States	United States	United Kingdom
Land holding system	State leasehold	Market freehold	Market freehold	Market freehold	Market freehold
Metropolitan population (1,000) 2010	7,053	36,933	20,104	4,634	8,923
Metropolitan area (km²)	1,104	13,752	11,642	3,424	1,623
Population density (metropolitan) (1,000/km²)	6.4	2.7	1.7	1.4	5.5
Population growth of metropolitan areas, 2000–10 (%) (annual)	4.0% (0.4%)	7.2% (0.7%)	12.7% (1.2%)	17.3% (1.6%)	8.5% (0.8%)
Population growth forecast of metropolitan areas, 2010–25 (%) (annual)	15.7% (1.5%)	4.7% (0.5%)	17.2% (1.6%)	22.3% (2.0%)	14.9% (1.4%)
Per capita GDP growth rate, 2007–11 (%)	-3.2%	-5.6%	-3.7%	-2.2%	-5.3%
GDP growth rate projection, 2008–25 (%) (annual)	58% (2.7%)	34% (1.7%)	36% (1.8%)	34% (1.8%)	45% (2.2%)
Real estate price annual growth rate	12.0% (house, 2008–12)	-4.6% (land, 2008–12)	-14.8% (house, 2008–12)	-16.6% (house, 2008–12)	1.4% (house, 2008–12)
Number of private car registrations (out of 1,000 population)	82	308	230	680	317 (2007–09)
Private car registration growth rate a year	3.4% (2005–10)	-1.1 % (2005–13)	0.4% (2008–12)	1,3% (2008–11)	1.3% (2002–09)
% of public transportation use	88%	51%	23%	37%	28%
Metro lines (existing) km	218	304	223	170	402
Number of stations (existing)	84	285	468	86	270

Sources: World Bank databases (http://data.worldbank.org), United Nations Statistics (http://unstats.un.org/unsd/default.htm), websites of transit agencies, and others.
Note: GDP = gross domestic product.

and local community livability with PPP-based infrastructure funding and property development. This is especially important to be borne in mind when development-based LVC schemes are used in very expensive HSR projects during redevelopment of former railway yards in global or regional capital cities of the developing world.

Notes

1. "Sending districts" can be defined as the areas from which development rights are transferred along with zoning regulations to address natural, scenic, recreational, architectural, or open land, or sites of historical, cultural, aesthetic, or economic values to be protected. "Receiving districts can be designated as the areas to which development rights are transferred mainly for desirable densification, including TOD. This means that the designation of receiving districts also call for careful analysis and planning on the availability and provision of public infrastructure and services in the areas influenced by new densification activities, such as transport, parking, water and energy supply, sewage, and fire protection" (Nelson, Pruetz, and Woodruff 2012; New York State 2011).
2. A new "transitional" zoning tool introduced, R15-30T (Arlington County Department of Community Planning, Housing and Development, Planning Division 2012); see Arlington County Department of Community Planning, Housing and Development, Building Arlington Division (2012).
3. A special taxing district is "an area defined by the local government where a new tax is assessed to businesses and perhaps other properties and the revenue generated by the new tax is dedicated to a particular use within the district. Special taxing districts can be used in several ways: to fund directly capital construction of public infrastructure at a TOD; to provide revenue or security for the repayment of a bond; or fund operating and maintenance costs such as management contract costs, utilities, cleaning, snow removal, and security services within the defined district" (Maryland Department of Transportation 2012).

References

AECOM. 2011. "Making the Case for Transit: WMATA Regional Benefits of Transit." Technical Report. Washington Metropolitan Area Transit Authority Office of Long Range Planning, Washington, DC, November. www.wmata.com/pdfs/planning/WMATA%20Making%20the%20 Case%20for%20Transit%20Final%20Tech%20Report.pdf.

APTA (American Public Transportation Association). 2013. "Public Transportation Investment Background Data 8th Edition." Washington, DC: American Public Transportation Association, December 12. www.apta .com/resources/reportsandpublications/Documents/Public-Transportation -Investment-Background-Data.pdf.

Arlington County Department of Community Planning, Housing and Development, Building Arlington Division. 2012. "Section 10A. 'R15-30T' Residential Town House Dwelling Districts." April. http://building .arlingtonva.us/wp-content/uploads/2012/04/Ordinance_Section10a.pdf.

Arlington County Department of Community Planning, Housing and Development, Planning Division. 2012. "40 Years of Smart Growth: Arlington County's Experience with Transit Oriented Development in the Rosslyn-Ballston Metro Corridor." Presentation by the Arlington County Department of Community Planning, Housing and Development, Planning Division, December 6.

Bertolini, Luca, and Tejo Split. 1998. *Cities on Rails: The Redevelopment of Railway Station Areas*. London: E. & F.N. Spon.

Butcher, Louise. 2011. "Railways: Channel Tunnel Rail Link (HS1)." Business and Transport Section, London, March 24. www.parliament.uk/Templates/BriefingPapers/Pages/BPPdfDownload.aspx?bp-id=SN00267.

Camden Council. 2006. "King's Cross Redevelopment Takes Next Step Forward." November 17. www.camden.gov.uk/ccm/content/press/2006/november-2006/kings-cross-redevelopment-takes-next-step-forward.en;jsessionid=684C5F167C509DBC45FE7220223FA13B.

Comptroller and Auditor General. 2005. "Progress on the Channel Tunnel Rail Link." National Audit Office, Department for Transport, London, July. www.nao.org.uk/wp-content/uploads/2005/07/050677.pdf.

————. 2012. "The Completion and Sale of High Speed 1." National Audit Office, Department for Transport, London, March. www.nao.org.uk/wp-content/uploads/2012/03/10121834.pdf.

Council of the City of New York. 2013. "Joint Statement by Council Speaker Christine C. Quinn and Council Member Dan Garodnick Re: East Midtown Rezoning Proposal." Press Release, Office of Communications, November 12. http://council.nyc.gov/html/pr/111213midtown.shtml.

Furman Center for Real Estate and Urban Policy. 2013. *Buying Sky: The Market for Transferable Development Rights in New York City*. New York: New York University, School of Law and Wagner School of Public Policy, Policy Brief, October. http://furmancenter.org/files/BuyingSky_PolicyBrief_21OCT2013.pdf.

Goldin, Steven. 2010. "Metro Streamlines Joint Development Process." *Urban Land*, September 13. http://urbanland.uli.org/Articles/2010/SeptOct/Goldin.

Gossop, Chris. 2007. "London's Railway Land – Strategic Visions for the King's Cross Opportunity Area." www.isocarp.net/Data/case_studies/940.pdf.

Guerra, Erick, and Robert Cervero. 2011. "Cost of a Ride: The Effects of Densities on Fixed-Guideway Transit Ridership and Costs." *Journal of the American Planning Association* 77 (3): 267–90. doi:10.1080/01944363.2011.589767.

King's Cross. 2014. "Heritage Buildings." London. www.kingscross.co.uk/heritage-buildings.

King's Cross Railway Lands Group. n.d. "King's Cross Railway Lands Group (KXRLG): Brief History." London. www.kxrlg.org.uk/group /history.htm.

Landis, John, Robert Cervero, and Peter Hall. 1991. "Transit Joint Development in the USA: An Inventory and Policy Assessment." *Environment and Planning C: Government and Policy* 9 (4): 431–52. doi:10.1068/ c090431.

LCR (London & Continental Railways). 2009. "Economic Impact of High Speed 1: Final Report." Colin Buchanan and Partners, Limited, London, January. http://www.lcrhq.co.uk/media/cms_page_media/32/HS1.final .report.pdf.

London Assembly Planning and Special Development Committee. 2008. "Who Gains? The Operation of Section 106 Planning Agreements in London." London, March. http://legacy.london.gov.uk/assembly/reports /plansd/section-106-who-gains.pdf.

London Borough of Newham Strategic Development Committee. 2011. "Planning Obligations Report." London, February 23. https://mgov .newham.gov.uk/documents/s38361/Planning%20Obligations.pdf.

Maryland Department of Transportation. 2012. "The Designation of Transit Oriented Development Projects: Frequently Asked Questions." Hanover, MD, January 23. www.mdot.maryland.gov/Office_of_Planning _and_Capital_Programming/TOD/Documents/Update_8_9_12/TOD _FAQ.pdf.

Mayor of London. 2004. "The London Plan: Spatial Development Strategy for Greater London." Greater London Authority, February. http://static .london.gov.uk/mayor/strategies/sds/london_plan/lon_plan_all.pdf.

McNeal, Alvin R., and Rosalyn P. Doggett. 1999. "Metro Makes Its Mark: Promoting Development near Metrorail Stations Helps the Washington Metropolitan Area Transit Authority Finance a Portion of the More Than $700 Million Required Annually to Just Maintain Operations." *Urban Land* 58 (9): 78–81, 117.

Morris, Eugene J. 1969. "Air Rights Are Fertile Soil." *The Urban Lawyer* 1 (3): 247–67.

MTA (Metropolitan Transportation Authority). 2013. "The MTA Network: Public Transportation for the New York Region." New York. http://web .mta.info/mta/network.htm.

Nelson, Arthur C., Rick Pruetz, and Doug Woodruff. 2012. *The TDR Handbook: Designing and Implementing Successful Transfer of Development Rights Programs*. Washington, DC: Island Press.

New York State. 2011. "Transfer of Development Rights." James A. Coon Local Government Technical Series, Albany, NY. www.dos.ny.gov/lg /publications/Transfer_of_Development_Rights.pdf.

New York Times. 1913. "New Grand Central Terminal Opens its Doors." February 2. http://query.nytimes.com/mem/archive-free/pdf?res=F70F1F FC385F13738DDDAB0894DA405B838DF1D3.

Omega Centre. 2008. "Channel Tunnel Rail Link Case Study: Project Profile." OMEGA Centre: Centre for Mega Projects in Transport and Development, London, August. www.omegacentre.bartlett.ucl.ac.uk /studies/cases/pdf/UK_CTRL_PROFILE_080808.pdf.

Parsons Brinckerhoff, Inc. 2010. "New York Avenue-Florida Avenue-Gallaudet University Station Access Improvement Study." Lead Agency: Washington Metropolitan Area Transit Authority, June. www.wmata .com/pdfs/planning/NY%20Ave-FL%20Ave-Gall%20U%20 Station%20Access%20Improvement%20Study%20Final%20Report .pdf.

————. 2013. "East Midtown Rezoning and Related Actions: Draft Environmental Impact Statement." New York, April 9. www.nyc.gov/html /dcp/html/env_review/eis.shtml#east_midtown.

Perkins, Stephen. 2005. "The Role of Government in European Railway Investment and Funding." Ministry of Railways of the People's Republic of China, Beijing.

Regional Plan Association. 2013. *Rail Rewards: How LIRR's Grand Central Connection Will Boost Home Values*. New York: Regional Plan Association, January. www.rpa.org/library/pdf/RPA-Rail-Rewards.pdf.

TIGER/Line Shapefiles (data set). United States Census Bureau. http://www .data.gov/.

U.K. Parliament. n.d. "London and Continental Railways." Parliamentary Business, Bound Volume Hansard—Written Answers, London. www.publications.parliament.uk/pa/cm199798/cmhansrd/vo980204 /text/80204w03.htm.

U.S. EPA (Environmental Protection Agency). 2013. *Infrastructure Financing Options for Transit-Oriented Development*. Washington, DC: Office of Sustainable Communities Smart Growth Program, January.

WMATA (Washington Metropolitan Area Transit Authority). 2012. "Proposed Fiscal Year 2013 Annual Budget." Washington, DC, January 12. www.wmata.com/about_metro/docs/ProposedFY2013Budget.pdf.

————. 2014. "Metro Records Available for Public Review." Washington, DC, January. www.wmata.com/about_metro/public_rr.cfm?.

WMATA Office of Property Development and Management. 2008. "WMATA Joint Development Policies and Guidelines." Washington, DC, November. www.wmata.com/pdfs/business/Guidelines%20 Revision11-20-08.pdf.

PART III

Emerging Development-Based Land Value Capture Practices in Developing Countries

CHAPTER 6

Financing a Metro with Development Rights of Public Land, Nanchang, China

China's public sales of development rights are a major funding source for local governments in delivering infrastructure projects. These sales have often led to the rapid conversion of rural agriculture land into urban land for industrial and residential uses but without an adequate economic rationale or planning. With increased concern over the negative impacts of such rural–urban land conversion, policymakers in reform-oriented cities have already started taking longer-term approaches in public sales of development rights, focusing on sustainable finances and urban development.

Nanchang is one of these cities. Its public land leasing scheme attempts to incorporate the principles of transit-oriented development (TOD) into new metro finance. As this scheme has not yet been fully implemented, it is too early to assess whether it will generate the desired outcomes. If successfully executed, however, Nanchang's development-based land value capture (LVC) schemes could provide a good model for other Chinese cities.

Urban Development Context

Population and Urbanization Trends

Nanchang's central location in southeastern China relative to the Pearl River and Yangtze Delta regions, and to the junctions of major highways, makes it a major transport hub (map 6.1). The provincial capital, Nanchang is also a regional center for agricultural production in Jiangxi province. The city has many manufacturing firms including those producing cotton textiles and yarn, paper products, processed food, agricultural chemicals and insecticides, and Chinese medicine and other pharmaceuticals. Annual gross domestic product (GDP) growth in 2007–11 was a very robust 16–22 percent.

Map 6.1 Location of Nanchang

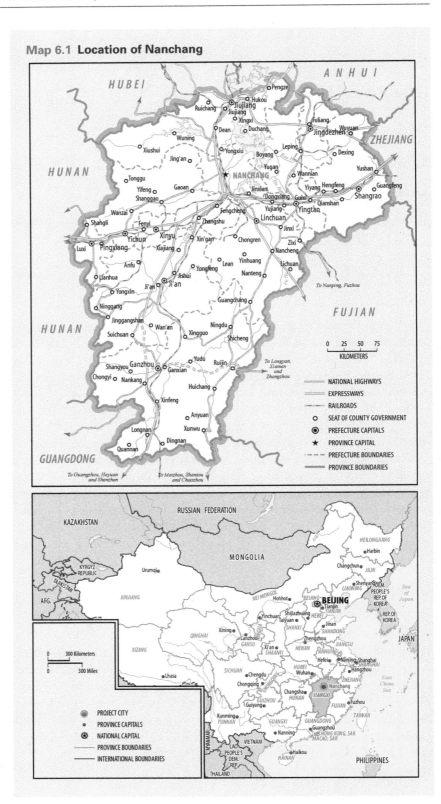

The strong growth triggered rapid urbanization. According to the United Nations Department of Economic and Social Affairs, Population Division (2012), the population in Nanchang's core city areas (330 square kilometers) increased from 1.6 million to 2.3 million from 2000 to 2010, or by 44 percent. It also projects that the population in the core areas will continue to grow, to 2.8 million by 2015 and 3.5 million by 2025 (figure 6.1). Due to rapid population growth in the city center, proper land use and transport planning is becoming crucial.

As in many rapidly urbanizing Chinese cities, traffic congestion in Nanchang is one of the major downsides of urbanization. Car ownership (at 120 per 1,000 people in 2012, according to ChinaAutoweb, June 25, 2013) is lower than most provincial capitals, but the share of motorized road trips (including those on public buses) grew from 22 percent in 2002 to 30.5 percent in 2010, according to traffic surveys (World Bank 2013). Public transport accounted for only 13.5 percent of total daily trips, which is lower than in cities of similar size and GDP such as Changsha (24.5 percent) or Wuhan (23.4 percent) (World Bank 2013). Roads in southern Nanchang and the four bridges across the river routinely see congestion with average driving speeds down to 11 kilometers an hour during rush hour. Roads built in the newly developed part of northern Nanchang are wide, favoring car use.

Urban Planning

Nanchang has a tradition of good urban planning. Its 1985 Strategic Plan aimed to develop the historic city center on the right bend of the Gan River

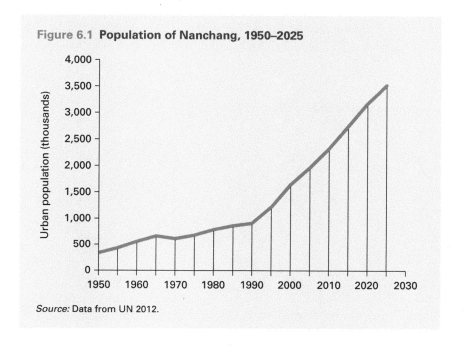

Figure 6.1 Population of Nanchang, 1950–2025

Source: Data from UN 2012.

(map 6.2); the left bend saw very little development at that time. As the city's industries continued growing, more space was needed.

In 1995, a new strategic plan was written to extend city development to the left bend. Industrial and residential development started on the northern part of Nanchang's city center. The goal then was to balance urban development on both sides of the river and to extend residential areas to the surrounding seven districts. This 1995 strategy is unchanged.

According to the 2005 Urban Comprehensive Development Plan, northern and southern Nanchang will form the city's future urban core, with new developments radiating out to surrounding districts and towns (see map 6.2). In southern Nanchang, the Nanchang municipal government (NMG) plans to decrease the population in the historic core, lower its development densities, lessen traffic congestion, and preserve historic buildings.

Metro Project

To achieve these goals and resolve the growing congestion, NMG has designed an extensive public transport system with fully integrated bus services and metro railway networks to facilitate travel between the newly planned areas and between the left and right bends of the Gan River. NMG plans to build five metro lines; two are under construction. Once complete, the metro railway network will be about 160–170 kilometers long with 128 stations (map 6.3). With a target completion date of 2020, lines 1, 2, and 3—60–70 kilometers in all—will form the basic structure of the metro railway network, connecting major business centers, the financial district, recreational areas, sport facilities, two industrial parks, and three universities.

Construction of Line 1 began in 2012 and will be completed in December 2015. This will connect the old city center to the new development areas on the left bend, helping redirect economic and residential investments from

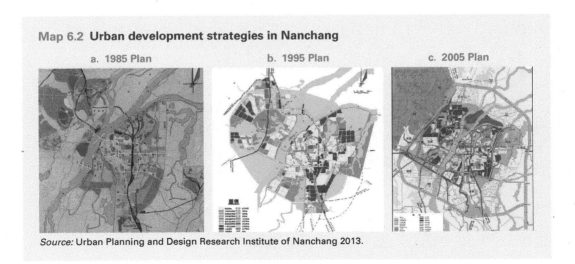

Map 6.2 Urban development strategies in Nanchang

a. 1985 Plan   b. 1995 Plan   c. 2005 Plan

Source: Urban Planning and Design Research Institute of Nanchang 2013.

Map 6.3 Lines 1–5 of the metro railway system, Nanchang

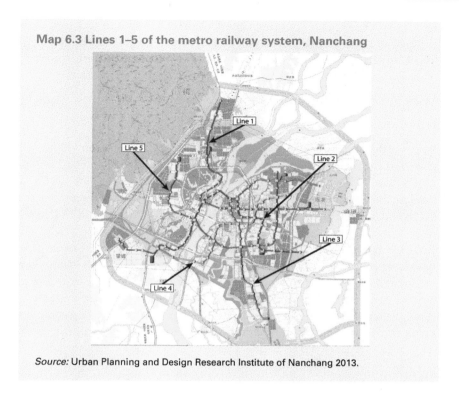

Source: Urban Planning and Design Research Institute of Nanchang 2013.

southern to northern Nanchang. On completion, Line 1 will be 28.7 kilometers long with 24 stations, one depot, and one parking yard. The average distance between stations will be about 1.2 kilometers.

Line 2's construction started in July 2013 and is partly financed by the World Bank. It goes from Zhan Qian Nan Da Dao Station to Xin Jia An Station and will be 23.8 kilometers long with 21 stations and one depot. NMG expects construction of Line 2 to be completed by 2016. Plans to build lines 3, 4, and 5, and Phase II of lines 1 and 2, are awaiting approval from the National Development and Reform Commission.

To feed the metro railway system, bus services will be reorganized. Several interchange locations between the bus and metro railway networks have already been designed for lines 1 and 2. More important, these interchanges are coordinated with better land use planning than in the past to allow retail stores and supermarkets to be built there.

Regulatory and Institutional Frameworks

In China, responsibility for city-level land use planning and investments in local infrastructure and services is delegated to municipalities. Strong leadership in Nanchang by the mayor and vice mayors ensures interdepartmental coordination and cooperation. NMG established the Nanchang Railway Transit Group Co. Ltd. (NRTG), wholly city owned, to build and operate the metro system. To better leverage the private sector's expertise, NRTG set up a special property management division with key staff recruited from the private sector to manage all real estate assets owned by the company. It also acts as a key liaison between government agencies to coordinate their planning and reviewing of metro railway investments and projects.

Nanchang Municipal Finance

In 2011, the budget of NMG was RMB49.7 billion ($8.1 billion). Land revenue was the major revenue source at RMB18.9 billion ($3 billion, 38 percent) (figure 6.2). The estimated cost for Line 2 is RMB1.48 billion ($2.42 billion), excluding interest charges, or equivalent to about 30 percent of the 2011 budget. During the construction phase, NMG will pay 37.3 percent of construction costs and interest each year. The largest expenses, about RMB1.4 billion ($230 million), will incur in 2017. On the revenue side, operating revenues in the fifth year are estimated to be RMB342 million ($56 million), resulting in a recovery ratio of 0.63. NRTG is expected to achieve breakeven in the 15th year. The debt service repayment and operational deficit will be filled by real estate development revenue (expected net profit of $166 million) and other land transfer fees. For land transfer fees, 25 parcels of 10,878 mu (7.2 square kilometers) out of an envisaged 50,000

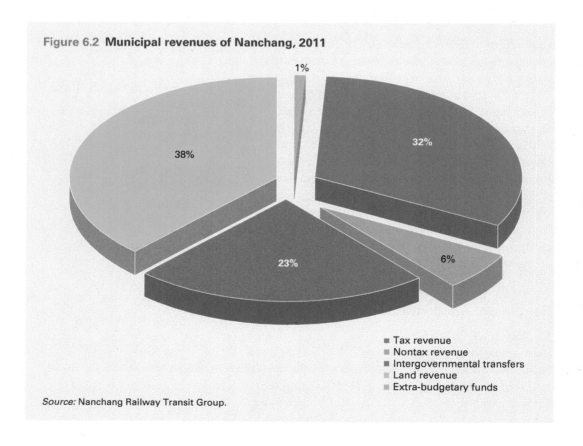

Figure 6.2 Municipal revenues of Nanchang, 2011

- Tax revenue
- Nontax revenue
- Intergovernmental transfers
- Land revenue
- Extra-budgetary funds

Source: Nanchang Railway Transit Group.

mu (33.3 kilometers) have been allocated to the metro system, representing a potential net contribution of RMB21.6 billion ($3.54 billion) to the metro railway construction program. Given that NMG needs to finance the five subway lines, NMG has to maximize revenues from real estate development or land transfer by adopting development-based LVC approaches.

Real Estate Market

Before discussing the LVC scheme designed by NMG, we examine the real estate market in Nanchang. The national government established a lease-hold system in 1978 to enable public and private exchanges of leasehold rights. Leases are long—residential land 70 years and commercial and industrial land 40 years. According to the Constitution, buildings on lease-hold land are private property. Under this legal framework, functioning real estate markets have appeared in many Chinese cities.

In 2008–09, the global economic downturn affected Chinese exporters and manufacturers, hurting land prices for commercial, commercial/services (mixed-use), and industrial land, which dropped back to 2006 levels (figure 6.3). Yet prices for other land types continued to rise, especially residential and commercial/residential mixed-use land. Hence, overall land prices declined by only 2 percent (table 6.1).

In 2009–10, prices soared in response to the central government's economic stimulus, which included a loosening of monetary policy and a lowering of mortgage rates. Prices for all land types increased by more than 50 percent, except industrial land. Commercial/residential mixed-use land prices more than doubled, and commercial land prices more than tripled (see table 6.1).

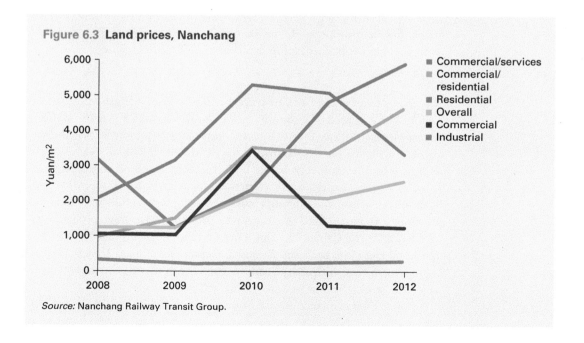

Figure 6.3 Land prices, Nanchang

Source: Nanchang Railway Transit Group.

Table 6.1 **Percent change of land prices in Nanchang, 2008–12**

	Commercial/ residential	Commercial/ services	Industrial	Commercial	Residential	Overall
2008–09	50%	−61%	−38%	−1%	52%	−2%
2009–10	134%	88%	24%	226%	67%	77%
2010–11	−4%	109%	−12%	−63%	−4%	−5%
2011–12	39%	22%	28%	−4%	−34%	24%

Source: Nanchang Railway Transit Group.

Concerned that real estate markets might be overheated, in 2010 NMG adopted certain measures: it passed a regulation allowing each family to purchase only one new housing unit—and prices for land designated for residential and commercial development dropped in 2011–12. Yet because the new law applied only to residential property, the price for commercial/ service land kept rising. From 2011–12, although residential land prices continued to drop, prices for other land types saw an upward trend, with the performance of land for mixed use such as commercial/services and commercial/residential land the strongest. On average, the aggregate land price climbed by 24 percent.

These are interesting outcomes because TOD is a strategy that promotes mixed land use. A typical TOD scheme will have office buildings clustered with residential properties and retail stores around a transit station. This design can both increase ridership and cross-subsidize transit development costs by capturing the increased land value generated by commercial and residential development. Rising land prices for mixed use is a favorable condition for adopting development-based LVC in Nanchang.

LVC

Nanchang's metro railway construction (60–70 km in length by 2020) will require large capital investment. Aside from transfers from the national government, local tax revenues, fares, and loans from international development agencies like the World Bank or domestic banks, NMG is also adapting the development-based LVC financing method to recoup land value increments generated by its metro railway investment to pay for some of the construction and operating costs. NRTG plans to fully use land value increments to partly fund metro railway investment via three procedures.

First, after the Urban Planning Bureau announces the City Master Plan and Land Use Plan, the Land Resource Center will acquire land for NRTG from landowners, with compensation, exercising eminent domain (compulsory purchase).[1] NRTG will pay for all acquisition costs.

Second, NMG will increase the floor area ratio (FAR) limit at the acquired sites and allow NRTG to either invest directly in land redevelopment or transfer the development rights to private investors to raise funds to finance metro railway construction. All land parcels within a 500–meter radius from a subway station will be qualified for upzoning with higher FARs. While the 500–meter criterion is uniformly applied to all station areas, some flexibility should be incorporated to accommodate varying market conditions. More important, the Urban Planning Bureau will also convert land use at these sites to mixed use to allow NRTG to promote TOD and to maximize land-related revenues.

Third, with the land resources in hand, NRTG will generate land revenue to defray metro railway development costs. For this, NRTG, through the Land Resource Center, will re-auction the land sites to developers at market value that reflects the increase in the development density and land use change and the improvement in accessibility due to the metro railway. The successful bidder will pay the bidding price (called a transfer fee) to the Municipal Finance Bureau, which will in turn deduct fees for six development funds related to education, agriculture, and other public services. These charges together are about 20 percent of the transfer fee. NRTG will receive the balance from the Finance Bureau and use the funds to finance construction of subway lines and stations.

NRTG can also develop the space above and below the metro railway stations, whether offices, recreational facilities, retail spaces, or residential units, all within the physical space of a metro railway station. Revenue from renting or selling residential and commercial properties will be used to partly finance metro railway investment or operating costs.

To illustrate these procedures in detail, we present the entire LVC financial arrangement of lines 1 and 2. Again, because these projects are in progress, we can only show how use of the LVC mechanism has been planned but cannot tell how much land value NRTG has actually captured.

LVC Financing of Lines 1 and 2

These lines' LVC financing will follow two methods: sale of development rights, and direct property development and management above or below the metro railway stations.

Sale of development rights. Line 1 (see map 6.3) is under construction and is planned to begin operating in 2015. The construction of Line 2 started in July 2013, and operations are expected to start in 2016.

NRTG has, through negotiated land sales, gained control over the development rights of 46 land sites with an area of 15,200 mu (10 square kilometers). About 2,600 mu (1.7 square kilometers) of the acquired land is close to the planned metro railway stations. NRTG also took part in public tenders of land and obtained the leasehold rights to 147 mu (0.1 square kilometers) of land for real estate development.

The total cost of developing the land resource was about RMB9 billion ($1.5 billion), including acquisition costs of RMB4.2 billion ($688 million) and demolition costs of RMB4.8 billion ($787 million). For the entire investment period (2012–20), estimated financial benefits derived from NRTG's planned real estate investment for own use and rental, or subleasing of land use rights to third parties, are about RMB22 billion ($3.6 billion). For 2012–16, these land benefits are estimated at around RMB14 billion ($2.2 billion).

Balancing the estimated costs and benefits of accumulating land resource, by 2016 NRTG will be able to generate a surplus of RMB5 billion ($820 million), equivalent to 15.1 percent of total construction costs of Line 1 (RMB18.1 billion, $3 billion) and Line 2 (RMB15 billion, $2.5 billion).

To assure projected land profits, NRTG has followed TOD principles. It combines development of the metro stations with improvements to surrounding neighborhoods. It has also designed the stations using one-stop-shop ideas and is financing their construction with revenue from mixed development above all subway stations. NRTG's strategy is to develop areas that are close to the city center first and then extend toward the suburbs (figure 6.4).

Direct property development: In 2012–15, NRTG plans to build 28 stations along lines 1 and 2 of two types. The first is mixed development on the ground above the metro stations; there will be 23 projects of this type. NRTG will invest directly in five of them and develop the other 18 stations with private investors. The second type is underground development at selected metro railway stations. There will be five projects of this type. NRTG will be the sole investor in three, with two co-financed and developed by other private investors.

These projects will cover 1,700 mu (1.1 square kilometers), with an estimated capital investment of RMB8.3 billion ($1.4 billion). NRTG is

Figure 6.4 Sequence and scale of station development along Line 1 in Nanchang

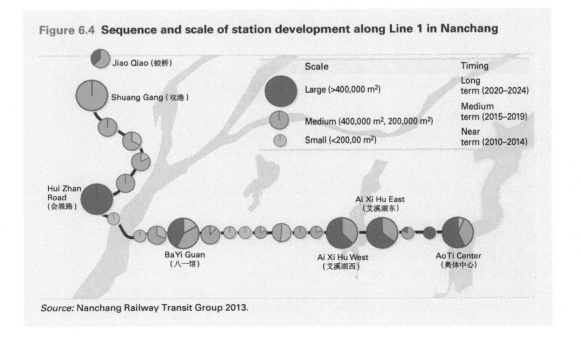

Source: Nanchang Railway Transit Group 2013.

expected to raise RMB6.8 billion ($1.1 billion) of the capital requirements between 2013 and 2015, mainly from commercial loans and bonds or the sale of leasehold rights.

Expected income generated from the investment includes: RMB3.5 billion ($574 million) from the sale of development rights; an estimated revenue of RMB8.9 billion ($1.5 billion) from selling 500,000 square meters of commercial property; and an average annual rental income of RMB400 million ($65.6 million), totaling RMB1.2 billion ($198 million) for three years. If these projections are fulfilled, property investments above or below the stations will bring a net profit of RMB6.8 billion ($1.1 billion) to the company by end-2015, equivalent to 20.5 percent of the construction cost of lines 1 and 2.

Development Cases

This section presents two metro railway property projects at station areas that follow development-based LVC in different floor uses and development parameters.

NRTG's Metro Mansion Station

NRTG is constructing a 45-story, 193-meter office tower with a FAR of 7.04 above the Metro Mansion Station on Line 1 in Nanchang's financial center. There will be underground parking on three levels. NRTG's headquarters and control center will occupy the first five floors of the tower, with the remaining office space rented to other tenants (figure 6.5).

Investment in land and construction comes to RMB1.3 billion ($213 million), financed in two ways. NRTG's real estate subsidiary will develop and sell some of its development rights, of which NRTG will get 80 percent of the revenue, or about RMB160 million ($25.8 million), to finance

Figure 6.5 Metro Mansion Station

  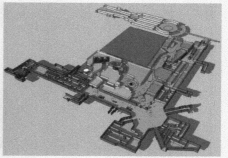

Source: Nanchang Railway Transit Group 2013. © Nanchang Railway Transit Group. Used with permission. Further permission required for reuse.

metro construction. The real estate subsidiary will also build 100,000 square meters of office space, of which 40 percent will be sold to NRTG on preferential terms.[2] The subsidiary, under this scheme, will only earn a net profit of RMB5.6 million ($918,000), renting the remaining 60,000 square meters and earning an annual rental income of about RMB39 million ($6.5 million). It has an option to sell the rental units for some RMB1.1 billion ($180 million), valued at project completion. This financial arrangement appears to generate enough income to cover the project's property investment cost.

Metro Time Square

Metro Time Square at Bayi Bridge West Station of Line 1 has a development area of 125.8 mu (83,867 square meters) with a built-up area of 388,827 square meters and a FAR of 3.5 (figure 6.6).

Construction began in 2012, with an expected date of completion of December 2016. The investment cost is RMB2.8 billion ($459 million). Project financing is through a joint venture between the real estate subsidiary of NRTG and a developer. The venture financed land acquisition costs and will develop the land with high-end residential apartments, retail stores, recreational facilities, and offices and then sell some of the properties. NRTG will receive profits in proportion to its shareholding. Eighty percent of the land use rights sales revenue of RMB880 million ($144 million) has already been allocated to NRTG to finance metro railway construction. In addition, 40,000 square meters of commercial space will be available for lease to private companies, and some of the rental income will go to NRTG, again in proportion to its shareholding.

Figure 6.6 Architectural design and site plan for Time Square Station

Source: Nanchang Railway Transit Group 2013. © Nanchang Railway Transit Group. Used with permission. Further permission required for reuse.

Conclusion

The following are major enablers for Nanchang's development-based LVC schemes and the associated risks. If implemented well, Nanchang's development-based LVC schemes could provide a good LVC model for other Chinese cities.

- Under a state leasehold system similar to Hong Kong SAR, China's, overall economic and urban environments are conducive to the development-based LVC approach. The city has experienced rapid economic and population growth coupled with fast urbanization. Not only will increases in income and population generate sufficient ridership for the metro railway, they can also help develop a buoyant real estate market, which is essential for LVC.
- Good urban planning helps, and Nanchang has played its part well. Land markets will behave erratically if land use regulations and planning are unpredictable. Public and private investors need to know with some degree of certainty when and where urban expansion will take place in order to invest. A well-designed master plan that allows for development flexibility serves this purpose.
- Nanchang's Urban Planning Bureau reviews its master plan every 10 years and makes additions and modifications as urban conditions change. Through this iterative process, NMG has established a vision for the future development of Nanchang that guides public and private investments.
- Well-integrated urban planning and public transport investments are other advantages. NMG has established a directive to use the metro railway as the backbone of its urban transport. The design of the system is based on facilitating the master plan. The number of metro lines and stations, with their locations and surrounding land uses, are specified for short- and long-term development.
- NMG and private investors understand the importance of mixed land use to make the idea of TOD and LVC work. NRTG's station designs provide strong evidence of this underlying principle. This is also reflected by sustained increases in prices for land designated for mixed use, showing that the market has caught on to the idea.
- NMG collects about 20 percent of the transfer fees of land use rights for the use of six development funds. This will allow NMG to use the revenues from development-based LVC for prioritized public investments other than metro investment.
- Key government agencies under the leadership of the mayor and the vice mayors fully support NRTG in reaching its financial goals under the LVC approach. This type of institutional backing is crucial for lowering transaction costs of land acquisition and regulatory changes.
- Cooperation from all government agencies can help engender synergies between public and private sectors to undertake the technically and financially complicated metro railway investments.

- Although Nanchang seems to possess the preconditions for applying development-based LVC, potential risks include overreliance on land financing that exposes NMG to overheated real estate markets; unaffordable housing due to gentrification of transit station areas; and lack of public-private experience in jointly delivering property development projects alongside complex TOD/LVC procedures in fast-moving real estate markets.

Challenges Faced by Other Chinese Cities with Development-Based LVC

Integrating metro investment with land management and incorporating development-based LVC in infrastructure finance and urban planning with cities' policies will be crucial for urbanization success, as metros offer another attractive mode of transport. If done well, Nanchang's approach combining TOD and LVC will increase the vibrancy and livability of the city, making it a model for other Chinese cities. Yet many barriers remain throughout China.

- Strict development parameters and site control plans are not conducive to maximize urban land values via TOD around stations and along corridors. They include excessive building setbacks; excessive road width; limited emphasis on mixed land uses; low differentiation in FAR, not reflecting accessibility of mass transit systems; limits to building height; and fire regulations limiting allowable FAR.
- Public land leasing programs are not designed in transit-supportive ways. Land development rights around stations cannot be formally transferred to mass transit agencies at the start of a project in a way that enables those companies to coordinate integration of mass transit investment with land management through public-private partnerships or to secure the sustainability of revenue streams from properties on and around stations. In Chinese practice, once land has been attributed to a developer, the developer cannot subdivide the land or transfer rights to subdevelopers. Additionally, the varying authorized land use periods for residential and commercial buildings make the combination of both in a single development difficult.
- Location priority is given to greenfield development rather than redevelopment of built-up areas, including brownfield. While most metro alignments go through existing city centers, fragmented property rights and complexities over the redevelopment of already built-up areas lead developers to favor greenfield development, limiting the application of TOD and LVC in potentially high-access and high-density districts. The lack of urban redevelopment schemes is a critical constraint for implementing TOD and LVC in mass transit investment at city- and regionwide level.
- Transit investment in China often lacks long-term financing. Revenues from the sale of development rights are the major funding source

for local infrastructure, yet they are only a one-time revenue source for cities, and they fail to (1) capture the long-term increase in value brought by mass transit, and (2) meet the need for recurrent financial support for operation, maintenance, and renewal. There needs to be a mechanism for mass transit agencies to share recurrent revenues fairly with developers, through development-rights arrangements or other financial instruments, to capture increases in land values over the long run, such as property taxes, impact fees, and betterment taxes.

- The scale of TOD in Chinese cities is small, while the superblock design for car traffic creates urban islands disconnected from other streets within cities. Transit agencies have difficulty in finding experienced developers who can design and develop well-integrated spaces at the neighborhood level, even though the development rights of public land have been secured.

Notes

1. If other needed land sites are still under NMG's control, NRTG can obtain these parcels via public auction. The Land Resource Center is in charge of leasing public land in Nanchang and usually leases development rights to investors through public auction or tender. NRTG can also take part in these auctions. Less than 1 percent of total land resources (16,426 mu) obtained by NRTG was secured through public auction.
2. RMB3,600 per square meter, while the actual construction cost is RMB13,000 per square meter.

References

Nanchang Railway Transit Group. 2013. "Utilizing Land Resource to Finance Nanchang Mess Transit Railway." Presentation made at the World Bank Land Value Capture Workshop, Nanchang, China, May 13–14.

UN (United Nations). 2012. *World Urbanization Prospects: The 2011 Revision*, CD-ROM Edition. New York: Department of Economic and Social Affairs, Population Division.

Urban Planning and Design Research Institute of Nanchang. 2013. "The Interaction between Nanchang's Urban Comprehensive Plan and Railway Transport Planning." Presentation made at the World Bank Land Value Capture Workshop, Nanchang, China, May 13–14.

World Bank. 2013. *Project Information Document (Appraisal Stage) for Nanchang Urban Rail Project*. Report PIDA854. Washington, DC: World Bank.

CHAPTER 7

A Tale of Two Metro Cities: Delhi and Hyderabad, India

Two cities in India exemplify contrasting institutional approaches to land value capture (LVC) in delivering new metro projects: a conventional government-led approach in Delhi and an innovative public-private partnership (PPP) in Hyderabad. As the National Capital Region, Delhi faces the complexity of policymaking and interest sharing among multi-layered governments and their agencies within its wide territory. Despite the national government's strong support and operational success of the extensive metro system, the Delhi regional government and its transit agency have been unable to fully use development-based LVC schemes as a strategic apparatus of infrastructure financing and urban development. This underutilization of land around metro stations is largely due to an inconsistent policy and regulatory framework and lack of coordination among stakeholders. In contrast, Hyderabad, the multinational corporate hub of South Asia, has advanced the world's largest PPP metro project, integrating development-based LVC scheme as its financing and urban development instrument. Under a clear and transparent institutional and regulatory framework, the new private rail lines attempt to reconfigure the city's business districts and streetscapes, spurring real-estate development along metro corridors and station precincts for commercial properties or offices connected to the stations through skywalk pedestrian bridges. These two cases highlight constraints and opportunities in applying development-based LVC in the fast-growing cities of the developing world, given the institutional and regulatory frameworks, many informal settlements, private expertise and resources available, and the market potential.

Urban Development Context, Delhi

Population and Urbanization Trends

The Delhi Metropolitan Area consists of the National Capital Territory of Delhi (NCTD) and the first ring of towns around the capital, including Ghaziabad, Loni, Noida, Faridabad, Gurgaon, and Bahadurgarh (map 7.1). It was home to more than 22 million inhabitants within 1,483 square kilometers in 2010 and is projected to increase to 33 million inhabitants by 2025 (figure 7.1). The NCTD's per capita income is 2.4 times higher than the national average (Rs 70,238/$1,545 versus Rs 29,524/$650 in 2006–07), so its population ratio below the poverty line is also around half the national figure (14.7 percent versus 27.8 percent in 2004–05) (Gladstone and Kolapalli 2007).

Delhi's economic supremacy comes mainly from trade, commerce, banking, finance, manufacturing, and tourism, which, however, accounted for only 15 percent of jobs in 2006, whereas government is the largest employer. Development policies, such as transport network extensions, large-scale slum redevelopment, and special economic zones, have gradually diminished the cohesiveness of traditional business activities around the city center. Delhi's regional territory already expands beyond the NCTD's original boundary (1,483 square kilometers) and has gradually engulfed the surrounding cities, towns, villages, and rural hinterlands. This has been spurred on by recent rapid motorization (the number of registered motor vehicles in Delhi climbed from 6.0 million in 2008–09 to 7.4 million in 2011–12), further complicating interjurisdictional coordination.

Regulatory and Institutional Framework, Delhi

Master Plans

Delhi's strategic planning exercise began with the Delhi Development Act of 1957, which was followed by the Master Plan of Delhi, 1962 (MPD-62). MPD-62 first formulated the government's land acquisition, development, and disposal scheme to extend the urbanized areas of Delhi from 172.9 to 447.8 square kilometers by 1981. It also promoted the first ring of towns within a radius of 35 kilometers of the capital, along with provision of public infrastructure and services. Between 1961 and 1981, 155.4 square kilometers was identified for public land acquisition. The initial procedure was highly government led with limited private participation in housing development (shelter provision) and infrastructure investment until the early 1990s. Thereafter, the Master Plan of Delhi, 2001 (MPD-2001), elaborated land use characteristics with a hierarchical planning system: master, zonal, and layout plans for specific development schemes within each zone. Nevertheless, the government has acquired only 39 percent of the land proposed for development in MPD-2001 (Delhi Development Authority 2013).

Map 7.1 Delhi Metropolitan Area

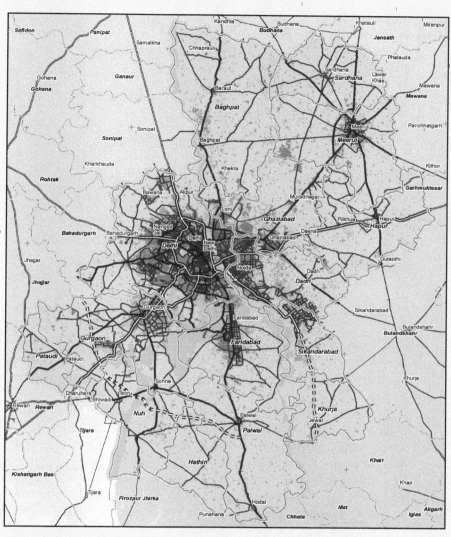

Land cover/land use		Transportation
■ Continuous Urban Fabric (U.F.)	■ Agricultural land	═══ Motorway
■ Discontinuous High Dense U.F.	■ Forest	═ ═ In construction
■ Discontinuous Low Dense U.F.	■ Other natural and seminatural areas	━━ Primary road
■ Industrial, commercial, and transportation		── Other road
■ Construction sites	■ Bare land	**Administrative**
■ Urban greenery	■ Water	▢ District border
	■ River bed	

Source: GISAT for European Space Agency/World Bank.

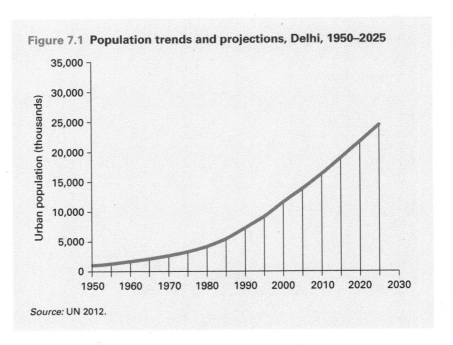

Figure 7.1 Population trends and projections, Delhi, 1950–2025

Source: UN 2012.

The latest version, the draft Master Plan of Delhi, 2021 (MPD-2021), takes into account the achievements and shortfalls of MPD-62 and MPD-2001. Several studies made for preparing MPD-2021 reveal that there had been substantial gaps between the land areas targeted, acquired, and developed due to the limitations of financial, physical, and human resources and various difficulties encountered in the course of land assembly.

The draft MPD-2021 thus stresses the importance of four approaches: improving the scheme of large-scale land acquisition and development, involving the private sector in the assembly and development of land and the provision of infrastructure and services, integrating land use planning and infrastructure investment, and promoting redevelopment and densification with more flexible land use and development codes (Delhi Development Authority 2013). MPD-2021 also envisages an integrated multimodal transport network for the overall structure of the city, including various guided transit systems, such as Metro Rail, ring rail, dedicated rail corridors for daily commuters, bus rapid transit corridors, and regional rapid transit system corridors.

The Mass Rapid Transport System (MRTS) is the most important transport mode, forming a roughly 250-kilometer network of underground, elevated, and surface lines across the territory by 2021. It is expected that after the full network is developed, about 60 percent of the urbanized area of Delhi will be no more than a 15-minute walk from MRTS stations. Such investments are also expected to generate greater opportunities for economic growth and employment by calling for selective redevelopment and densification of the existing built-up areas given local conditions and informal settlement patterns such as land pockets of slum and Jhuggi Jhoppadi (a cluster of slum colonies). In the MPD-2021 framework, therefore, it is recommended that a comprehensive redevelopment scheme of the catchment areas of MRTS stations be made with multiple land use categories and floor area ratios (FARs) (map 7.2).

Zoning and Land Administration

Delhi's zonal plans aim to detail the policies of the master plan and lead to the practices of the layout plan. Between the master plan and layout plan, Delhi's urban area is divided up into planning zones A through P, whose population and housing capacities are to be enhanced with target densities for redevelopment projects, especially along some sections of the rail corridors. Like many other large cities in India, the FAR of Delhi's central business district has been kept much lower than those of global megacities in developed countries (1.12–3.5 versus 12.0 in Hong Kong SAR, China, 15.0 in New York City, and 20.0 in Tokyo) (World Bank 2013b). In addition, the FAR for the properties of the Delhi Metro Rail Corporation Limited (DMRC) at its station sites has been capped at 1.0, which does not allow DMRC to maximize revenues from property development.

Map 7.2 Land use plan of the draft Master Plan for Delhi-2021

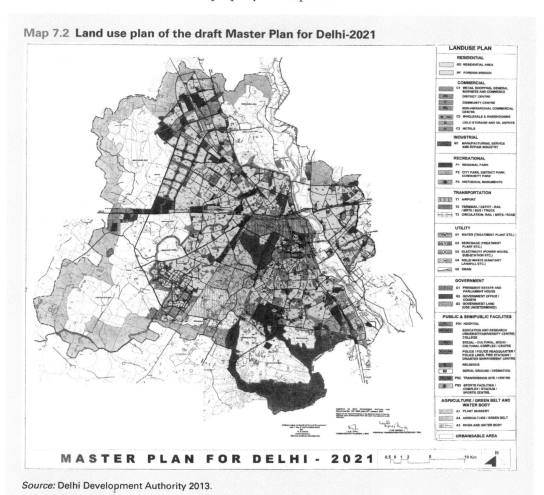

Source: Delhi Development Authority 2013.

The Delhi Development Authority (DDA), set up in 1957 and in charge of the master plans, proposes to greatly raise FARs in Delhi under MPD-2021. A 500-meter wide transit-oriented development (TOD)/multi-use zone would be overlaid on both sides of the metro corridor to encourage a mix of commercial and employment-generating activities along with residential developments. Higher FARs would be permitted subject to certain setback and height restrictions. One redevelopment package will be included in the influence zone if more than 70 percent of the site area falls inside the 500-meter buffer. Property developments around the MRTS stations, up to a maximum area of 3.0 hectares, will be allowed in all use (mixed land use) zones, with some exceptions. This flexible land use coordination could lead to a mix of residential and commercial uses as well as densely built-up areas, but whether this actually triggers redevelopment along the corridor remains to be seen.

In practice, other regulatory impairments have impeded property development in the influence zones besides a low FAR limit. For example, the delivery of property development projects around the MRTS stations is subject to the approval of multiple statutory bodies as well as statutory clearance from local municipalities and related agencies, a process that can take several years. In addition, approvals of any development activities in the influence zones are granted only after the start of the MRTS extension projects, which blocks planners, developers, and operators from coordination and physical integration between public spaces, private properties, and station facilities (Delhi Development Authority 2013).

The private sector is expected to mobilize financial resources for land acquisition of slum areas, resettlement, and redevelopment through capital markets, while the government agency (DDA) enforces development controls, such as higher FARs and targeted land use planning, to achieve broader social objectives. In Delhi, the local government has set up mandatory provision of housing units for "economically weaker sections" (EWS) by exercising slum redevelopment to the extent of 15 percent of the permissible FAR, or 35 percent of the dwelling units on the plot. After private developers complete construction, EWS housing units are handed over to the government agency and are allotted to beneficiaries. Slum rehabilitation requires a minimum lot size of 2,000 square meters and an FAR of 4.0 for residential use. The FAR for remunerative use (mixed and commercial use) is up to 10 percent of the permissible FAR for residential areas. A minimum proportion of squatter resettlement area is 60 percent of the total areas for the residential use, while a maximum proportion of area for the remunerative use has to be up to 40 percent of the total area.

The practice of land banking in Delhi started in 1961, allowing DDA to take control of land designated for urban development and management. However, despite its financial success, fundamental issues remain with implementation. First, land acquisition is often difficult due to an outdated land valuation system. Second, land disposal has reallocated a high share of land resources to a small number of wealthy groups rather than a large number of low-income people. Third, DDA has been unable to provide affordable housing units to low-income people and new immigrants, which has generated yet more informal settlements beyond the city boundaries. Fourth, land values have escalated as DDA has deliberately limited the release of DDA-owned sites to land markets (Nallathiga 2009; Gladstone and Kolapalli 2007).

MPD-2021: Guidelines for TOD

The term TOD has become increasingly popular across Indian cities, yet even as TOD standards for Indian cities are still being set up and executed, they face new challenges in urban land markets. In response, the current draft MPD-2021 attempts to provide guidelines for TOD practices that aim to reduce private automobile dependency through urban design and policies and to maximize public transport access through enhancing connectivity and densifying. It states that "the MRTS influence zone may catalyze the private sector into cross subsidizing and providing the various public amenities, greater affordable housing stock and high-quality public transport" (UTTIPEC 2012).

The draft MPD-2021 proposes that the influence zones of MRTS stations be further classified into three zone categories with certain location thresholds (table 7.1 and map 7.3). The total area covered by these TOD zones will be around 44.1 percent of Delhi, or 665.1 square kilometers. Applying the principles of TOD to Delhi would probably require more diversified approaches (including redevelopment, infill, and greenfield development) and using incentives and restrictions within the intense and standard zones.

Table 7.1 Three transit-oriented development zones around Mass Rapid Transport System stations

Zone categories	Location thresholds
Zone 1: Intense TOD	• 300 m influence zone of all metro stations • 800 m (10 minutes' walking) influence zone of regional interchange station (that is, interchange between rail and metro or two different metro lines)
Zone 2: Standard TOD	• 800 m (10 minutes' walking) influence zone of all metro stations
Zone 3: Nonmotorized transport	• 2,000 m (10 minutes' cycling) influence zone of all regional interchange stations and metro stations • 300 m influence zone of all bus rapid transit corridors • Zones within intense or standard TOD influence zones, which are not permitted for redevelopment but need enhancements in public realm

Source: Adapted from Delhi Development Authority 2013.
Note: TOD = transit-oriented development.

Map 7.3 Example of drawing the 300-m, 800-m, and 2,000-m catchments of Mass Rapid Transport System stations

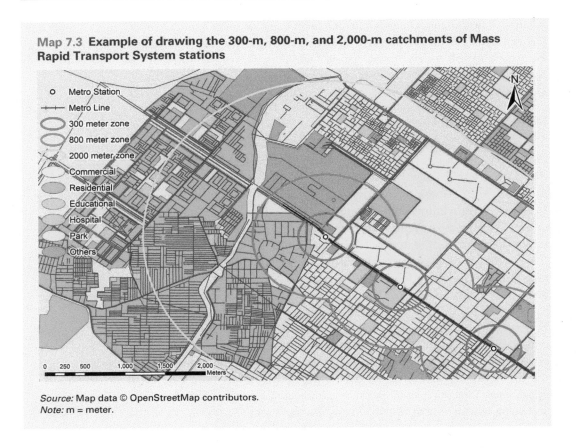

Source: Map data © OpenStreetMap contributors.
Note: m = meter.

Any development practices in the zones are intended to be flexible, subject to development parameters and land use criteria: minimum site area of 6 hectare or 5,000 residents, minimum gross density permissible for TOD of 250 dwelling units per hectare, no universal cap on the FAR, minimum 30 percent residential and 30 percent commercial/institutional use of the FAR, and minimum 15 percent of the FAR to be allocated to rental or for-sale housing with unit sizes no larger than 25 square meters (table 7.2). However, the TOD zones and criteria listed are still inconsistent with the land use map shown in the MPD-2021 (map 7.4). MPD-2021 implies that DDA will continue to restrict the FAR for DMRC's properties at its station sites up to 1.0.

The guidelines also encourage integration of multimodal public transport at key interchanges, with a checklist of interchanges, public facilities and open spaces, urban designs, and parking locations/policies over the 300-meter influence zone of MRTS stations. Similarly they target pedestrian and cyclist access to public transport systems, with street connectivity, housing density, and job-home accessibility standards (Delhi Development Authority 2013). The guidelines present a range of opportunities to tap developable sites around target interchanges and create greater benefits to

Table 7.2 Proposed permissible floor area ratios and density for transit-oriented development

Gross FAR (site)	Net FAR (block)	Minimum permissible density (with ±10% variation)	
		Residential-dominated (FAR ≥ 50%), dwelling units per hectare	Less residential (FAR ≤ 30%), dwelling units per hectare
Below 1.0	Below 2.0	Underutilization of FAR not permitted	
1.1–1.5	2.1–3.0	300	250
1.6–2.0	3.1–4.0	400	350
2.1–2.5	4.1–5.0	500	450
2.6–3.0	5.1–6.0	600	550
3.1–3.5	6.1–7.0	700	650
3.6–4.0	7.1–8.0	800	750

Source: Adapted from Delhi Development Authority 2013.
Note: FAR = floor area ratio.

Map 7.4 Inconsistencies between Master Plan for Delhi-2021 and proposed transit-oriented development zones

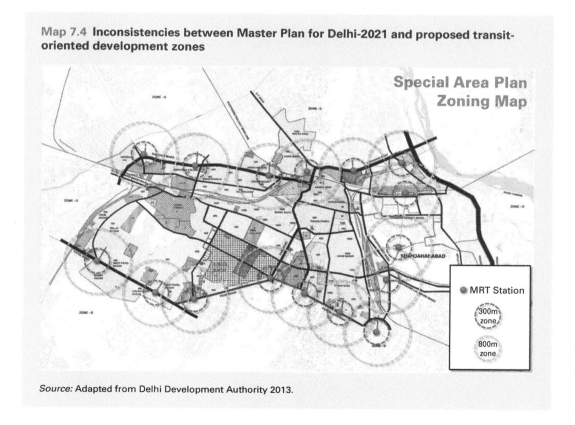

Source: Adapted from Delhi Development Authority 2013.

several transport bodies, but the plethora of development-related bureaus in Delhi's multilayered government rather inhibits seamless decision making and joint development.

A Complicated Government Structure

Delhi is statutorily distinct from other Indian cities. It is the seat of the national government, which heavily involves itself in managing urban affairs. Multiple government bodies over multiple jurisdictions often overlap territorially and functionally (figure 7.2). Unlike other Indian city-states, Delhi has no metropolitan planning committee—the NCTD has no control over its urban development. Instead, DDA administers land acquisition, disposal, and development within the NCTD. It started institutionalizing the TOD concept in 2007 for MPD-2021, while the Unified Traffic and Transportation Infrastructure Planning and Engineering Centre (UTTI-PEC), established as one branch of DDA in 2008, is responsible for TOD policies and projects.

Transport, nationwide, is the domain of multiple government agencies. For example, since 1986 the Ministry of Urban Development has been the nodal body for planning and coordinating urban transport. Major transport projects in 65 Indian cities are sanctioned under the Urban Infrastructure and Governance component of the Jawaharlal Nehru National Urban Renewal Mission (JnNURM), launched in 2005 and administered by the Ministry of Urban Development. The writ of the Unified Metropolitan Transport Authority runs in all municipalities with more than

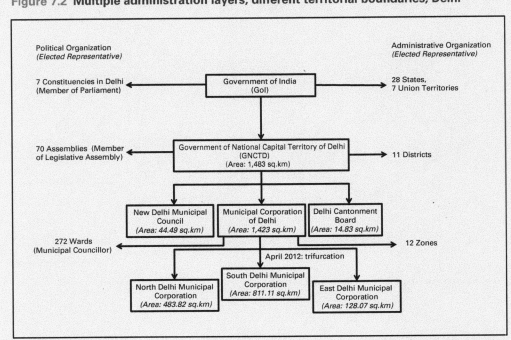

Figure 7.2 Multiple administration layers, different territorial boundaries, Delhi

Source: World Bank 2013a.

1 million people, such as Hyderabad, Bangalore, Chennai, Mumbai, and Jaipur. Beyond that, with the Dedicated Urban Transport Fund (funded by a green surcharge on petrol, "a green tax" on registered personalized vehicles, and an urban transport tax on purchase of new cars at national government level), state- and city-level transport agencies attempted to raise their own capital funds from revenues from the increased FAR, enhancement of property tax, and parking charges.

In Delhi, matters are even more complicated. Three major bodies—DDA, National Capital Region Board, and DMRC (see just below)—are under the national Ministry of Urban Development, whereas several transport-related branches, such as the Delhi Transport Corporation, Delhi Integrated Multi-Modal Transit Systems, and IFDC Foundation, are also involved in coordinating fares and services, operating bus transit, integrating multimodal activities, and funding infrastructure under the government of Delhi.

Still, India may be one of the few developing countries to have adopted a national urban transport policy. Its objective is "to ensure safe, affordable, quick, comfortable, reliable and sustainable access for the growing number of city residents to jobs, education, recreation and such other needs within our cities" (Ministry of Urban Development 2006). The policy thus encourages municipal governments and transit agencies to "raise funds, through an innovative mechanism that taps land as a resource, for investments in urban transport infrastructure" (Ministry of Urban Development, Government of India 2006).

DMRC

DMRC was established as a state-owned company in 1995 through an equal partnership between the national and Delhi governments, specifically for building and operating MRTS in the National Capital Region and beyond. It has powers of decision in railway business practices, while the exercise of land development rights remains with government authorities—the Ministry of Urban Development often intervenes in DMRC's station plans with property development projects.

Since its beginning, DMRC has held a strong position in public infrastructure and urban mobility services. Due in large part to the financial difficulty faced by its initial operations, it was allowed to carry out property development projects and generate real estate revenues from the sites granted by the national government in and around its station facilities (map 7.5). The DDA and other municipal authorities agreed on such development practices to support the implementation of the DMRC's railway projects in the early years. However, the DMRC was also exempted from paying most taxes levied by the national and Delhi governments—a source of conflict between the Municipality of Delhi and DMRC. The municipal agencies eventually refused to sanction some plans for commercial development on land granted because the DMRC was exempted from property taxes on some projects that were not directly related to MRTS operations.

Map 7.5   Delhi Metro Rail Corporation Limited network phases I (1995–2006), II (2006–11), and III (2011–16)

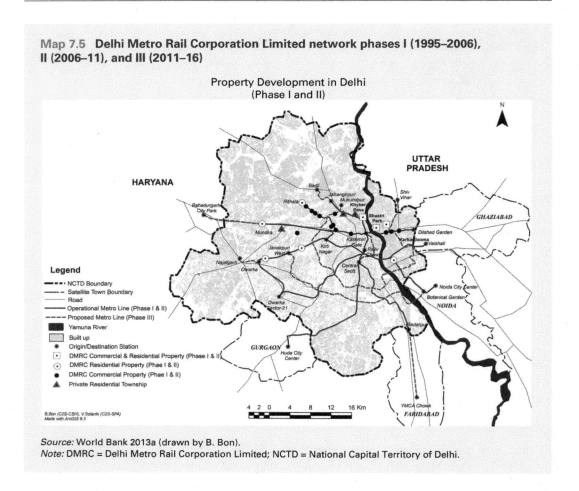

Source: World Bank 2013a (drawn by B. Bon).
Note: DMRC = Delhi Metro Rail Corporation Limited; NCTD = National Capital Territory of Delhi.

DMRC has to get statutory clearance from multiple government stakeholders at NCTD level: for architectural and conceptual plans, from the Delhi Urban Arts Commission; land use changes—DDA; building plans—municipal authorities; no objection certificates—the Land and Development Office and DDA; archaeological surveys—the Archaeological Survey of India; fire-fighting clearance—Delhi Fire Service; and environmental clearance—the Ministry of Environment.

This slow and convoluted process (requiring two or three years a project) is often held up by DMRC and by private developers as the main barrier to delivering property development projects on MRTS station sites (see the second bullet in the Delhi "Conclusion"). Nevertheless, the process of generating revenues from property development in Delhi has been generally recognized as a metro finance model for other Indian cities.

Land Value Capture, Delhi

Funding Arrangements

The current and proposed Delhi MRTS network combined is about 293 kilometers long and has three project phases (table 7.3). The national government's direct participation in project funding in the three phases was required to secure concessional Japanese yen loans (30 years, including a 10-year grace period, with an interest rate of about 1.8 percent) from the Japan International Cooperation Agency (JICA).

The land parcels belonging to the various bureaus, agencies, and municipalities were transferred to DMRC at intergovernmental transfer rates decided by the Ministry of Urban Development for a 99-year lease. The

Table 7.3 Mass Rapid Transport System financing

Phase I (1995–2006)

Project completion cost (in crores Rs): 10,891 ($3,472 million)

- Government of India equity: 14%
- Government of Delhi equity: 14%
- Subordinate debt of government of India: 2.5%
- Subordinate debt of government of Delhi: 2.5%
- Interest free subordinate debt representing land cost: 7%
- JICA loan: 60%

Phase II (2006–11)

Project completion cost (in crores Rs): 19,390 ($4,304 million)

- Government of India equity: 17%
- Government of Delhi equity: 17%
- Subordinate debt of government of India: 3.26%
- Subordinate debt of government of Delhi: 3.26%
- Interest free subordinate debt representing land cost: 4.35%
- JICA loan: 55.13%

Phase III (2011–16)

Project completion cost (in crores Rs): 35,242 ($7,889 million)

- Government of India equity: 10.6%
- Government of Delhi equity: 10.6%
- Subordinate debt of government of India: 7.2%
- Subordinate debt of government of Delhi: 7.2%
- Interest free subordinate debt representing land cost: 4.50%
- JICA loan: 40%
- Others: 19.9%

Source: DMRC 2001, 2010, 2013b.
Note: JICA = Japan International Cooperation Agency.

Delhi government is essentially in charge of acquiring private lands for public projects and then transferring them to DMRC. In some locations, DDA also provides the land for free to DMRC. The cost of land acquisition is treated as a premium to be recovered as an interest-free subordinate debt over a 25-year period in the fund allocation schemes.

From 2006 to 2012, DMRC gained more passengers (about a 285 percent increase in daily ridership), leading to operational cost recovery of about 247 percent in fiscal year 2011–12 (DMRC 2013a). However, this exceptional outcome can be explained by tax exemptions (see above), preferential power tariffs, and low-cost labor. The recurrent income from traffic operations, which accounts for 57 percent of total corporate revenue in fiscal year 2011–12, is a primary source for DMRC to pay back the low-interest foreign loans.

Property Development

In 1996 during phase I, DMRC was granted a mandate from the union cabinet to raise 7 percent of the total cost of the first phase of the metro project through property development. Its property division, set up in July 1999, deals with smaller commercial properties inside the MRTS, reserved developable land parcels close to stations, and larger residential and commercial property projects on the sites initially acquired for constructing depots and maintenance buildings. This funding approach—development-based LVC, in other words—was followed by phases II and III, but the capital proportion from property development fell (table 7.4).

Most residential development projects on depot and standalone plots with 90-year leases generate substantial upfront payments, whereas commercial properties within station buildings with short (6–12-year) leases and on large plots outside stations with medium-term (20-year) leases produce more recurrent revenue streams. DMRC's recurrent income from real estate accounted for about 30 percent of the total over seven recent years (figure 7.3). Yet the financial contribution from the real estate practice has been minor for the last few years (such as only 6 percent in 2011–12).

Table 7.4 Capital share funded by property development, Mass Rapid Transport System

Phase	Metro Rail Project cost (crores Rs)	Funded by property (crores Rs)	(%)
I	10,891	762.37	7.00
II	19,390	843.46	4.35
Subtotal	30,291	1,605.83	5.30
III	35,242	1,586.00	4.50
Total	65,523 ($12,049 mn)	3,191.83 ($587 mn)	4.87

Source: World Bank 2013a.

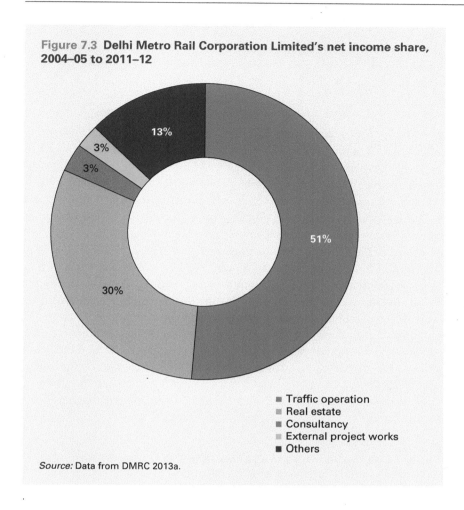

Figure 7.3 Delhi Metro Rail Corporation Limited's net income share, 2004–05 to 2011–12

- Traffic operation
- Real estate
- Consultancy
- External project works
- Others

Source: Data from DMRC 2013a.

Sales of development rights are in two steps. After it gets the land transfers from multiple government agencies, DMRC usually invites shortlisted bidders to make concession agreements with successful tenders for the development rights. Only DMRC selects the developer and sets the lease terms. Yet inefficiencies in implementation remain at the site level. An audit report of the Comptroller and Auditor General of India (2008) highlighted weak responses and poor performance on the amount of development realized at a reasonable price. From a private developer's standpoint, two impediments stand out: restrictive clauses for land use in the allotment letter and stringent technical criteria fixed through the bidding process; and inadequate FAR and plot size to generate a profit.

Development Cases, Delhi

To illustrate Delhi's TOD and LVC practices at the site level, this short section presents two current Delhi cases. Both sites are being mainly developed with large-scale properties: one by UTTIPEC based on the TOD principle, the other by a private developer without a TOD-planning framework and control. Their experiences reveal some of the potentials and barriers to these practices.

Case 1: TOD Pilot Project, Karkardooma Metro Station

In 2010, the DDA decided that UTTIPEC would conduct a TOD pilot project at MRTS stations. The UTTIPEC team drafted a project for a group housing complex around Karkardooma Metro Station (photo 7.1). The area has more than 30 hectares of developable land connected to Vikas Marg Station and the new MRTS Line III that stretches from Yamuna Bank to Anand Vihar Terminal and points to huge accessibility benefits from the multiple metro lines, commuter rail, and feeder services.

UTTIPEC is attempting to demonstrate TOD principles, which aim to improve neighborhood connectivity and reduce automobile trips. It proposes mixed-use developments with a variety of housing types (including EWS units) and civic amenities, all intended to encourage affordable and walkable communities around a multimodal transport node. The area is surrounded by informal housing clusters. Yet the implementation of such an ideal TOD proposal would require drastic changes and several modifications to the strict FAR and coverage regulations, zoning and design codes, and painstaking clearance procedures (table 7.5). Worse, there has been no coordination between UTTIPEC and DMRC on the metro station area's

Photo 7.1 Group housing site and Mass Rapid Transport System extension around Karkardooma Metro Station

Source: © Jin Murakami. Used with permission. Further permission required for reuse.

Table 7.5 Proposed transit-oriented development project around Karkardooma Metro Station

Project period	2010–present
Distance to central business district	9 km
Population	24,800 (projection)
Site area	30.72 ha
FAR	2.0
Floor area use	Residential: 43% Commercial: 38% Social: 19%
Parking requirement	34% less
Key stakeholders	DDA; UTTIPEC
Financial figures	Not available[a]

Source: World Bank 2013a.
Note: DDA = Delhi Development Authority; FAR = floor area ratio; UTTIPEC = Unified Traffic and Transportation Infrastructure Planning and Engineering Centre.
a. Because the project is a pilot, financial figures have not been published, and official financing data was not available as of May 2013.

land use and layout plans, design parameters, multimodal facilities, feeder services, and travel and property demand estimates, even though these conditions will determine the financial feasibility of the project and the metro line extension.

Case 2: Sales of Development Rights for High-End Residential Complex, Khyber Pass Metro Depot

The Khyber Pass Metro Depot is located 9 kilometers north of the city center near the Yamuna River and a series of major roads that were originally selected by the Delhi government for building a new bridge. In 1999, more than 37 hectares of land were transferred from the Land and Development Office to DMRC for more than Rs 210 million ($4.9 million) with an annuity of 2 percent of this amount. In 2003, DMRC invited tenders for much of the depot site. It received six bids for a residential condominium package and two for a shopping mall. The developer Parsvnath won the bid for residential development at about Rs 194 crores ($40 million) for a long-term leasehold of 99 years (property development rights); the up-front payment was 94 percent higher than the reserve price set by the DMRC. Parsvnath then sold the leasehold rights to high-end housing units to private buyers. To finance the project, the developer raised Rs 115 crores ($24 million) from a private investment company for a 22 percent stake in the property package.

Parsvnath's residential condominiums are mainly three- to five-bedroom units with about four parking spaces per household along the depot (figure

7.4). But the layout is not connected to the nearest MRTS station—making it a typical transit-adjacent development (TAD) for DMRC's financial gain rather than a TOD. Still, a social component of the project is housing

Figure 7.4 Layout of residential complex property development around Khyber Pass Metro Depot

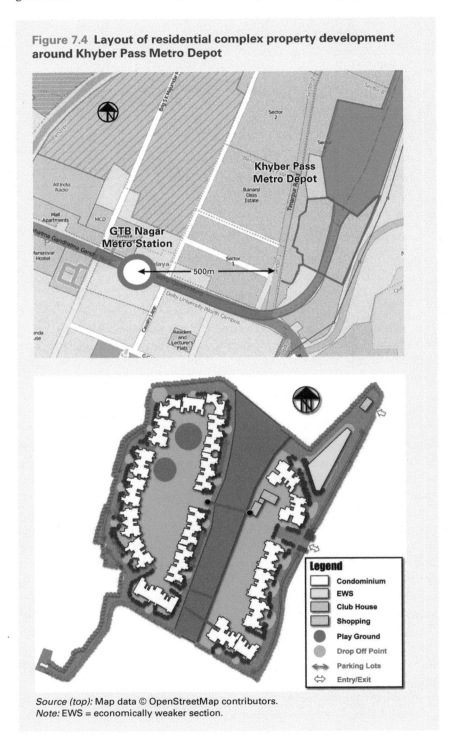

Source (top): Map data © OpenStreetMap contributors.
Note: EWS = economically weaker section.

reserved for economically weaker sections (EWS) of society: the MPD-2021 stipulates that large housing projects must reserve 35 percent of their units for EWS residents (table 7.6). This development includes 273 such units. Yet the physical configuration between the condominium and EWS units raises questions whether this public requirement will promote social inclusiveness.

Urban Development Context, Hyderabad

Population and Urbanization Trends

Hyderabad, the capital of Andhra Pradesh, has long been the international corporate hub for India's driving businesses since the arrival of modern infrastructure—railway and education—in the late 19th century. Hyderabad's economy is once more restructuring, transitioning from low-cost manufacturing to services- and knowledge-based activities. Information technology (IT) and IT-related services, with the biotech industry, have formed new business clusters largely in the northern part of the Hyderabad Metropolitan Development Area (HMDA), helping make it the fourth-largest exporter of software in the country (GHMC 2013).

More than 7.5 million people live within the 7,257 square kilometers of the HMDA, which includes the Greater Hyderabad Municipal Corporation (GHMC). Hyderabad's metropolitan population is projected to grow to more than 11.6 million by 2025 (figure 7.5), of which the major development and population growth are likely to occur in the surrounding municipalities. Hence, there is a need to think long term about public infrastructure investments and land use regulations, reflecting population growth patterns and the emerging industrial clusters across the whole metropolitan area (GHMC 2013).

Table 7.6 Residential property around Khyber Pass Metro Depot

Period	2003–present (99-year lease)
Distance to central business district	9 km
Population	2,000
Site area	16.8 acres
Total units	507 excluding EWS units
EWS units	273 (35% of total units)
Car parking	1,500 spaces
Key stakeholders	Land and Development Office; DMRC; Parsvnath (developer); Private Investment Company
Financial figures	Rs 210 million (DMRC to Land and Development Office); Rs 194 crores (Parsvnath to DMRC); Rs 115 crores (investment company to Parsvnath)

Source: World Bank 2013a.
Note: DMRC = Delhi Metro Rail Corporation; EWS = economically weak sections.

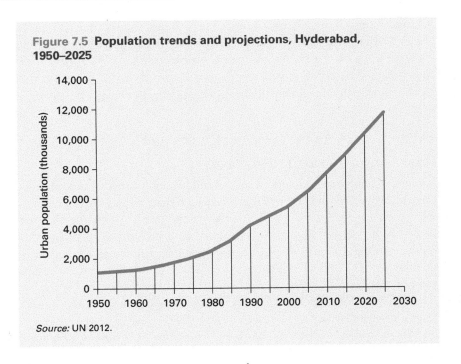

Figure 7.5 Population trends and projections, Hyderabad, 1950–2025

Source: UN 2012.

Regulatory and Institutional Framework, Hyderabad

Master Plans

Hyderabad's master plans have been updated to address emerging population growth patterns and business location shifts for the long term. The latest Metropolitan Plan-2031 for the outer areas (that is, outside the outer ring road) encourages the clustering of economic and social activities within built-up areas and along target transport corridors for more compact development (map 7.6). The metro rail has never been integrated into any of the master plans, and so there were no studies on the impact of the new metro system on adjacent areas. The metro network development in the central area was in fact a standalone project in the broader metropolitan development strategy. Once the metro development plan was complete, the master plan of the GHMC was amended by the state government to introduce a 300-meter wide "multi use zone (mixed land use)" on both sides of the metro corridor to promote commercial and office use, which can also benefit from transit services.

Government Structure

Hyderabad used to have many municipalities and administrative organizations, though it has recently consolidated them. The overarching spatial unit is the HMDA, which was set up in 2008 as an umbrella authority after five authorities were merged (map 7.7). This unit is in charge of planning,

Map 7.6 Metropolitan Development Plan-2031, Hyderabad

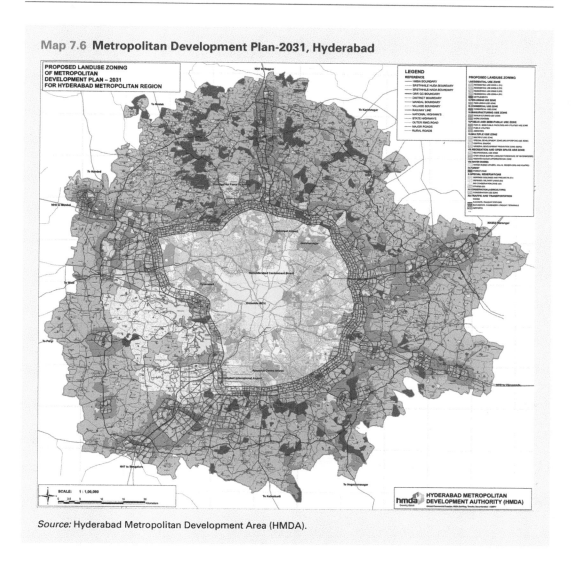

Source: Hyderabad Metropolitan Development Area (HMDA).

coordinating, supervising, promoting, and securing the development of the HMDA by allocating development funds for amenities and infrastructure.

Within the outer ring road growth corridor is the Greater Hyderabad Municipal Corporation (GHMC), with an area of about 650 square kilometers, formed by the merger of the Municipal Corporation of Hyderabad with 12 municipalities and eight *gram panchayat* of two neighboring districts in 2007 (except Secunderabad Cantonment Board, which has camps of the Indian Army and Indian Air Force). The GHMC is divided into five zones (north, south, central, east, and west) and 18 circles that contain 150 municipal wards. Each ward is headed by an elected "corporator." The corporators elect the city mayor, the titular head of GHMC, though its executive powers lie with the municipal commissioner, appointed by the state government.

Map 7.7 Merged jurisdictional boundaries, Hyderabad

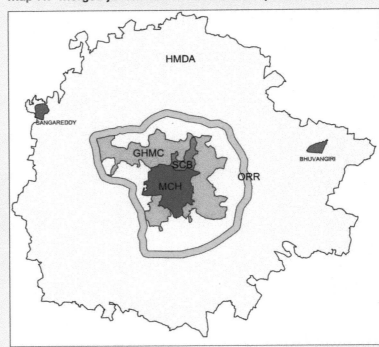

Source: Based on information provided in the report on Development Plan for Hyderabad Metro Rail Limited (drawn by S. Ballaney).
Note: GHMC = Greater Hyderabad Municipal Corporation; HMDA = Hyderabad Metropolitan Development Area; MCH = Municipal Corporation of Hyderabad; ORR = Outer Ring Road; SCB = Secunderabad Cantonment Board.

Public-Private Partnership

Hyderabad runs the world's largest metro PPP project, in an entrepreneurial model established after reviews of worldwide best practices, as for example, Bangkok; Hong Kong SAR, China; London; Singapore; and Tokyo (Hyderabad Metro Rail Limited, 2010 information). The state government is attempting to provide a rail system for 71.16 kilometers on elevated structures in Hyderabad via design-build-finance-operate-transfer. In 2009, it invited proposals from eight consortium bidders shortlisted for undertaking the project with a maximum 10 percent viability gap fund (a subsidy from the national government to fill a PPP's financing gap).

Among the three finalists, Larsen & Toubro Limited (L&T) won the bid as it asked for the lowest viability gap funding (VGF) (Rs 1,458 crores/$230 million) and signed the concession agreement with the state government for the project over 35 years, of which 5 years are for construction. Hyderabad Metro Rail Limited (HMR) was set up as a special-purpose vehicle. In this framework, HMR is an intermediary ensuring that

L&T gets the right of way for the metro construction, coordinating with the GHMC, traffic and police departments, and utility agencies for multiple clearances. Essentially, all heads of major departments are on the board of the HMR, and the core members of the HMR were selected from the state government, which tries to make the painstaking task of obtaining various clearances easier. The HMR has acquired about 269 acres (108.8 hectares) of land for property development. Where road widening in certain sections was required, the land parcels were acquired at market rates.

The L&T Hyderabad Metro Rail Private Limited (L&T Metro Rail)—the concessionaire of the Metro Rail Project—assisted by international consulting firms has been entitled to undertake development, operation, and maintenance of real estate along corridors, with the right to sublicense any or all parts of those properties. Two important obligations of the concessionaire are to achieve integration with the surrounding landscape by engaging architects and town planners and to design the metro system to accommodate interchange facilities with other transport modes and new corridors.

Land Value Capture, Hyderabad

Funding Arrangements

The first phase of the Metro Rail System is still under construction (photo 7.2 and map 7.8). The length of the three metro rail lines will reach 71.16 kilometers with 66 stations roughly 1 kilometer apart. Most of the area of the former Municipal Corporation of Hyderabad will be covered by the

Photo 7.2 Metro construction in progress: Cutting across the built-up areas of Hyderabad

Source: © Hyderabad Metro Rail Limited (HMR). Used with permission. Further permission required for reuse.

Map 7.8 First phase of the Hyderabad Metro Rail Limited

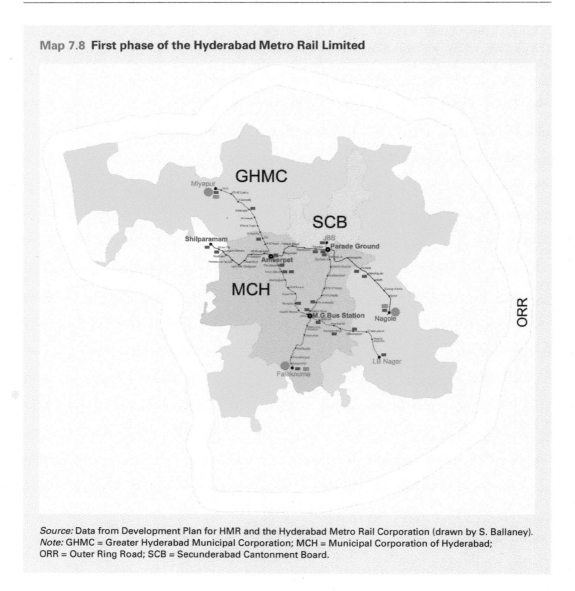

Source: Data from Development Plan for HMR and the Hyderabad Metro Rail Corporation (drawn by S. Ballaney).
Note: GHMC = Greater Hyderabad Municipal Corporation; MCH = Municipal Corporation of Hyderabad;
ORR = Outer Ring Road; SCB = Secunderabad Cantonment Board.

network. The entire system is elevated and positioned in the center of the right of way of the roads because the underground basements are too rock-strewn to construct subway structures.

In accord with one of the bid conditions, the government meets 40 percent of the project costs—half from the national government and half from the state government. The balance of 60 percent has to be provided by L&T Metro Rail. A consortium of 10 banks led by the State Bank of India provided financing. The debt to equity ratio set out for this rail project was 2:1. L&T Metro Rail foresees around 50 percent of corporate revenue coming from fares, about 45 percent from real estate development, and 5 percent from adverts and parking fees.

The proportion of L&T Metro Rail's real estate revenues is therefore much higher than DMRC's (see table 7.4 for DMRC's real estate contribution rate). The total project costs are \$3.07 billion, which include \$0.41 billion for real estate development along the metro rail corridors (L&T Metro Rail, 2013 information).

Property Development

Based on Hyderabad's PPP scheme, L&T Metro Rail is pushing through with several real estate development projects at depots and stations. The three depots' area of development is nearly 86 hectares, with a maximum floor area of about 1,161,000 square meters, which would be structured at and above first floor level by earmarking 70–80 percent of the ground floor for maintenance and stabling of trains and other depot facilities. Also, some 20 percent of the floor area of each station will be used for real estate. (The sites under tracks are not considered for computing the floor area.) L&T Metro Rail is entitled to use the stations' parking and circulation spaces for real estate development on the 25 sites, accounting for 23 hectares, and with a maximum floor area of 557,000 square meters. Many of the developable sites are former government facilities for nonresidential use near future metro stations and include government quarters, hospitals, and colleges. If any of the land parcels earmarked are not made available, the government will provide alternate sites on a comparable scale.

L&T Metro Rail is expected to provide public amenities, specifically where a 300-meter wide band from the metro corridor is envisaged for TOD at higher densities. In the TOD scheme, it is also essential to provide good feeder bus services and build well-connected foot and bike pathway networks around the new metro stations. However, the costs of such infrastructure and services are not included in the original concession agreement. For the intermodal integration objective, additional project funds need to be arranged from other transport sources such as JnNURM.

Conclusion

Delhi and Hyderabad are two Indian cities that have applied the value capture concept and schemes, having learned from other cities' experiences, to finance their new metro rail projects and to transform their urban structure with transit. The two cities have adapted different institutional and regulatory frameworks. Based on their experiences, they are adjusting these frameworks to overcome existing barriers, as seen in the proposed new TOD guidelines in Delhi. Even though it is early, some constraints and opportunities are now summarized.

Delhi's Experience

- DMRC began its first property development in 1999, though the contemporary MPD-2001 did not consider MRTS stations in its zoning systems, partly as Delhi's planning concept had, since World War II, been automobile oriented. Political and financial support from the national government could only start bearing fruit after a series of master plans was launched, which integrated the key position of new metro stations in the long-term development strategies and zoning systems.

- The FARs for DMRC's first property development were kept very low because DDA was initially concerned about the extra commercial activities inside metro stations generating serious congestion there. DMRC tried hard to get DDA to allow higher FARs by referring to Hong Kong SAR, China's, successful practice. But DDA did not relent because it recognized that DMRC properties would attract more people than the properties outside—controlled by DDA. For this reason, any proposals made by the DMRC for changes in land uses, approvals of building controls, and other clearances have been often held up for a long period. While DDA has proposed to significantly increase FARs in the metro influence zone in the draft MPD-2021, it seems that DDA will continue to limit FARs for DMRC's properties at station sites to 1.0. Beyond congestion, it seems that DDA's obstruction originates from a fundamental disagreement on how to share the development benefits generated by multiple property developments in metro impact areas among itself, DMRC, and other stakeholders.

- To increase broader public interest in India's first metro project, land parcels along the routes were transferred from various national government departments, agencies, and municipalities to the DMRC at far less than market prices. However, DMRC began using part of the land for real estate businesses without paying property taxes. The profits of development should have been shared with the land contributors and other benefit generators, including DDA. And so the regulatory tools have been used by DDA, not to support DMRC's property development projects, but to resist DMRC's monopolistic position.

- To solve the conflict of interest, the property development programs around metro stations should be conducted jointly by the DDA and DMRC. Yet they also have big differences in working cultures and methods. DMRC as a transport agency gives more attention to the efficiency of the metro system with certain privileges provided under the Indian Railways Act, which cannot legally be shared with DDA and other municipal agencies. Unlike the MTR of Hong Kong SAR, China, and several railway companies in Tokyo, DMRC's property division has not yet been given a strong business mandate because the major funds for its metro projects have been raised by the national government, including yen loans. While passenger services have increasingly generated substantial corporate profits in recent years, the lack of adequate expertise in real estate and town planning has diminished DMRC's motivation to explore joint development opportunities and create greater profits with DDA and other stakeholders.

- The TOD parameters set out by the UTTIPEC seem extremely similar to those introduced from U.S. urban planning and design schools but realistically they would not be able to perform well for residents and passengers in the real estate and transport markets unless DDA and DMRC work together on the master layout plan. The world's best LVC practices suggest that the parameters be determined not based on fixed standards but on local site conditions, networkwide node characteristics, and market-based demands. Despite the importance of private entities' participation in implementing large TOD projects, the opportunities have been limited thus far for developers to put greater knowledge and resources into a variety of housing properties around metro station areas.

Hyderabad's Experience

- In the innovative business climate of Hyderabad, the world's largest metro PPP scheme has involved several municipal agencies and multinational corporate parties. The procedure has been very smooth because of the clear-cut concession agreement that spells out public-private obligations and provides a list of the land parcels for real estate development with specifications of public facilities. In accord with the obligations, the government has hastily acquired land parcels along the city's main corridors, and the private partner has been building bridge pillars, railway segments, and depots.
- The latest master plan for the Hyderabad Metropolitan Area includes neither specific development strategies nor strict land use restrictions along the new metro lines that will serve the central area of Hyderabad. Instead, 300-meter buffer areas from the target corridors have been set up as TOD zones at the municipal government level to work with PPP-based metro projects. Such relaxed and localized policies raise the question of how the short- and mid-term project outcomes in the PPP framework will meet the long-term urban development goals at the metropolitan scale.
- A list of the real estate development packages being proposed by L&T Metro Rail contains mainly commercial properties within the small plots awarded for financial gain. Associated with rash land acquisition and clearance processes, TOD principles have not yet been incorporated in the PPP-based development practice. Additional time, knowledge, and experience are needed for the Metro Corporation to embark on larger mixed-use development projects with elevated pedestrian networks and to gradually harmonize metro facilities into the surrounding districts for wider social interest. Such a scenario may not be too optimistic, as Hong Kong SAR, China's, MTR Corporation took a similar approach after the initial stage of R+P implementation in the 1980s.

References

Comptroller and Auditor General of India (CAG). 2008. "Performance Audit of Phase I of Delhi Mass Rapid Transit System by Delhi Metro Rail Corporation Limited, 2006–2007." New Delhi.

Delhi Development Authority. 2013. *Draft Master Plan for Delhi–2021*. Delhi. www.dda.org.in/planning/draft_master_plans.htm.

DMRC (Delhi Metro Rail Corporation Limited). 2001. *Annual Report 2000–2001*. New Delhi.

———. 2010. *Annual Report 2009–2010*. New Delhi.

———. 2013a. "Delhi Metro Corporation Limited Year Wise Revenue." New Delhi.

———. 2013b. *Annual Report 2012–2013*. New Delhi.

Gladstone, David L., and Kameswara Sreenivas Kolapalli. 2007. *The Urban Development Effects of Large-Scale Public Sector Landowners in India: A Comparative Study of Delhi and Bangalore*. Cambridge, MA: Lincoln Institute of Land Policy.

GHMC (Greater Hyderabad Municipal Corporation). 2013. "Hyderabad Urban Agglomeration: Demography, Economy and Land Use Pattern." Hyderabad, India. www.ghmc.gov.in/downloads/chapters%202.pdf.

Ministry of Urban Development, Government of India. 2006. *National Urban Transport Policy*. New Delhi.

Nallathiga, Ramakrishna. 2009. "Potential of Land and Land Based Instruments for Infrastructure Development in Urban Areas." In *India Infrastructure Report 2009: Land—A Critical Resource for Infrastructure*, edited by 3iNetwork Infrastructure Development Finance Company, 218–26. New Delhi: Oxford University Press.

UN (United Nations). 2012. *World Urbanization Prospects: The 2011 Revision*, CD-ROM Edition. New York: Department of Economic and Social Affairs, Population Division.

UTTIPEC (Unified Traffic and Transportation Infrastructure Planning and Engineering Centre). 2012. "Transit Oriented Development: Policy. Norms. Guidelines." New Delhi (Draft).

World Bank. 2013a. "World Bank Guidebook on Incentive-Based Value Capture Mechanism for Transit in Developing Countries: Draft Case Report Delhi Metro Case Study." Washington, DC.

———. 2013b. *Urbanization beyond Municipal Boundaries: Nurturing Metropolitan Economies and Connecting Peri-Urban Areas in India*. Directions in Development. Washington, DC: World Bank.

CHAPTER 8

Air Rights Sales, São Paulo, Brazil

São Paulo is Brazil's land value capture (LVC) pioneer, as without large fiscal resources it has explored LVC instruments to raise funds for urban infrastructure investment. Yet having urbanized heavily and owning few developable lands—and so, unlike Chinese or Indian cities, unable to sell or lease public lands—the local government has explored air rights sales as an integral part of urban redevelopment. It has attracted private real estate investments into its designated urban redevelopment areas, called "Urban Operations" (UOs), and raised funds for urban infrastructure by auctioning out tradable air rights—Certificados de Potencial Adicional de Construção (Certificates of Additional Construction Potential, or CEPACs). CEPACs have rarely financed transit or transit-oriented development (TOD)–related investments in São Paulo but could be used more to finance this type of project elsewhere in Brazil, as Curitiba has done. CEPACs are not without problems, however, due to downzoning, which seems to have unintended negative impacts on urban development patterns.

Urban Development Context: Population and Urbanization Trends

São Paulo is pivotal for the development of the Southeast and Midwest Regions of Brazil. Many of the municipalities in its metropolitan area have evolved from small villages along the major rivers that were used as regional transport corridors during the colonial era. The first period of intensive growth was in the 19th century when the region's coffee production and trading businesses extended with the construction of railroads from the Port of Santos to the City of São Paulo and its hinterlands. The second phase was during industrialization in 1940–80. While the city's gross domestic product increased 10 times, the population quintupled, up to about 12.1 million. But since the 1990s, São Paulo's economy has heavily deindustrialized.

The high pace of income and population growth linked to unstable political and financial conditions, as well as inadequate implementation of a spatial development vision and strategy in past years, have led to urban expansion (map 8.1), including massive informal settlements on the periphery. Currently, 86.5 percent of São Paulo is urbanized (World Bank n.d.). The urban agglomeration is projected to have around 23.1 million inhabitants by 2025 (figure 8.1), even though developable land is in short supply.

While the city-region boundaries persistently drive outwards, the central area presents a high concentration of job openings, educational activities, public services, businesses, and entertainment activities. These have generated excessive commuting patterns between the city center and surrounding municipalities, where the majority of people live. Lately, however, central urban areas have once more seen the return of residential populations, similar to other global cities like Tokyo, New York, and London. Such urban regeneration trends could have been used better to provide opportunities to adapt value capture instruments in association with rail transit investments over the last decade.

Map 8.1 São Paulo's metropolitan region

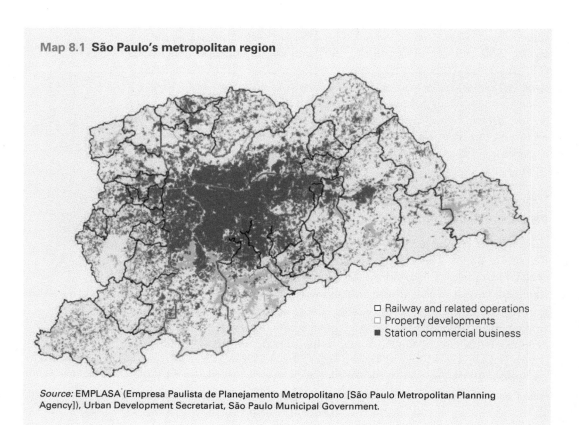

□ Railway and related operations
□ Property developments
■ Station commercial business

Source: EMPLASA (Empresa Paulista de Planejamento Metropolitano [São Paulo Metropolitan Planning Agency]), Urban Development Secretariat, São Paulo Municipal Government.

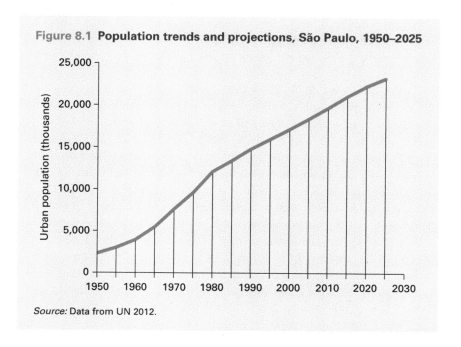

Figure 8.1 Population trends and projections, São Paulo, 1950–2025

Source: Data from UN 2012.

Regulatory and Institutional Framework

Laws and Master Plans

Several laws and master plans guide São Paulo's urban development and transit investment across federal, state, and municipal governments. At the federal level, the City Statute (Federal Law 10.257/2001) defines the legislative principles to guide governmental actions for controlling the processes of urban land development and management, complemented with municipal by-laws (Fernandes 2010). The City Statute also defines the obligations of municipalities with more than 20,000 inhabitants and the functions of UOs to be implemented through partnerships between municipal governments and private developers, among other instruments. The City Statute also underlines the social function of property by distinguishing between the ownership of land and the right of use. This means that land ownership does not immediately promise complete freedom of site use, as landholders have to obtain development permits with conditions from their local government. In accord with the City Statute, municipal governments in Brazil ensure the public interest of property through land development approvals as well as air rights sales. This provides the legal background for air rights sales by municipal governments.

The National Plan of Logistics and Transport was prepared by the Ministry of Transport to guide public-private transport infrastructure investments and integrate multiple transport modes over the medium and long term. The Urban Mobility Program was developed by the Ministry of Cities, with action plans for policymakers and practitioners to promote urban transport projects in their own cities, such as bus rapid transit (BRT) and urban improvements along commuter and metro rail lines. The Ministry of Cities has also published guidelines for urban mobility projects and related programs.

At the state level, PITU 2025 (Integrated Urban Transport Plan 2025) (STM 2006) proposed a well-integrated transport development strategy that aims to balance the supply of and demand for urban mobility. The latest revision in 2006 stressed the integration of land use policies with transit infrastructure investments, aiming to promote the relocation of business activities and lessen excessive commuting trips to and from the central business district. Some of the railway projects proposed in PITU 2025 have already been delivered, such as the construction of the new Marginal Pinheiros station, the modernization of rail line 9, the extension of metro lines 4 and 5, and the installation of new BRT lanes. By 2025, the entire network is expected to comprise 110 kilometers of commuter rail and metro systems, including express services to Guarulhos International Airport (map 8.2).

At the city level, the latest Strategic Master Plan of 2002—Plano Diretor Estratégico (PDE)—incorporated the urbanization instruments defined by the City Statute in its spatial development strategy. The PDE also emphasized the integration of transit and land development that could be achieved through market incentives for high-density and mixed-land use development, creation of new business clusters along metro lines, redevelopment

Map 8.2 Proposed transit network, Integrated Urban Transport Plan 2025

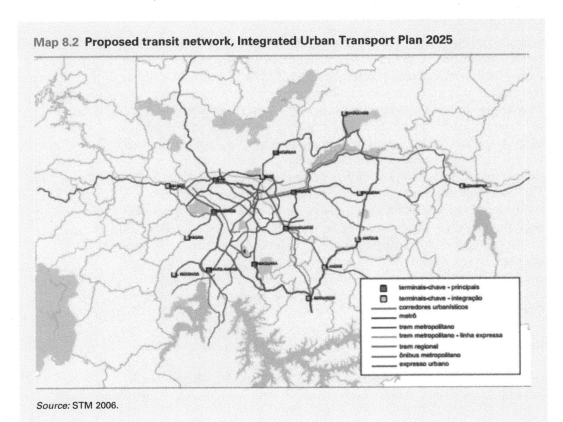

Legend:
- terminais-chave - principais
- terminais-chave - integração
- corredores urbanísticos
- metrô
- trem metropolitano
- trem metropolitano - linha expressa
- trem regional
- ônibus metropolitano
- expresso urbano

Source: STM 2006.

of built-up areas, and use of existing transport infrastructure. Many of the directions in the PDE are consistent with those in PITU 2025. Since 2013, the PDE has been undergoing revision through civic consultation, after which the strategic development districts in São Paulo will be redefined, based on future urban transit investments and current land market conditions.

A document, São Paulo 2040, was prepared by City Hall in 2012 to share a longer-term vision of the city. A notable outcome was the "30 Minutes City" (Cidade de 30 Minutos), to get urban residents closer to their daily activities, in time and space, by improving urban transit quality and extending the metro network to 264 kilometers by 2040.

UOs

"An urban operation (Operacion Urbanisica/UO) is defined by the City Statute as a tool to promote the restructuring of large areas of the city through land-based incentives offered to public-private partnership (PPP), including local public authorities, developers, landowners, and other stakeholders as independent investors" (Montandon and de Souza 2007). UOs are implemented through instruments called Operações Urbanas Consorciadas (Consortia Urban Operations). The urban infrastructure investments in UOs will be financed by the incremental value created by public investment, land use, and zoning change (Sandroni 2010), as recouped through air rights sales (described below).

The first UO in São Paulo was Anhangabaú in 1991, later expanded under the new name of Centro. Two other UOs were Faria Lima around a business district, and Água Branca on a former industrial site (map 8.3).

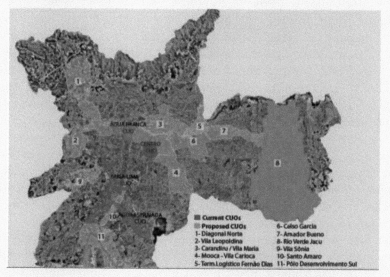

Map 8.3 São Paulo's 15 current and proposed urban operations in the Plano Diretor Estratégico of 2002

Source: Urban Development Secretariat, São Paulo Municipal Government 2002.
Note: CUO = Consortia Urban Operations.

Only a few months after the City Statute was approved, Água Espraiada was designated a UO, based on the new 2001 standards. The 2002 PDE recognized the four current UOs and proposed 11 new UOs. The city-level plan also reiterated the need to update existing UOs to meet the requirements of the City Statute, as the four initial UOs did not have CEPACs. The amount to be paid for additional air rights used to be assessed based on the valuation report prepared by professional auditors for each real estate project. The new system was applied to update Faria Lima in 2004. A study to update Água Branca began in 2008, and its revision was sent to the City Council in 2012, though it is still waiting for official approval.

Government Structure and Roles

Federal, state, and municipal governments all have a hand in executing the PDEs and transport master plans for São Paulo. The federal government is responsible for formulating normative criteria on urban planning and TOD projects belonging to the city and surrounding municipalities. It is also in charge of managing the federal road, rail, and waterway systems more broadly. The federal Ministry of Cities is given an instructive role to guide urban development processes, taking into account the benefits of integrating multitransport systems across cities. Its recommendations cover multiple states and municipalities to consolidate their own ideas.

The state government is accountable for the metro rail and integrated transport network across the metropolitan area, while the municipal agencies control parts of the urban transport systems within their jurisdictions, as well as land use planning.

State and municipal governments have formed multiple departments and agencies for regional and local transport systems. The state Secretariat of Metropolitan Transport (STM) has three operating companies: São Paulo Company of the Metropolitan (METRO), São Paulo Metropolitan Trains Company (CPTM), and Metropolitan Urban Transportation Company (EMTU). Within the STM, the tasks for public transport and traffic management are split between SPTrans (São Paulo Transporte S.A.) and CET (Traffic Engineering Company). As a primary transit agency, SPTrans coordinates all municipal bus services, which are operated by eight private companies within the city of São Paulo. Important transit projects are being undertaken by two units: STM and the Municipal Secretariat of Urban Development. The latter works mostly on urban planning and design around new transit corridors and terminuses, controls land regulations, and oversees the municipal urban development company (São Paulo Urbanismo).

State and municipal governments and agencies face onerous financial requirements for the transit investments proposed in recent master plans (table 8.1). According to the latest report of the São Paulo state government, total public expenditure for FY2013 was R$173 billion (US$88.7 billion), of which about R$24 billion (US$12.3 billion) was for transport investments. New investments in the São Paulo metro accounted for R$4.8 billion (US$2.5 billion), of which R$3.5 billion (US$1.8 billion) was financed by the State Treasury and R$1.3 billion (US$0.7 billion) by METRO. The São Paulo municipal government had a total budget of R$42 billion (US$21.5 billion) of statutory spending by Brazilian municipalities on health, education, debt servicing, and operations for FY2013, of which R$2.6 billion (US$1.3 billion) was allocated to transport projects and related urban programs.

Land Value Capture

Funding Arrangements for Transit Investments

The funding for most transit projects in the city of São Paulo and surrounding municipalities relies heavily on local government resources, especially São Paulo state government's general budget for metro, commuter rail, and intercity bus transit investments. The federal government provides financial support to some projects (such as the construction of 150 kilometers of new bus corridor projects in the city since April 2013). According to a study on the financial feasibility of public investments (called SP 2040), São Paulo's

Table 8.1 Summary of transit projects proposed in recent master plans

Project	Agencies	Objective
BRT	Prefeitura Municipal de São Paulo (PMSP)	Implementation of new bus corridors (150 km)
Intercity Bus Corridors–Itapevi–São Paulo	STM/EMTU	30.4 km of bus corridor and integration with metro line 4
Intercity Bus Corridors–Guarulhos–São Paulo	STM/EMTU	24.8 km of bus corridor
New lines for the Railway System	STM/CPTM	Line ABC Express (will run parallel to line 10) and Line 13 Jade/Airport express
Extension of Railway System	STM/CPTM	Extension of line 8 (Diamond) and 9 (Emerald)
Metro Line 4 Yellow	STM/METRO	Extension of 12.8 km, with 6 new stations
Metro Line 6 Orange	STM/METRO	New line with 15.3 km and 15 stations
Metro Line 18 Bronze VLT São Paulo SBC	STM/METRO	14.2 km of monorail line with 12 stations
Metro Line 20 Pink	STM/METRO	New line with 12.3 km and 14 stations
Metro Line 5 Lilac	STM/METRO	Extension between Largo Treze and line 2 Green—19.9 km
Metro Line 15 Silver	STM/METRO	25.8 km of monorail line and 18 stations
Metro Line 17 Gold	STM/METRO	7.7 km of monorail line connecting Congonhas Airport to the CPTM—line 9

Source: Based on data from Cartão BOM (http://www.cartaobom.net), METRO (http://www.metro.sp.gov.br), and SPTrans (http://www.sptrans.com.br), 2013.
Note: BRT = bus rapid transit; CPTM = São Paulo Metropolitan Trains Company; EMTU = Metropolitan Urban Transportation Company; km = kilometer; METRO = São Paulo Company of the Metropolitan; SBC = São Bernardo do Campo (municipality); STM = State Ministry of Transportation, São Paulo; VLT = light rail.

municipal government does not have enough fiscal resources to deliver and maintain the capital-intensive transit systems enumerated in several master plans.

To raise the capital funds required in the coming decades, PITU 2025 examined financing scenarios for transit investments based on conventional tax resources and innovative financing schemes, including value capture. According to the funding arrangement models analyzed in the master plan, substantial development benefits could be captured by air rights sales in "urban intervention areas" and in "urban operations or consortia urban operations," accompanied by PPP initiatives and congestion charges (*pedágio urbano*) (table 8.2).

Value Capture Instruments

The city of São Paulo has played a pioneering role in value capture instruments since the early 1990s, including CEPACs adapted under UOs. Many municipalities' LVC regulatory frameworks and schemes have been derived from São Paulo's experience. The key features of the main LVC instruments in Brazil are now discussed and are summarized in table 8.3.

Additional building charge (Outorga Onerosa do Direito de Construir/ OODC) is the sale of floor areas that enable landholders to make use of their own sites up to the maximum floor area ratio (FAR) defined by law. Under OODC, the landowner's property right is limited to a basic FAR that is different from "the maximum FAR the area could support" (Smolka 2013). In São Paulo, the city planning department sets the "basic" FAR for the city at 1.0–2.0, though specific FARs within this range depend on

Table 8.2 Funding schemes for transit investments in Integrated Urban Transport Plan 2025 (R$ million)

Funding scheme	2007–12	2013–25
State government—treasury contribution	7,700	13,200
State government—financing	600	2,800
Federal government—federal tax return	1,000	2,000
Federal government—Contribution of Intervention in the Economic Domain	600	1,200
Municipal government—property tax	300	1,000
Municipal government—financing	300	0
Municipal government—urban tolls	0	3,000
Private (PMSP and others)—urban concessions	500	4,500
Private—PPPs with state and municipal governments	5,400	4,000
Private—operators' operating margin	200	400
Total	16,600	32,100

Source: STM 2006.
Note: PMSP = Prefeitrua Municpal de São Paulo; PPP = public-private parternship.

Table 8.3 **Land value capture instruments in Brazil**

Instrument	Mechanism	Paid by	Delivered by	Applications
Property tax	Property taxation	Property owners	Municipal government	General budget use
Betterment levy	Charge on public improvement	Property owners getting benefit from public investments	All government levels	Public investments
OODC	Air rights sale	Property owners	Municipal government	Urban Development Fund (finances prioritized public urban investments including slum upgrading within city boundary)
CEPAC as an integral part of UOs	Air rights sale	Property developers and owners	Municipal government	Predetermined public urban investments including slum upgrading within UO
Urban intervention area	Air rights sale	Property developers and owners	Municipal government	Not implemented
Urban concession	Development rights sale and power of eminent domain	Property developers and owners	Municipal government	Infrastructure investment

Source: Maleronka and Pires 2013.
Note: CEPAC = Certificate of Additional Construction Potential; OODC = Outorga Onerosa do Direito de Construir; UO = urban operation.

location and land use (table 8.4). If landowners want to build above the free basic FAR up to the maximum allowable FAR (1.0–4.0, also depending on location and land use), they have to buy additional FARs. The free basic FAR in certain areas has become lower than the preexisting basic FAR. The revenues generated from the sales of OODC are deposited in the Urban Development Fund (Fundo de Desenvolvimento Urbano), which finances public urban investments including slum upgrading within the city boundary. The PDE 2002 established an inventory of all air rights in the municipality, except those tradable within the UO that are subject to federal law.

CEPACs are a market-based instrument to finance public urban investments through air rights transactions within designated UOs. Through CEPACs, municipalities can raise infrastructure investment funds by selling the bearer additional building rights, such as a higher FAR and possible land use changes, that should induce private investments in the transformations wanted by urban development policy. One advantage is that municipalities can obtain revenue before the project starts and can finance

Table 8.4 Change of basic floor area ratios in São Paulo, before and after 2002

Changes in FAR Coefficients in São Paulo, 2002–04					
Land Use Zones Established by the Strategic Development Plan in 2002	Land Use Zones before 2002	Basic FAR			
		FAR up to 2002	In 2003	From 2004 on	Maximum FAR
Exclusive Residential Zones (ZER)	Strict horizontal single-family residential zone (Z1)	1.0	1.0	1.0	1.0
Mixed Use Zones (ZM)	Predominant horizontal residences zone (Z9)	1.0	1.0	1.0	1.0
	Predominant low demographic density residential zone (Z2)	1.0	1.0	1.0	2.5
	Predominant low demographic density residential zone (Z11, Z13, Z17, Z18)	1.0	1.0	1.0	2.0
	Predominant medium demographic density residential zone (Z3, Z10, Z12)	2.5	2.0	2.0	4.0
	Mixed use zones and medium high demographic density zone (Z4)	3.0	2.5	2.0	4.0
	Mixed use zones and high demographic density zone (Z5)	3.5	3.0	2.0	4.0
	Special use zones (Z8 007-02, -04, -05, -08, -11, -12)	3.0	2.5	2.0	4.0
	Special use zones (Z8 007-10, -13)	2.0	2.0	2.0	4.0
	Special use zones (Z8 060-01, -03)	1.5	1.0	1.0	2.5
	Mixed use with predominance of commerce and services zone (Z19)	2.5	1.5	1.0	4.0
Industrial Zones under Restructuring (ZIR)	Predominant industrial zone (Z6)	1.5	1.0	1.0	2.5
	Strict industrial zone (Z7)	1.0	1.0	1.0	2.5

Source: Smolka 2013.
Note: FAR = floor area ratio.

infrastructure construction without creating a deficit or public debt or using budget resources (Sandroni 2010). Another is that market forces determine the price of undeveloped air rights, though the municipality can reject prices offered below its minimum prices. (The CEPAC mechanism is detailed in the next section.)

Although unused because application laws are still pending, *urban intervention areas* in the PDE are areas where the city intends to promote urban development. In the designated areas, landholders can develop their own sites beyond the basic FAR in accord with their master plans. The revenues gained from air rights sales go into the Urban Development Fund to finance public works throughout the city.

Urban concessions (UCs)—not yet implemented—are another public-private development mechanism, under which a municipal government delegates site-specific master plan implementation to a private developer. Whereas the master plan needs to be developed by the municipal government through consultation with the public, one private entity, selected through the bidding process, becomes the concessionary of real estate development in a UC area. The concessionary is entitled to expropriate land required for the master plan and to generate revenues from the associated real estate development. In this framework, the municipal government requires the concessionary to provide public facilities, green spaces, and social housing units, which are funded by the revenues generated from real estate development in the UC area.

CEPAC Mechanism

CEPACs—tradable air rights—created by municipal governments are auctioned on the Brazilian stock exchange, which means that they are regulated not only by the City Statute but also the Securities and Exchange Commission of Brazil (CVM), under CVM Instruction 401, published two years after the City Statute. CVM Instruction 401 requires municipal governments to set the minimum price of the CEPAC to keep the city's real estate business competitive. For price valuation of CEPACs in São Paulo, the virtual land method was applied. It assumes that the private revenue gained from a property project must comprise development costs, land acquisition costs, real estate margin, and the added land value premium. The CEPAC price can be estimated as the residual land value between two

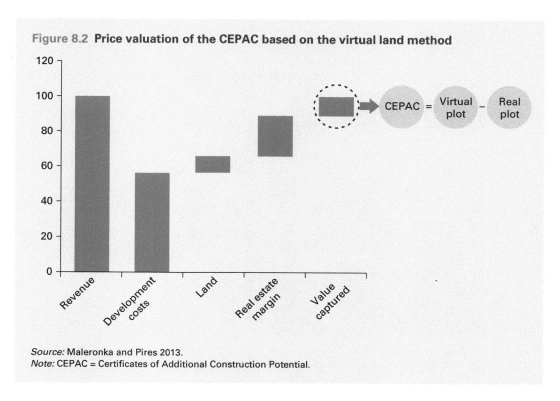

Figure 8.2 Price valuation of the CEPAC based on the virtual land method

Source: Maleronka and Pires 2013.
Note: CEPAC = Certificates of Additional Construction Potential.

different situations: the actual plot with the full benefits of additional air rights and the plot without any additional air rights (figure 8.2).

The municipal government is required to update the minimum price as well as the amount of CEPACs offered for each public auction. The final sale price is determined at auction. In theory, CEPACs can be traded in the securities market, though a secondary market has not yet developed. The amount of the CEPAC to be issued corresponds to the additional square meters that the present and future urban infrastructure in the designated UO can support. That quantity is based on program feasibility analysis that takes into account existing infrastructure and all additional construction work foreseen in the UO. The CEPAC can be used only at construction sites within UOs that exceed the standard FAR set by land development legislation, up to the maximum fixed by the UO law (figure 8.3).

Revenues from CEPAC auctions are deposited in a special escrow account because they are earmarked for improving the UOs as defined by the prospectus of each UO. This means that each of the CEPAC auctions is intended to finance predetermined public works projects. In São Paulo, the priority of public works for each CEPAC public offering is decided by the UO's administration committee, composed of municipal government officers and civic representatives.

Although air rights sale instruments are available in major Brazilian cities with fiscal constraints and limited land, the CEPAC instrument has been rarely used to finance transit projects to pursue TOD.

CEPAC-Funded UO Case: Água Espraiada, São Paulo

Água Espraiada occupies about 1,425 hectares of the UO, approved in 2001. Although it looks like an expansion of Faria Lima's business district, Água Espraiada contains many slum housing units between high-rise office

Figure 8.3 CEPAC use in urban operations

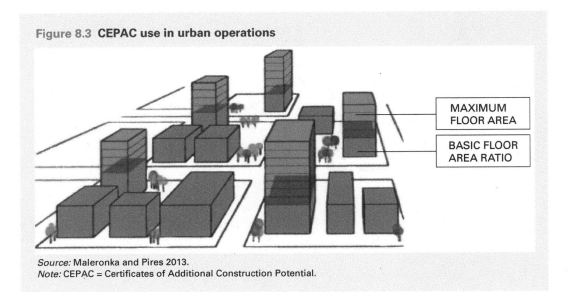

MAXIMUM FLOOR AREA

BASIC FLOOR AREA RATIO

Source: Maleronka and Pires 2013.
Note: CEPAC = Certificates of Additional Construction Potential.

buildings, two highways, and one metro line. The initial number of CEPAC units authorized was 3.75 million, of which 2.39 million units had been sold on the stock exchange as of February 2013. The air rights sold were used for 136 property developments in 2004–12. The revenue generated by the Água Espraiada through January 2013 was R$3,282 million (US$1,683 million) with expenditures of R$978 million (US$502 million), accounting for net public income of R$2,303 million (US$1,181 million).

The list of major projects to be funded by that net income included high-amenity public open spaces, 8,000 social housing units for families affected by the UO, construction of viaducts, and a bridge over the Pinheiros River. While the UO's prospectus lists up to an R$82 million investment in the metro and monorail line projects (according to the Memorandum of Understanding between São Paulo's state government and city hall), CEPAC transactions in the real estate market have not yet generated TOD.

In the UOs, air rights are not distributed freely or evenly. To attain desirable spatial development targets (such as articulated densities and mixed uses), a sector map and corresponding equivalence table have been prepared for each UO (table 8.5 and map 8.4). In accord with the unique zoning system and specific floor area conversion ratios, the CEPAC should have been allocated strategically through transaction processes. However, CEPAC operations have not always resulted in desirable spatial development in all parts of the UOs (photo 8.1). The market responses to UO designation remains to be seen, as CEPACs are relatively new.

Photo 8.1 Undesirable built environment predominantly filled with car parking around the train station in Faria Lima Urban Operation

Source: © Jin Murakami. Used with permission. Further permission required for reuse.

Table 8.5 Example of CEPAC coefficient table

Sector	CEPAC coefficient
Jabaquara	3 m^2
Brooklin	1 m^2
Berrini	1 m^2
Marginal Pinheiros	1 m^2
Chri Zaidan	2 m^2

Note: m^2 = meters squared. The table shows the amounts of floor space that can be purchased by one Certificate of Additional Construction Potential (CEPAC) in different sectors.

Map 8.4 Sector map of Água Espraiada

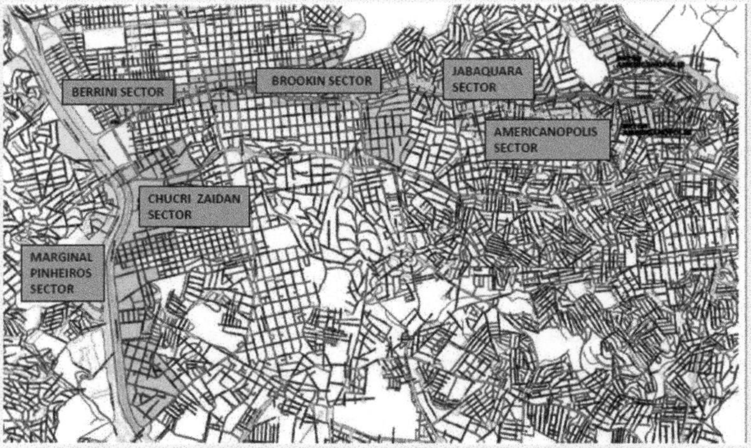

Source: São Paulo Urbanismo (Municipal Urban Planning Agency). http://www.prefeit ura.sp.gov.br/cidade/secretarias/upload/desenvolvimento_urbano/sp_urbanismo /arquivos/ouae/AE-Perimetro.pdf

Unintended Negative Impacts of OODC and CEPAC on Urban Development Pattern

To create higher demand for air rights to be sold through OODC or CEPAC, São Paulo initially reduced the basic (free) FAR of the entire city area to the range of 1.0 to 2.0. Under the new FAR scheme, current owners who want to rebuild their old buildings have to pay OODC or CEPAC for additional FAR exceeding the free FAR limit, on top of demolition and construction costs. Aside from the difficulty in achieving consensus on reconstruction, the newly imposed free FAR limitation may discourage current owners from rebuilding older properties built under the previously higher FAR allowance. Seeking a high return on investment, developers intending to build high-rises via an OODC or CEPAC generally focus on high-end properties such as offices, shopping malls, and luxury residential buildings in the city center. This results in a limited supply of affordable housing in the city center where most jobs are found, in spite of the municipal government's efforts to construct social housing in the center using the revenues from OODCs, CEPACs, and the general budget, as well as incentivize the construction of residential buildings by allocating FAR higher than regulations typically permit. Thus low- and lower-middle-income people, who account for the majority of the city's population, live in the suburbs far from the city center and deal with long commutes in crowded trains or buses.

The maximum FAR that can be bought through an OODC or CEPAC in São Paulo is limited to 4.0, even in the central business district. Other megacities allocate much higher FARs: in Tokyo, for example, from 1 to 20; in Hong Kong SAR, China, from 1 to 12; and in Seoul, from 8 to 10 (Suzuki, Cervero, and Iuchi 2013). São Paulo would seem to share characteristics with many metropolitan areas in developing countries—namely high population densities and low FARs, which usually leads to urban sprawl (photo 8.2).

Photo 8.2 Low- or lower-middle-income household areas, São Paulo

Source: © Hiroaki Suzuki. Used with permission. Further permission required for reuse.

Institutional Barriers

In São Paulo, rail transit (metro and suburban rail) and bus services are under the responsibility of the state government and the municipal government, respectively. Except for a few minor investments, CEPAC revenues have not been used for metro construction. In addition, CEPACs within UOs have often not been allocated to the precinct of the railway or bus station areas to promote TOD. CEPACs have not therefore always captured the increments of land value attributed to transit investments.

Further, political factors (such as control of the state and municipal governments being under different political parties) make coordination difficult between transit agencies and the urban planning department (which allocates CEPACs). Even in the same transport sector, railway transit companies owned by the state government and bus companies owned by the municipality seem to be competing rather than collaborating. Due to lack of coordination between transit agencies and the city planning bureau, as well as transit agencies' railway-centered engineering approaches, transit agencies often miss out on opportunities to explore the use of air rights above stations to generate revenues. For instance, given the tight budget situation and legal restrictions, metro company engineers tend to design metro stations according to minimum structural specifications requiring the least investment—yet these cannot support the type of multipurpose terminal building that can generate sizable lease revenues and increase transit ridership.

Opportunities for Adapting Development-Based LVC for Transit-Oriented Development

Despite the above challenges, São Paulo has great potential to adapt development-based LVC for transit investment and to develop articulated densities suitable for TOD. CEPAC revenues partly financed the investment costs of the Linha Verde (Green Line) UO in Curitiba, where a major national highway was converted into an urban avenue along with the extension of a bus rapid transit green line and promotion of higher-density land uses (Smolka 2013).

São Paulo's city planners are considering reducing overcrowded commuting between suburbs and city centers by developing subcenters to balance business and residential densities across the city (such as Região da Jacu-Pêssego as a new commercial center and Região da Cupecê for commercial and residential use), based on the TOD concept where developable lands are still available. Demand for good housing in the mid-market segment is very high because of fast-rising household incomes, and so land prices close to transit stations could climb.

If the municipal government and transit agencies collaborated with investors and developers, as their counterparts in Hong Kong SAR, China, and Tokyo, Japan, do, they could raise revenues to recoup a portion of the transit and other TOD-related investment costs. The municipal government can redevelop these areas by directly selling land or selling CEPACs. Even if these lands are occupied, developers would likely be interested in rebuilding high-density properties by purchasing land together with CEPACs, because of their low land costs relative to the city center.

To maximize revenues and at the same time promote TOD, the municipal government would need to allocate many CEPACs to station areas, if possible with much higher FARs, designating these areas as urban intervention areas. It could also encourage residents to live and work in TOD areas by changing zoning from single to mixed land use. Finally, by using development-based LVC-generated revenues, it could finance the construction of much needed social housing as a part of its development programs.

Conclusion

Air rights sales may be innovative development-based LVC, but few Brazilian cities have used them to finance transit investment projects and promote TOD, missing an opportunity to move their cities' transit development to the forefront of global practice.

A summary of São Paulo's experience is as follows:

- The greatest advantage of tradable air right sales is that local governments in developing countries with limited developable lands can produce substantial upfront cash flows for capital intensive urban infrastructure projects without increasing their public debt.
- In São Paulo, limiting the basic free FAR to 1.0–2.0 over the city artificially raised demand for tradable air rights, thus increasing revenues from sales. However, this downzoning seems to have led to unintended negative urban development impacts.
- São Paulo's spatial development pattern has progressed as high urban densification in a relatively unarticulated manner, partly because the city government has not established a strong land assemblage system for infill development with air rights sales schemes inside UOs. Additionally, government officials lack experience with the new LVC mechanisms and air rights market. It is hard for financial and planning practitioners to estimate an appropriate value of tradable air rights and designate effective zoning codes that lead to TOD. In São Paulo, the designations of UOs with the CEPAC auctions have not resulted in transit-supportive urban forms, though the master plans may have benefited from innovative value capture schemes for new metro projects.
- The lack of integration between metro-rail investments and value capture applications is due in large part to institutional barriers between state and municipal agencies for intergovernment funding allocations. For multiple government entities working together using revenues from air rights sales, the world's best value capture practices suggest that they need to develop a transparent project finance scheme with clear rules and mechanisms to share profits and risks among multiple agencies, local government, transit agencies, landholders, residents,

developers, and investors, as well as coordination mechanisms between them in planning, financing, and implementing transit and urban development. These moves also require strong political leadership at the highest level.

Annex table 8A.1 Data on case study cities in developing countries

City	Nanchang	Delhi	Hyderabad	São Paulo
Country	China	India	India	Brazil
Landholding system	State leasehold	Market freehold	Market freehold	Market freehold
Metropolitan population (thousand), 2010	2,331	21,935	7,578	19,649
Metropolitan area (km²)	617	1,943	881	7,947
Population density (metropolitan) (1,000/km²)	3.8	11.3	8.6	2.5
Population growth in metropolitan areas, 2000–10 (%, annual)	41.5% (3.5%)	39.4% (3.4%)	39.2% (3.4%)	14.9% (1.4%)
GDP per capita growth, 2007–2011 (%, annual)	12.4%	8.7%	5.2%	-2.8%
GDP growth rate projection, 2008–25 (%, annual)	13% (2011–15)	189% (6.4%)	193% (6.5%)	102% (4.2%)
Real estate price growth (%, annual)	19.5% (2008–12, land)	14.3% (2007–12, housing)	-2.1% (2007–12, housing)	18.7% (2008–12, housing)
Number of private cars registered (of 1,000 population)	57 (2010)	143 (2011)	13 (for Andhra Pradesh)	410
Private car registration growth rate (%, annual)	24.9% (2007–)	8.3% (2006–11)	10%	5% (2005–10)
Public transport use (%)	13.5%	42%	44%	36.8%
Metro lines (existing) km	—	190	—	74.2
Number of stations (existing)	—	144	—	64
Metro lines to be constructed (km)	168	120	72	205 (by 2030)
Number of stations (to be constructed)	128	81	66	94 (by 2016)
Estimated metro construction cost (US$ million)	2,421 (line 2)	11,701 (Phases I–III)	3,440 (Phase I)	14,000 (for extension)
Contribution of land value capture financing (US$ million and %)	168 (7%) (line 2)	570 (5%) (Phases I–III)	Modeled as 45% of revenue	N/A

Source: World Bank databases; UN Statistics; websites of transit agencies; and others.
Note: GDP = gross domestic product; N/A = Not available.

References

Fernandes, Edesio. 2010. "The City Statute and the Legal-Urban Order." In *The City Statute: A Commentary*, edited by Celso Santos Carvalho and Anaclaudia Rossbach, 55–70. São Paulo, Brazil: Cities Alliance and Ministry of Cities.

Maleronka, Camila and Domingos Pires. 2013. "Consultancy Work for Preparing a Guidebook on 'Development Incentive'-based Land Value Capture Mechanism for Transit in Developing Countries: São Paulo Case Report." Prepared by P3urb, São Paulo, Brazil, for the World Bank. World Bank, Washington, DC.

Montandon, Daniel T., and Phelipe F. de Souza. 2007. "Land readjustment e operações consorciadas." Ronmano Guerra Editora, São Paulo, Brazil.

Sandroni, Paulo. 2010. "A New Financial Instrument of Value Capture in São Paulo: Certificates of Additional Construction Potential." In *Municipal Revenues and Land Policies*, edited by Gregory K. Ingram and Yu-Hung Hong, 218–36. Cambridge, MA: Lincoln Institute of Land Policy. www.lincolninst.edu/pubs/2064_A-New-Financial-Instrument-of-Value-Capture-in-S%C3%A3o-Paulo.

Smolka, Martim O. 2013. *Implementing Value Capture in Latin America, Policy Focus Report.* Cambridge, MA: Lincoln Institute of Land Policy.

STM (State Secretariat for Metropolitan Transport, São Paulo). 2006. *PITU 2025—Plano Integrado De Transportes Urbanos.* São Paulo, Brazil. www.stm.sp.gov.br/images/stories/Pitus/Pitu2025/Pdf/Pitu_2025_08.pdf.

Suzuki, Hiroaki, Robert Cervero, and Kanako Iuchi. 2013. *Transforming Cities with Transit: Transit and Land-Use Integration for Sustainable Urban Development.* Washington, DC: World Bank.

UN (United Nations). 2012. *World Urbanization Prospects: The 2011 Revision*, CD-ROM Edition. New York: Department of Economic and Social Affairs, Population Division.

Urban Development Secretariat, São Paulo Municipal Government. 2002. "Plano Diretor Estratégico" (Strategic Master Plan). São Paulo, Brazil.

World Bank. n.d. "Urban Development." Washington, DC. http://data.worldbank.org/topic/urban-development.

Index